THE FIRST YEAR OF HOMESCHOOLING YOUR CHILD

MORE HOMESCHOOLING TITLES

LINDA DOBSON

The First Year of Homeschooling Your Child

YOUR COMPLETE GUIDE TO GETTING
OFF TO THE RIGHT START

THREE RIVERS PRESS • NEW YORK

Published by Three Rivers Press, New York, New York.
Member of the Crown Publishing Group, a division of Random House, Inc.
www.randomhouse.com

THREE RIVERS PRESS and the Tugboat design are registered trademarks of Random House, Inc.

Originally published by Prima Publishing, Roseville, California, in 2001.

All products mentioned in this book are trademarks of their respective companies.

Cover photos copyright © Comstock

Printed in the United States of America

Library of Congress Cataloging-in-Publication Data
Dobson, Linda.
    The first year of homeschooling your child : your complete guide to getting off to the right start / Linda Dobson.
        p. cm.—(Prima home learning library)
    Includes index.
    1. Home schooling—United States—Handbooks, manuals, etc. I. Title: First year of home schooling your child. II. Title. III. Series.

LC40.D635   2001
371.04'2—dc21   2001021318
ISBN 0-7615-2788-5

10 9 8 7 6
First Edition

For Emily Caelin

Whose twinkling eyes, sweet smile, and affinity
for my keyboard are at once my hurdles
and my greatest rewards

What is most important and valuable about the home as a base for children's growth into the world is not that it is a better school than the schools, but that it isn't a school at all.

JOHN HOLT

CONTENTS

INTRODUCTION

$\mathcal{A}$RE YOUR PALMS sweating? Are you shaking in your boots? Welcome to your first year of homeschooling!

Relax. Here it's understood that you're at least a little—or perhaps a lot—apprehensive about your ability to enjoy and succeed in homeschooling. Your apprehension puts you in good company. Although the number of homeschooling families continues to swell, I daresay only a small minority of families begins with certainty, and even fewer are completely confident of success. Like most folks new to the idea of teaching your own, you're probably asking some form of the question "Will homeschooling work for *my* family?"

> Like most folks new to the idea of teaching your own, you're probably asking some form of the question "Will homeschooling work for *my* family?"

Just as a doctor can't recommend a single prescription for what ails all of his patients, no one can widely prescribe an educational option for all children. The answer to the question, then, depends largely on you. More specifically, whether or not homeschooling will work for your family is subject, to a great degree, to your willingness to be flexible. Flexibility is built in to the homeschooling process, so it's only a matter of how well you bend and shape homeschooling until it fits your family. But it also requires that you limber up and increase the flexibility of your thinking about education itself so that you may comfortably unify everyday life and learning.

The first year of homeschooling has often been described as feeling like a leap off a cliff. If you, too, feel this way right now, consider this book the friendly push you might be needing to discover that you, like so many other homeschoolers, have wings.

WHO IS HELPING YOU?

WHEN PRESENTED with the challenge to put together a book specializing in information most useful and important to the brand-new homeschooling family, I turned to the "experts" in the field—scores of families practicing homeschooling in myriad ways who could look back on their own first years to share with you what they learned. I was gratified and humbled by their willingness to share, their candor in doing so, and their deep insight into and devotion to the homeschooling lifestyle.

Their information and advice felt like a warm arm around the shoulders, the same hug your favorite aunt gives you while explaining that your baby won't be teething forever and your next good night's sleep is just around the corner.

What is the essence of their message to you?

- ✦ Yes, we made our share of mistakes.

- ✦ Yes, some days are hard—not all homeschooled children run off to help with chores, whistling while they work.

- ✦ Yes, there were many things we would prefer to have known before starting, but things turned out okay.

- ✦ Yes, we're just like you, and it was possible to build a lifestyle we preferred because of homeschooling.

- ✦ Yes, as so well put by respondent Allison Dodrill, "The rewards, so far, are astounding."

Anyone so moved was invited via e-mail to respond to one or all topics addressed in this book. This narrowed the field, in that the majority of responses came from those connected to national, state, or local homeschooling support via computer. An impressive number of responses, however, arrived via snail mail. Thanks to this shotgun approach, we've tapped into the experience of a wonderfully eclectic group of homeschoolers. While their differences are noted, it's their similarities that will lead you to the best homeschooling has to offer.

WHAT'S INSIDE?

IN TALKING to countless parents considering or new to homeschooling, I noted that a most pervasive underlying cause of trepidation became clear. When education takes place in the confines of a particular building (an institutional one, at that), options and choices are few; there's not much to think about. Along comes the notion of homeschooling, and suddenly education leaves the confines of an institutional concept and bursts into the "big wide world." A parent has a whole lot more to ponder when the educational options and choices mushroom to such immense proportions.

> Along comes the notion of homeschooling, and suddenly education leaves the confines of an institutional concept and bursts into the "big wide world."

This is where *Your First Year of Homeschooling* begins.

Laying Your Homeschooling Foundation

A home needs a foundation in order to stand. A happy homeschooling experience for your family similarly must include some attention to its foundation before you start building it. Basic to that foundation is thoughtful attention to the reasons you are considering homeschooling. An overview of the many reasons families turn to homeschooling will help you think about the very personal motives you bring to the decision. Your motives can guide you to start the process of bending homeschooling toward your child's unique needs.

Next we'll take a deeper look at some of the choices presented to you through homeschooling. When you observe your child for answers to questions about decisions on educational schedule, method, and organization, your discoveries can further lend direction to the way *you* might bend homeschooling. At the same time, you'll learn how looking at homeschooling as an educational experiment, as opposed to a cliff jump, keeps all of these important decisions in perspective.

Building Your First Year of Homeschooling

Many potential homeschooling parents are surprised to learn that there is no single first step for all. Rather, we're going to make you your homeschooling experiment's first "guinea pig" and show you how to gather your own research to decide your own first step. You'll begin building your own educational philosophy, understand the laws that govern homeschooling where you live, decide how you will assess your child's progress, and keep spending to a minimum.

Next we'll visit educational readiness, multiple intelligences, learning styles, and, because of their proliferation, learning disorders and tie these in to your homeschooling decisions. After that, you're encouraged to begin homeschooling (now!) in whatever way makes you comfortable today, while understanding that you can easily turn homeschooling in another direction if you discover that a different homeschooling approach better fills your child's needs. To help you consider what those other directions are, we summarize nine different homeschooling methods and peek at what a week of learning looks like for each.

Myths about homeschooling (and homeschoolers) abound. Now that you have a deeper understanding of the educational freedom inherent in the act, it's time to reexamine half a dozen of the most persistent myths to see them for what they are.

Some readers will begin homeschooling with little ones who have never attended school; others are removing children from school after they've spent some time within the system. We'll cover some of the experiences all new homeschooling families have in common, then address the specific experiences each type of home-schooling family may encounter.

Inspiration for Continued Building

Finally, we offer a rebuttal to the criticism that books about home-schooling paint too rosy a picture. Scores of respondents shared the hurdles they faced in their first years so you'll know everything hasn't been all sunshine and lollipops. Your inspiration will come from their ability to solve their problems (and then—sorry, critics—their ability to move on with smiles on their faces!), as well as from the chapter devoted to "gold-medal hurdlers." These families very well may make your own experience seem like a walk in the park by comparison.

And That's Not All!

Appendix A contains resources from books to Web sites, from free-ware for kiddies to information on college admissions—everything you may need to get your homeschool building project started.

There's more. Scattered among the pages you'll find kid-tested, mother-approved learning activities that experienced homeschoolers remember as their favorites. Use their ideas in your own home-school, wholesale or as springboards to create new activities that become your family's favorites.

Sprinkled throughout you'll also find what may just be this book's most precious gems. Don't overlook the gifts that seasoned homeschoolers have presented by sharing their "What I wish some-one had told me during my first year of homeschooling." So much wisdom packed into brief, brilliant answers, they're sure to entertain and enlighten.

May your family's life together be graced with as much joy, laughter, love, and learning as have the lives of those who have gone before you.

The First Year
of Homeschooling
Your Child

1

THINKING ABOUT HOMESCHOOLING?

In This Chapter

✦ Getting what your child needs
from homeschooling

✦ What all types of homeschoolers have in common

© EyeWire

"I wish someone had told me that it is better to jump in, get started, and learn from your mistakes than to sit worrying and trying to decide what to do and how to do it perfectly."

—Karyn Scallorn, Stanley, Wisconsin

So you're thinking about homeschooling, are you? Finding more information than you could read in a month of rainy days? Afraid you'll ruin your child's mind forever if you don't homeschool exactly the right way?

Welcome to the growing number of parents who right now are facing the same feelings, thoughts, and fears. I know the odds are good that you're thinking about homeschooling solely in terms of how your child will be educated, and that's fine for now. I just want to give you Linda Dobson's homeschooling equivalent to the surgeon general's warnings: Homeschooling can—and most likely will—cause permanent changes to your family's priorities and lifestyle.

"Homeschooling will not just bring education back into the home," says homeschooling mom Laurae Lyster-Mensh, of Warrenton, Virginia, and she notes that new homeschoolers probably are not ready to hear this at first. "The whole experience of stepping out into the unknown requires such a feisty and independent nature that we are often far more in need of an ear than ready to listen in that first, exhilarating year."

> That homeschooling will change your lifestyle is as inevitable as night following day.

Even if you are the new homeschooler Laurae is talking about, I hope you can listen for just a moment anyway.

That homeschooling will change your lifestyle is as inevitable as night following day, and while you may not believe it right now, folks almost unanimously say that these changes are much more important benefits of homeschooling than the grandest of academic achievements.

Today chances are better than ever that you're considering homeschooling before you have children, while pregnant, or while still nursing your precious little one. Maybe your child's kindergarten registration deadline is approaching and it's decision time. You might be joining parents of teen children who are bored or turned off by attendance at school.

Yours could be a family spending so much time on homework that you figure you might as *well* be homeschooling. Or a family traveling a lot. Or a family simply concluding that you'd like to be there when your child reads his first sentences or to watch in wonder as a butterfly emerges from its cocoon.

Whatever reasons brought you to this point, they are good and valid ones, regardless of what others may say to the contrary. No one else on earth knows your child as well as you do, or cares as much about the experiences that fill her time. Preparing food for her mind and heart is no less worthy of your time and attention than preparing food for her body.

GETTING WHAT YOUR CHILD NEEDS FROM HOMESCHOOLING

CONSIDER THIS chapter a primer to help ensure that your family gets what you need from homeschooling, according to your motivation for doing so. While reasons for homeschooling are as wonderfully diverse as the families who practice it, they tend to fall into four roughly defined categories. Folks come to homeschooling proactively, reactively, reluctantly, or temporarily. We're about to take a closer look within these contexts at reasons to homeschool.

Experienced homeschoolers not only share the reasons their families came to homeschooling but also reveal the route their homeschooling took as a result of their reasons. In other words, you'll get a glimpse at how they shaped homeschooling to provide exactly what they needed.

If you realize from the get-go that homeschooling doesn't *have* to mean "school at home," if you understand that love for your child will see you through, and if you realize that homeschooling can fit a wide variety of family circumstances and needs, this crash course will get your wheels turning in the right direction and help you discover

LEARNING ACTIVITY

Begin with Baseball
(across the curriculum; early and middle years)

Each family member chooses a team at the beginning of baseball season. On a map you can find the teams' hometowns and all the places they will play that year. Figure out the distance between cities and the best route. Write letters to the teams and to some favorite players (they write back!). Read biographies of Babe Ruth, Hank Aaron, Mark McGwire, and more. Keep charts and graphs, do "baseball math," write news reports, and finish up by going to a game. This unit scores a home run.

—ANN CURRIE

early on how you, too, can get the most out of your homeschooling experience.

Homeschooling Proactively

Are you a parent who was just plain smitten with the idea of homeschooling from the moment you heard of it? For some, the idea of sharing learning by sharing life together just feels so right. Other parents find easy philosophical agreement with the notion that freedom and individuality are inherent in homeschooling, and they're eager to fashion a lifestyle that incorporates them. Still others find that they question the efficacy of the latest educational trends—such as increased standardized testing, school-to-work, and other outgrowths of Goals 2000—and want to remove their influence from their children's education.

"We first heard of homeschooling when our eldest was but a few months old," says homeschooling dad Jim Henderson. "We were quite intrigued. We had philosophical concerns about public school, including low standards and complete lack of parental control. When arbitrary age rules precluded our academically prepared son from entering public school kindergarten, we began homeschooling, half thinking that if it didn't work out, we'd just put him in kindergarten the next year. Homeschooling worked fabulously, though, and we'd never consider doing it any other way.

"We've since discovered additional benefits," Jim notes. "It's much more efficient, it's more tailored to the individual student, and it provides a consistent and flexible curriculum. As a military family we move every one to three years," he explains. "Having little concern for the quality of school districts in new places widens our assignment possibilities and removes one consideration when looking for a house. We don't have to worry about whether the new district is ahead of or behind a previous one, and we don't have to schedule our moves for summer or Christmas break."

It was through work as a librarian and tutor before the birth of her first child, in 1993, that Deb Baker found philosophical agreement with homeschooling. "I helped out at the library during the hectic after-school hours," says Deb. "So many of the children grumbled about homework, teachers, and other school-related topics. Studious children were sometimes teased and taunted. The girl I tutored in phonics understood it all, but she hated the repetitive work and was shy about singing the silly phonics song in class. I wondered if she'd end up like the kids I saw at the library, more interested in which kids were currently 'in' than in which books were a good read.

"Then a patron came in and asked about books on homeschooling," continues Deb. "I'd never heard of it, but while helping the patron, I grabbed a book, too, the Colfaxes' *Homeschooling for Excellence*. Everything in it rang true, and I wondered if homeschooling could prevent the indifference toward learning that I witnessed in the after-school crowd at the library."

Deb concludes, "When we talk about homeschooling today, we're amazed at how many people agree that they didn't learn much in

WHAT I WISH SOMEONE HAD TOLD ME DURING MY FIRST YEAR OF HOMESCHOOLING

First, I wish someone had explained that every day would not be perfect but that they all have value. Actually, I heard this basic message in a few different places, and read nearly the same words. But no one I knew seemed to experience any low moments, so even though I understood deep down that we would not have magical moments every day, I felt really bad when we had a less-than-stellar day.

I felt especially sensitive to this on days when I was finding myself trying to explain homeschooling to someone who didn't quite get it. Or after I read lots of anecdotes in books and magazines about amazing things that other homeschoolers are doing.

Lately I have tried to find something to cherish in every day, even if it is simply a hug or kiss from my kids. I have found that as I worry less about having picture-perfect days, I am more able to enjoy good days and live with bad ones. I am also better able to see that my kids are learning even when things don't go smoothly.

—DEB BAKER, BELLEVUE, WASHINGTON

school, that school teaches kids to pass the test and move on rather than explore and investigate and inquire, that school can be very damaging to tender emotions, and that it can harm healthy social development."

Your reasons to homeschool may be closer to those of Lynn Foster, who homeschools two "early years" sons in Smithville, Indiana, after having discovered homeschooling when her mother searched for an educational alternative for her younger sister. "Because my sister was having major health problems, because I had

had them in the past, and my son had started as well, I couldn't help but wonder whether Nicholas would be sick all the time in public school," says Lynn. "I began learning all I could and, in the learning, fell in love with the whole concept.

"I liked the idea of being with my kids," she continues, "being free to teach them Bible, being able to have a flexible schedule, learning as our interests prod us. We've homeschooled for over a year on a preschool level and love it! I have really gotten to *know* my sons and myself. I learn right along with my preschooler as I pick up on his enthusiasm and natural curiosity."

Washington's Sarah Rose explains how proactive reasons to homeschool can blend with reactive ones even as the reasons change with time and experience. Sarah was attracted to homeschooling because she had hated school until she went to college. She stresses, "The one reason we did *not* have was to isolate our children from the 'real world.'" She adds, "However, as the years went on, that reason came to be more important than we originally thought."

Sarah also wanted to share life's fun and "little things" with her own children. "I couldn't imagine missing the excitement of learning to read, write stories, do science experiments, go on field trips," she says.

There's more, though. Sarah continues: "Our oldest boy was six kinds of difficult, and I knew if we put him in school, he would be labeled and possibly go on to become *real* trouble. At the age of two, he spent two mornings a week in a parent co-op preschool, and it was way too much stimulation for him. For our family, homeschooling solved problems and provided me with a way to have a solid influence in my children's lives."

I admit I have a favorite proactive reason for homeschooling, and many respondents proved this reason is still alive and well. Susan, who homeschools with her family in Wisconsin, shares a story that proves homeschooling children are themselves frequently its best advertisements.

"We were often in the company of a family we enjoyed very much," she says. "The youngest child was about the same age as our

WHAT I WISH SOMEONE HAD TOLD ME DURING MY FIRST YEAR OF HOMESCHOOLING

I wish someone had told me that your first year of homeschooling is your hardest, no matter what. If you pull your children out of school, you and they have to get used to the differences, and you think, "Why didn't I homeschool from the beginning, then this would be so much easier?" If you start when your oldest is compulsory school age, you may be expecting, have a baby or a toddler, and you think, "How can I homeschool when I can't keep the little ones out of the dog food while I'm teaching?" The truth is that no matter your situation, the first year is a big challenge and a big change. You don't even know the questions to ask. It gets easier.

—SARAH ROSE, MOUNTLAKE TERRACE, WASHINGTON

oldest. It took me a while, but one day, out of the blue, I realized that the oldest child was 'school-aged' and not in school. When I asked his mother about this," Susan explains, "she told me about homeschooling. Because we really liked and respected this family, we took their ideas to heart and read the books they gently recommended. We were convinced immediately."

Homeschooling Reactively

Reasons to homeschool hit a high in the reactive category. School's "dumbed-down academics" were mentioned frequently, as was the opposite end of this spectrum: the inability of a classroom situation to address children's different learning styles, creating problems for those who don't learn in "the school way." Concerns about overt lessons—or covert insinuations—about values brought home many families, whether or not they were homeschooling for religious reasons. Parents made note of school bullying by both students and teachers, personality-altering peer dependence, disenchantment with learning, stress and resulting irritability, scheduling and transportation issues, and, of course, safety concerns.

"I was reacting to the overwhelming pressures on children these days—both morally and otherwise," explains Amy Cooper, from Wilmore, Kentucky. "We could probably be called 'reverse snobs,' in that we avoid—at all costs—the 'latest and greatest' in clothing, entertainment, and everything else."

Amy's children had experienced public and private school, and homeschooling seemed like a terrific idea for the children and the entire family. "Children are so impressionable, and it would be almost impossible to compete with the barrage of messages they receive in school and the world to conform to whatever happens to be 'in.' Frankly," Amy says, "our family can't afford that, financially or otherwise. Our children enjoy the simple life, and each other. School would not encourage either."

A part-time, work-at-home typist and editor, Barbara Paquin brought home two sons in the middle of second and fifth grades two-and-one-half years ago. The second grader, termed a "good reader" by his teacher, could not read simple four-letter words. Math was too easy, and his handwriting was growing worse. The fifth grader, "an introverted eccentric concrete random," according to his mom, was humiliated by teachers for not conforming. His sloppy work received A's, in part because it was often corrected by other students, "who made mistakes on nearly every paper they corrected." The teacher was still teaching phonics and handwriting to the fifth-grade class, because the students didn't have them down yet.

> The second grader, termed a "good reader" by his teacher, could not read simple four-letter words. Math was too easy, and his handwriting was growing worse.

LEARNING ACTIVITY

Extreme Chocolate (language arts/life skills; all ages)

My six year-old, Ali, loves cooking and constantly asks people for recipes. To encourage this, we are reading *The Chocolate Touch,* a fun children's novel about a boy who turns into chocolate everything his lips touch. She uses the computer to find simple chocolate recipes, her first Internet research experience. She is learning how to copy and paste text and how to save files to her own disk. We make the recipes and of course use fractions and math skills. We rate the dishes with three stars (good, very good, and great). When the chocolate collection is complete, we'll turn it into her very own recipe book. We also found out where chocolate is grown, its natural habitat, and where most of the world's chocolate farms are located.

—SUSAN BROWN, MUSCLE SHOALS, ALABAMA

While researching the learning disabilities she thought her second grader might have, Barbara happened on the idea of homeschooling, and she figured she couldn't do a worse job educating her own children. "One day I casually mentioned homeschooling to my fifth-grade son," recalls Barbara.

"Can I do that, too?" he asked immediately. The Paquin family has since concluded the second grader had no learning disabilities. Mom notes, "I spent a month teaching him phonics, and now he reads three years above grade level."

When Thyne Rutrough, of Richmond, Kentucky, figured out that day care for three children was costing more than she was making as a part-time university teacher, she became a stay-at-home mom. When given the choice, her oldest child, Abby, chose kindergarten attendance over homeschooling. Abby grew progressively more unhappy, though, after Christmas break, when the teacher began training children "to sit still and listen—otherwise they'll never be able to learn."

Having observed that Abby, like her two younger siblings, learns best when engaged in activity of her own choosing, the teacher's methods didn't make any sense to Thyne. "The last straw came when the kindergarten class spent the better part of a week taking standardized tests 'for practice,' since they'd have to take tests that really counted (in terms of the school's funding!) come *fourth* grade." Thyne continues, "Meanwhile, we'd planned to homeschool Isaac for kindergarten, so we just notified the school both children would be at home the following year."

Cindy Allas, of Fairfield, California, decided to keep her daughter out of school for first grade, because she felt Natalie wasn't ready. "In kindergarten Natalie needed extra help, which she didn't qualify for because there were too many others in the class who needed help more than she did," Cindy begins. "We put her back in first grade after a year off. She was placed in a kindergarten–first-grade combination class that only had two other girls in it (in addition to the boys). One of her girl 'friends' began saying hurtful, mean things to Natalie every day. I had Natalie write a letter to the teacher about this. When there was no response, Natalie came home."

Cindy's son, Travis, was still in the school's special education program when it was decided he would receive his work assignments from the regular teacher instead of the special education teacher. "We were concerned about this because in his special education past there had been many pockets of information not taught, and we worried that with the new arrangements Travis would be behind his classmates," says Cindy. Despite her concerns, the teachers made the change.

Travis's class had a test the first day, and the next day it was returned. All the special education children had failed. "The teacher

LEARNING ACTIVITY

Word Squares (reading; early and middle years)

My son loves secret codes and playing spy, so I explained that any written language, even plain old English, is a code for spoken language. Then I capitalized on his excitement with this game.

On squares of paper I write out a sentence or silly rhyme, one word to each square. (I try to draw rebuses on some squares to make it look more like a secret code.) I number the squares, then hide them around the house, telling him only how many squares he is looking for. His little sister is his assistant spy and helps search. While trying to determine how many squares are missing at any given time, he's doing the math. When he's found all the squares, he puts them in order on the kitchen table and reads one square at a time. Voilà, he's reading long sentences!

—DEB BAKER, BELLEVUE, WASHINGTON

gave ice pops to the children who had passed and lectured the others in front of their classmates that 'they needed to do better unless they wanted to be in resource for the rest of their lives.' My son," Cindy explains, "was in resource because of a diagnosed developmental disorder and had come further than expected in his education. I was furious; I pulled him out of school the next day."

Residing in a rural area, Diane Burton's children were spending one-and-one-half hours riding a school bus each day. The teacher in their Mays Landing, New Jersey, school also complained that Diane's six-year-old son needed to "slow down," as he would complete papers before she finished passing them out to the rest of the class. But the red flag went up for Diane when the same teacher started dropping hints about placing the boy on a prescription of Ritalin.

"Our life was full of stress and chaos," Diane says. "I never in my wildest dreams pictured myself as a homeschooling mom, but when I went to my first homeschooling seminar and heard the term 'dumbed-down,' I immediately thought of the teacher's comments about my son. I knew I was in the right place, because my child was expected to be 'dumbed down' so he could fit in and not be such a disturbance to his teacher or class."

Diane also has a ten-year-old daughter who, she observed, was quickly learning to do only what was expected of her and no more. "Another main concern was her homework. I felt like my children were growing up and away and I wasn't enjoying any of it. I hated the fights over homework," Diane recalls.

"I felt confused, frustrated, and overwhelmed that the teacher was telling her how to do subjects in school, and I was supposed to know what method was explained and help my child where they left off. The only problem is I wasn't present during the lesson, and asking a ten-year-old to explain how it was explained to her at school is next to impossible. If she knew, we wouldn't be having this conversation—or argument—in the first place!

"Public school was hurting my children more than helping them grow," Diane concludes. "Now I'm on the inside with my children, learning and sharing their day, instead of on the outside looking in and feeling very left out."

Homeschooling Reluctantly

You could very well be one of many parents reluctantly considering homeschooling. You're checking into it because your child is habitually truant. Maybe he dropped out of school or stands in jeopardy of dropping out. You may have a child who is angry, rapidly losing self-esteem, bored, or overwhelmed by textbook learning, or suffering

WHAT I WISH SOMEONE HAD TOLD ME DURING MY FIRST YEAR OF HOMESCHOOLING

I wish someone had told me you can't force a child to learn. My daughter was in kindergarten, and I was so afraid I wasn't going to do it right that I bought a very expensive, accredited curriculum that was approved by the state board of education. Everything was laid out for the teacher, including what to say to the child for each subject. This curriculum also required tests and samples of work to be mailed to a counselor every six weeks, whereupon they would grade and return them with a report card.

I forced my poor daughter to do every single bit of work that was required with this curriculum, whether she was ready for it or not, and nearly destroyed her

other problems you suspect are school-induced. (Obviously, parents of older children seem to fall into this category frequently.) Some parents reluctantly consider homeschooling because of a child's extended illness and/or need to recuperate. Many reluctant homeschoolers are just plain scared, for all the same reasons you can think of to be scared.

Rhonda Conner, of Rapid City, South Dakota, quit a full-time job to be with her son, because "he is my child, and it is my responsibility and pleasure to raise him," she says. "I started dreading the idea of his going to school when he was two years old, partly because of the schools themselves; they are horrible places."

With a son who Rhonda saw was ready for kindergarten academics at the age of four, the homeschooling option frightened her. "I was reluctant to become my child's academic teacher and had no idea how to do so," she explains. "I didn't have a choice, so I completely immersed myself in homeschooling and learned all I could.

desire to learn. If she was supposed to write an entire page of uppercase and low-ercase D's, then that's what she had to do—even if it took her two hours. Then, upon receiving her graded work back from the counselor, she would cry if she did not receive a smiley face or 100 percent on everything. I cannot tell you how miserable my daughter became and how frustrated I was—all for the sake of teaching her "the right way."

By the time I began homeschooling my son in his kindergarten year, my daughter was in the fourth grade and we had begun using unit studies. What a difference! I admit that teaching my son the basics was much more pleasurable, because I taught at his pace and there was no pressure to meet outside standards or requirements. Thankfully, my daughter has recovered from the tyrant that I was and is learning quite well, in spite of having been used as a guinea pig!

—TERRI BANDALOS, FREDERICK, MARYLAND

He will never go to public school. Today he finished kindergarten and will move on to first grade. I am so excited and so happy with the way he is enjoying life and learning so much."

Carol Moxley readily admits she came to homeschooling "kicking and screaming," as it was her husband's idea. "I was expecting our first child when he asked me to do some research and let him know what I found out. I decided to get right to it and stack up my arguments against homeschooling well before my due date."

> Many reluctant home-schoolers are just plain scared, for all the same reasons you can think of to be scared.

The soon-to-be mom collected every piece of information she could—which, eight years ago, didn't take nearly as long as it would today. Carol even visited a homeschooling support group "and convinced a couple of families to let me visit their homes during 'school time.' That was very eye-opening," reports Carol. "I talked with homeschooled kids and

WHAT I WISH SOMEONE HAD TOLD ME DURING MY FIRST YEAR OF HOMESCHOOLING

No matter how much information you have, I think everybody has to live through first-year uncertainties anyway. You're never sure you're doing it right, you think the school district is going to find a mistake in your paperwork and come after you, and it takes a while to find a format and schedule that work for you.

During her six-and-a-half years in school, Zoe was a very conscientious student, and her first act after leaving school was to make a formal schedule for herself. She insisted on allotting time for every subject she had studied in school. I at least convinced her that she wouldn't need as much time as school allowed for each one, since she was working on her own; so she allotted a half-hour for each

exchanged e-mail with one in particular, whose unschooling approach totally blew me away."

When it came time for Carol to assess her research, "held next to each other, my list of pros looked like Santa's list of good girls and boys, while my con list had but one item: 'I'm scared to death!'"

After eight years of homeschooling, Carol says, "I'm still scared. Two wonderful children later, I'm still learning more every day—mostly from my kids now. It terrifies me to see that the more I learn about learning, the more I realize how little I truly know." She continues, "It's scary how perceptive the children are, how passionate they can be in their pursuit of knowledge, how intense in their natural curiosity, how quickly they assimilate information, how astute their little minds. I also live with a daily fear that I'm not doing enough, yet I know in my heart that I'm doing what's best. There would be much more kicking and screaming involved were I to ever attempt to stop homeschooling."

subject, which still left her with half the day free. She quickly realized that she could cover way more material than she would have covered in school in way less time than even the half-hour she had thought it would take.

It only took a couple of weeks for her to abandon this effort altogether. One-and-one-half years later, as she recently stated it to one of her uncles, her philosophy is, "Spend as much time as possible on what you really enjoy and as little time as needed on all the other stuff." What she loves is reading, writing, listening to music, and learning the guitar. We do only enough intentional math, science, and social studies to satisfy reporting requirements (which is very little, as we can usually explain a lot of our unschooling activities as those subjects). As comfortable as she is with her life now, it took a long time to get there, even with lots of information and support.

—LINDA JORDAN, NOTTINGHAM, NEW HAMPSHIRE

When the Jordan family was forced to consider homeschooling, mom Barb worked full-time while Dad stayed home on disability. A twelve-year-old son remained in public school while Valerie, a sixteen-year-old daughter, came home to a dad not quite overjoyed with the idea. The county's high schools had switched to "the block system," in which classes were held for one-and-three-quarter hours with just four classes per day. (A block system approach is one of the educational trends of the day. The extended time for a subject is great in theory—and, indeed, appreciated in homeschooling, so that a child may study as long as interested or necessary—but hasn't seemed to translate well when applied to a "system.")

The trouble for the Jordans was that Valerie was bored. "Learning slowed down immensely," Barb explains, "because the class did not proceed until all had the gist of the class. A relatively bright child was allowed to sit and be bored for over an hour. Talk about 'dumbing down'!"

The school didn't offer accelerated or college preparatory classes. "She would have to get to a large metro area to take these classes, and this was not a desirable option at all," says Barb. "It was going to have to be homeschooling."

Kathy Triolo, of Fremont, California, was so reluctant to homeschool she spent years swinging back and forth through educational options, an increasingly common phenomenon in homeschooling families' histories. Her son, Chris, now thirteen years old, had a predetermined future, according to Kathy: "Private Catholic schools until college, at which point he would attend Stanford, Purdue, or a similar college," she says. Chris made it through Catholic kindergarten, then a private religious school halfway through third grade. After half a year of homeschooling, he was back to school, this time a private one for students with learning disabilities. Chris stayed here for two-and-one-half years—"struggling with the other kids and macho male teachers," Kathy notes—when he again came home for a full year of homeschooling. He recently finished seventh grade and will spend eighth grade, at least, at home too.

"We came to homeschooling because there was nothing else educationally available for Chris," Kathy explains. "He can't sit still in a classroom and has always had difficulties with lecture style learning. Having a high IQ while being emotionally young, he's the first one bullied in any situation with that potential."

She adds, "I *never* wanted to grow up and be a teacher. I'm only doing this because I love my son and want to provide an emotionally safe and educationally appropriate environment for him." She adds, "He'll still go to college, just not by the usual paths."

Homeschooling Temporarily

Some families see homeschooling as a temporary endeavor, merely a stopgap measure intended to help a child prepare for more schooling in the future, to provide a break from undue peer pressure, or even to give a younger child time to mature physically, mentally, or emotionally. Still other families are afraid to commit for the long haul, choosing instead a homeschooling trial period during which they will test everything from their ability to spend increased time with their children to their children's ability to learn without a classroom teacher's pointing every step of the way. While some families apply homeschooling as a problem solver and then move on, others appreciate the results of the trial period and, search as they may, can find no good reason to stop.

Believing that preschool attendance at age three would help Paul, her shy firstborn, Kristi Schrampfer, of Appleton, Wisconsin, didn't hesitate to enroll him. "By the time he reached kindergarten age," says Kristi, "we realized he was very bright. While he benefited from an excellent teacher, he remained quiet and reticent about change and new situations. We continued with public schooling until second grade."

> While some families apply homeschooling as a problem solver and then move on, others can find no good reason to stop.

Then Kristi heard about homeschooling, read up on the subject, and felt encouraged. "Even though he was reading at the fifth-grade level, Paul was so timid he could have easily fallen through the cracks at school. My husband, Kurt, was a bit difficult to convince, but, knowing my son as well as I did, I thought I could provide much more academic challenge," she says. "As he was always comfortable and secure in his home environment, it *seemed* an ideal situation. We decided on a one-year trial of homeschooling."

The Schrampfer family grew to include four children, all of whom now homeschool. "Our experiment was a success," Kristi affirms. "At the beginning I wondered about the social aspects of homeschooling, but with neighborhood friends, outside music lessons, and a homeschooling support group, our concerns disappeared. Now Paul and our other children are quite socially competent for children their age. They have relationships with children and adults of all ages, are respectful of their elders, and enjoy being with people. Best of all," she concludes, "they are *learning* and enjoying it."

Mary Mullenbach sought a temporary, yearlong homeschooling trial because she couldn't stand living on antacids any longer. After her family moved to Indiana, her oldest child, Tim, diagnosed with anxiety disorder, depression, and attention deficit hyperactivity disorder, was having trouble in second grade.

"He was stressed, not pleasant at home, and losing his innate love of learning," explains Mary. "Because he couldn't focus in school, he was bringing home two hours of homework—every day! He had no social life. I drilled him on homework constantly, even while he was in the shower, and had little to show for it."

In addition, the little boy was sent to the principal's office several times each week when, emotionally overwhelmed by the school experience, he had "outbursts." Tim's parents decided to bring him home for a year.

Now, *two* years later, Mary describes a "pleasant, well-educated boy. No one even believes me when I say we had problems. While his standardized test scores came in at the 52nd percentile two years ago, this year his core total was 86 percent. It has gone so well Tim's younger brother begged to come home at the end of last year. I'm more stretched than ever (although those homeschool moms teaching six children would probably laugh at me), but I love being with them and having all day long to share spiritual growth."

WHAT ALL TYPES OF HOME-SCHOOLERS HAVE IN COMMON

WHILE MANY respondents were kind enough to pin a label on their reasons to homeschool, by and large they revealed that their reasons rarely fit neatly into one category and often changed over time, most notably from reactive to proactive.

You, too, will likely find that your own reasons to consider homeschooling blur the boundaries between categories. With such a wide variety of reasons to homeschool to choose from, we need to look a little more deeply for what all these folks have in common. What is it about the act of homeschooling that draws people from every political, philosophical, economic, ethnic, religious, and geographic quarter?

+ They recognize a need in their children's lives—be it physical, mental, emotional, or spiritual—and homeschooling fills it.

+ They recognize a need in their family life—time to be together to share what they value, be it physical, mental, emotional, or spiritual—and homeschooling fills it.

Give some time to figuring out *why* you are thinking about homeschooling. Examine your reasons, because they'll provide a good starting point for "homeschooling as grand experiment."

2

HOMESCHOOLING AS GRAND EXPERIMENT

In This Chapter

✦ Put the scientist's skills to work

✦ Eliminating school attendance from your life

"I wish someone had told me to throw out all of my preconceived notions of what education is and to focus on the intricacies of my children's minds. When we first decided to homeschool, I never pondered what was driving my children to have problems in school and to dislike school. Once I considered how the children learn best, we did much better.

"To do this, we spent a lot of time that first year learning to love one another again and to work as a unit."

—Kate Montanio, Austin, Texas

*N*OW THAT YOU'VE examined your unique blend of reasons for starting to homeschool, it might help if you think of the experience as a grand experiment whose purpose is to find the way your individual child best goes about the act of learning.

PUT THE SCIENTIST'S SKILLS TO WORK

AS YOU conduct your experiment, it will help greatly to develop some of the skills that any good scientist brings to investigation. What are these traits, and how will they help your family?

An Open Mind

Be especially willing to consider learning beyond the narrow context of schooling, especially if you are turning to homeschooling because of school-induced problems. The best way to do this is to make learning about alternative educational approaches your new hobby. In this way you can open-mindedly consider and compare the many alternatives.

Observation Skills

Learn to really watch your children—preferably without interruption—as frequently as possible. This will help you discover their likes and dislikes, natural inclinations, and more. (To learn more about observing and using clues, see *Homeschooling the Early Years: Your Complete Guide to Successfully Homeschooling the 3- to 8-Year-Old Child* [Prima, 1999].) Quantum physics now verifies that the observer does indeed have an effect on the observed. For your homeschooling family, this creates a nice balance between head and heart, between science and art. It's a balance unachievable in any other educational situation. (More on balance in chapter 4.)

Curiosity

Get back in touch with the curiosity you had as a child. Dare to ask why, how, and what if. The more inspired the questions you ask, the more quickly and easily your answers will come.

Flexibility

An experiment means the results can be (and often are) a surprise. Limber up now so that when your experience blows your preconceived notions out of the water, you'll land on your feet, ready to move on to discover something new.

> It will help greatly to develop some of the skills that any good scientist brings to investigation.

Creativity

Great and useful inventions exist because folks either look to use existing materials in a brand-new way or within their minds conceive of something entirely new. Exercise your creativity muscles, and you'll be doing the same for your children's education.

Patience

I almost didn't add this to our list, as there is much misunderstanding regarding the patience required to be a homeschooling parent. The mistake is considering patience in terms of spending a lot of time with one's child, or getting him to sit still and read textbooks all day. Any effort to further develop patience is better spent on realizing that your experiment is a work in progress and will never be "finished," for just as you reach a comfortable fit between child and education, life will throw you another variable. Your child grows older, her interests change, your family moves, someone gets sick, you take a new or different job. The list is endless; thus so is your experiment.

ELIMINATING SCHOOL ATTENDANCE FROM YOUR LIFE

WHEN YOU first come to homeschooling, you discard something known—attendance in a school "system." Until this point the system has imposed on your family its own

+ schedule

+ organization

+ teaching method.

These requirements are placed on your family by compulsory school attendance laws, and by default they dictate a large portion of your family's lifestyle. Discard the notion of school attendance (a seed that has been planted deep in you, most especially if you yourself compulsorily attended school), and you create a huge void. Not only do you create a void, but you are now responsible for filling it!

Huge voids in life tend to scare us humans, especially when we begin with no clues as to how we will go about filling them. Could this be why some parents say the decision to homeschool feels like stepping off the side of a cliff?

Before you can make educated decisions about how you will fill the void, let's take a moment to examine what is suddenly missing when you do away with school attendance and how life-directing these few essential elements are.

Missing: School's Schedule

If your child has attended school, you're well aware of its schedule. How many family life decisions has this externally imposed schedule controlled?

+ How early your child must wake up in the morning

+ How late your child may stay up at night

SAMPLE OF GAMES HOMESCHOOLERS LIKE FOR FUN AND LEARNING

24	Hive Alive	Presto Change-o
Checkers	Labyrinth	Take Off
Chess	Learning Wrap-Ups	Tangrams
Chutes 'n' Ladders	Mancala	Set
Dominoes	Monopoly	Uno

- ✦ What time your child eats breakfast, lunch, dinner
- ✦ Number of hours available to your child to pursue personal interests
- ✦ Number of hours available to your child to contribute to household upkeep
- ✦ Your choice of family vacation dates and destinations determined by amount of time you're "allowed" to be away—and when
- ✦ Your ability to visit distant relatives and friends
- ✦ Time available to enjoy job or apprenticeship opportunities
- ✦ Time available to enjoy travel opportunities
- ✦ Attendance at performances, lectures, workshops, and classes limited because that would leave your child too tired for morning school attendance

Your first year of homeschooling, the grand experiment, will include just as much observation time as you can possibly devote. For practical purposes it does not matter whether that's half an hour or half a day at a time, as those with less daily time to observe will just take a little longer to figure things out. That's okay.

One of the pieces of information you'd like to gather from observation is your child's best time for learning. Have you ever known an adult who loves to get up before the sun, or one whom you'd call a night owl? When free to follow the sleep/awake/optimal time to learn patterns that come naturally to them, youngsters are as variable in their preferences as adults are.

Scientific research is finally catching up with this reality. In March 2000, *USA Today* reported on a National Sleep Foundation poll. Of 1,154 parents of teens, 36 percent reported that their adolescents were difficult to get to bed, and 38 percent said they were difficult to wake up in the morning.

> Your first year of home-schooling, the grand experiment, will include just as much observation time as you can possibly devote.

The problem may be "ill-timed" sleep. Sleep researcher Mary Carskadon, professor of psychiatry and human behavior and adjunct professor of psychology of E. P. Bradley Hospital and Brown University School of Medicine (Providence, Rhode Island), sees indications that teens are "biologically programmed to stay up later and wake up later than preteens." Children who don't get sleepy until midnight, then wake at six A.M. for school, are rising in the middle of their "biological night," according to Carskadon. Evidence suggests that teens' bodies are in "sleep mode" until about eight A.M, so Carskadon is encouraging junior and senior highs across the country to consider starting school later.

Experiment with different schedules to find your child's best times to sleep and to wake. (If you have more than one child, don't be at all surprised to find that your children are "opposites" in this regard.)

When should your child eat? The simple answer is "when he's hungry." Since hungry children aren't shy about sharing this knowledge, you shouldn't have to observe long to figure this one out.

Watch how long your child can entertain herself, following interests during time not occupied by other pursuits. Does she seem to need lots of time to complete activities? Does she seem to need less time for activity and more time interacting with you or others?

LEARNING ACTIVITY

For the Child Who's Gotta Move (spelling; middle years)

Say a spelling word, then bounce a ball to your child. Your child then bounces the ball as he says each letter in the word. When done, your child bounces the ball back to you as he says the word.

—TAMMY CUTSHAW, INDIANAPOLIS, INDIANA

If you feel that learning how to care for oneself and one's environment is important, watch for clues as to how much time your child has available to contribute to household upkeep then help him learn by doing. Not only does this help your child grow in responsibility toward eventual independence; it also goes a long way toward nourishing the spirit of "we're in this dance of life together" prevalent in so many homeschooling homes.

Do you happily choose to take your family vacations or visit loved ones during traditional travel peaks, sometimes competing with a peer in the office for rights to a popular vacation time, only to hit the highways when record numbers of cars are doing the same? Would you rather choose a time when popular destinations are much less crowded, and possibly discounted? Maybe you could even take a couple of extra days and head to a destination previously out of reach? Whenever and wherever you decide, now you don't have to spend your time on crowded highways if you don't want to.

Jobs, apprenticeships, and travel opportunities your child or family can easily and intelligently arrange for yourselves are important learning opportunities. Does the school schedule allow your child the chance to take advantage of them, or does school attendance shut the door on these opportunities? Should your child spend some time in these pursuits?

WHAT I WISH SOMEONE HAD TOLD ME DURING MY FIRST YEAR OF HOMESCHOOLING

I wish I'd known that you never have all the answers. Homeschooling is much more like parenting than it is like teaching school, and your child changes constantly—sometimes as a result of what you are doing and sometimes for unknown reasons. What worked on Tuesday won't work on Friday. What works with the first won't work with the second. What you think homeschooling will be like has as little resemblance to real homeschooling as that fantasy of nursing your newborn in a rocking chair has to colicky screaming at 3:00 A.M. Don't start that first year thinking you know what homeschooling is because you have a friend who homeschools. Learn everything you can and, as with parenting, let love take care of the unknowns.

—SARAH ROSE, MOUNTLAKE TERRACE, WASHINGTON

How about all those wonderful learning experiences available only through attendance at performances, lectures, and workshops not associated with school? Do you not even consider them now because participation would leave your child too tired for morning school attendance, or take him out of town on a compulsory attendance day or two? Could you choose to fill the void with these alternative approaches to education? You could—it's your choice now.

Missing: School's Organization

Every school has a curriculum, a course to follow, that dictates subjects of study. All children attending that school must sit in classes for all subjects in the lower grades, and some subjects are mandatory when the children reach high school. They must sit in these classes whether or not they are actually learning anything. Most high schools offer electives, or a menu of additional courses to follow, from which children can choose to fill in the remaining time they must be in school.

How has mandatory study shaped your child's learning life?

- ✦   Has it limited topics of study to only those the school offers?

- ✦   Has it turned off your child to the joy of learning?

- ✦   Has it presented to your child subjects he is not physically, mentally, or emotionally ready for?

- ✦   Has it addressed nonacademic subjects you would prefer to cover at home, or addressed these nonacademic subjects prematurely?

- ✦   Has its resultant homework crowded out the time necessary for your child to pursue a special interest?

- ✦   Have you seen indications of a special talent or gift wither with disuse?

Chances are, like many parents, you have simply accepted a mandatory course of study for your children. This course is so well-trodden that every child typically jumps right on to begin running in the same direction as everyone else. When you choose to homeschool, suddenly the course is missing, creating an exceptionally large void when thinking in terms of academic pursuits.

There are as many new courses of study to be laid out as there are people to conceive of them. What are your thoughts about an ideal situation? Are you imagining what learning organization would have been ideal for you if only you could have created it? If so, do you think your vision would be appropriate for your child? Appropriate if modified a bit? (Remember, schools today have problems that are both more numerous and dangerous than when you attended school.)

Remember, too, there is nothing magical about the curriculum your local school subscribes to. The school chose a curriculum it felt

WHAT I WISH SOMEONE HAD TOLD ME DURING MY FIRST YEAR OF HOMESCHOOLING

I wish someone had told me that it is okay to take time off during those more difficult moments. I felt like I needed to stick to a routine, feeling guilty every time I was ready to crumble and decided to skip school for a period of time. I took off the entire month of December but felt guilty. Now I know that it's okay to take a day, week, or more as needed; to recuperate, to get my head on straight, to give the kids a break—whatever is necessary to keep things rolling smoothly. I definitely needed to loosen up more and not worry so much about routines, schedules, and commitments but instead spend more time focusing on the truly important things, like quality time with my children, Bible studies, and plain old fun.

—STEPHANIE ROMERO, MILWAUKEE, WISCONSIN

would best meet the needs of the greatest percentage of a large number of children doing the same thing at the same time. Check with a different school and you'll get its version of curriculum which it, too, felt would do the best job for the majority of its students.

In homeschooling you aren't playing a numbers game with many students, hoping enough of them will get good scores on standardized tests, hoping it really is just a minority that falls through the cracks. Your curriculum can be custom-made for your child's needs that you are right now observing to discover. You can now organize learning, which is what a curriculum really does, based on your answers to the questions above.

With homeschooling, your child's curriculum can include subjects he's interested in, subjects that may not be available in a typical school curriculum. For example, did you know that by studying

Scout merit badges of interest, your child can quite nicely cover many curriculum basics? At the same time, your young Scout moves ever closer to requirements needed to advance in the program. (*Psst,* I just gave you your first clue as to why you hear about so many wonderful accomplishments by homeschooled children—they often busily kill two birds with one stone. Additionally, when approached this way, learning is not then separate from life.)

> There is nothing magical about the curriculum your local school subscribes to.

If your child has been experiencing problems with one subject, or a combination of subjects, chances are the bad experiences are overshadowing the good. It's hard to keep alive the joy of learning as its own reward under these circumstances. Your observations are revealing the way your child best goes about learning, and you will be able to apply this useful knowledge to choices about what subjects to study and how to study them.

Often, children have school problems because they are not physically, mentally, or emotionally ready for the curriculum's content. Besides laying out the subjects, a curriculum determines when a student learns a particular "piece" of the subject. Not only are homeschoolers discovering that children have their own internal timetables regarding physical, mental, and emotional maturity and ability; they know that if they watch for clues as part of daily life, their children reveal their personal readiness. This makes the timing of learning easier and more meaningful for the children.

Many of the topics today mandated for school curricula are nonacademic, and parents increasingly question whether and/or at what age schools should address moral values, sex, drugs, and other subjects they'd rather save for family discussions and, most especially, for when their children are older.

I can't count the numbers of families turning to homeschooling after observing that much family time—and too much of a child's free time—is devoted to after-school academics, better known as

LEARNING ACTIVITY

3-D Cell
(science; early and middle years)

My older son, Quinn, remembers making a cell as a great learning activity. When he was about eight years old, we studied living things, and he was to use whatever he wanted to create a 3-D representation of a cell. He decided on a zip-close plastic bag filled with a film container nucleus, and cotton balls, glitter, yarn scraps, macaroni, and more representing elements of the cell. It exceeded my expectations, and to this day he remembers a cell's structure.

—SARAH ROSE, MOUNTLAKE TERRACE, WASHINGTON

homework. Some families wonder what goes on in school if so much fundamental work needs to come home with their children.

The consequence of so much homework is that family time slides to the back burner, an unhealthy situation for any child. Additionally, a child who spends an inordinate amount of time within and outside school on work he "has" to get done has far too little time to discover or pursue personally meaningful learning. This too often leads to distaste or even a mental "shutdown" regarding learning in general, because it's all so overwhelming, joyless, and full of drudgery.

> The consequence of so much homework is that family time slides to the back burner, an unhealthy situation for any child.

Many homeschooling parents have discovered that it's those very topics that a child seems internally driven to learn about—be it sports, music, animals, or Pokémon—that nurture special talents and gifts. When talents and gifts are not exercised, when they are constantly set aside because someone else thinks other activities are more important, they wither. The cost of these lost gifts to our society, and to the happiness of individuals, can never be measured.

Missing: School's Teaching Method

Most of us have been there: sit quietly at your desk; pay attention to teacher; take notes; read textbook; study for test; take test; promptly forget anything you thought you knew.

Given that so many of us were exposed to this scenario around six hours each day, 180 days each year, for an average of twelve years, it's no surprise that this singular teaching method is so readily accepted and unquestioned. Not only does school attendance establish the subjects and types of material we can study (or not study) and when; it also utilizes a specific method in teaching these subjects. But is this the only method? Is it the best method?

How has school's teaching method impacted your child?

- ✦ Has your child experienced boredom associated with school attendance?
- ✦ Has your child "turned off" to learning anything outside a classroom or beyond school hours?
- ✦ Has your child been made to feel like a failure?
- ✦ Has your child been caused to feel superior to others?
- ✦ Does your child believe that the only valuable study is that done in school?
- ✦ Does your child believe he must have a teacher in order to learn something?
- ✦ Do you spend a lot of time at home teaching your child what you feel she should be learning at school?

Consider thirty randomly selected individuals receiving an unseen, rigid, one-size-fits-all baseball cap. You can expect the cap to be too big for one-third of the recipients, too small for another third of its recipients, and just right for the remaining third. Some of those for whom the cap is too big or small will make do and quietly suffer any resulting discomfort. For a much larger portion of those for whom the cap is too big or too small—almost two-thirds—the lack of fit will render the cap useless.

The school's teaching method was chosen to accommodate large numbers of students. Since it is basically a rigid, one-size-fits-all method, there are just as many for whom the learning method is a "misfit" as there are those who can't wear the one-size-fits-all baseball cap. If your child experiences boredom in school, chances are good that he's one of many who just can't make the method fit. Children for whom the classes move too quickly or too slowly are bored, and the minds of bored children wander. Children from both of these categories do well with homeschooling.

Some children get so turned off to learning when exposed to the wrong method, they resist learning *anything* once school is out for the day. Of course, we are always learning, whether consciously or not, but how many doors do children refuse to open because something sounds a little too much like the schooling they've learned to dislike?

An ill-fitting method can also leave its mark psychologically. Exposure to it can leave children feeling like failures, for no other reason than they don't best learn via the way schools teach. The resulting lack of self-esteem slowly but surely touches every aspect of life. Conversely—and equally harmful—children who excel with school's method quickly realize that others don't, and the grading system that accompanies the method "proves" them superior. Overinflated self-esteem can be as crippling as no self-esteem at all.

If not turning down learning opportunities because they sound like school, your child might be one who believes that learning can occur only in the trappings of school and that autonomous learning isn't possible, because a teacher is essential to the process. The school's method hammers this belief home because controlling the dispensation of knowledge is essential to its practices. After all, if

WHAT I WISH SOMEONE HAD TOLD ME DURING MY FIRST YEAR OF HOMESCHOOLING

I wish someone had warned me not to compare myself to other homeschool families. It is so easy to imagine that the people on those glossy magazine covers are oh-so-well-organized and have all their laundry folded (and probably starched and ironed too!) and that their children never misbehave! This can lead to a sense of failure when my family doesn't measure up. It wasn't until I met other homeschoolers in person that I realized that homeschool parents are real people and that homeschooled children don't automatically become perfectly behaved, brilliant, or willing to take the initiative on household chores.

—BETH NIEMAN, CARLSBAD, NEW MEXICO

children realized that they could learn anywhere, and further understood that anyone could share knowledge, why would they sit quietly in an institution all day?

Many families who turn to homeschooling note just how much teaching they'd previously been doing at home after their children had spent a full day in school. Some reported that their children hadn't been understanding the lessons taught, and others were flabbergasted that their children's teachers had sent home notes requesting that they teach skills once learned in school. Either way, the school's method was not working.

The Nature of Experimenting

When Thomas Edison set about to illuminate the world, he tried many methods that didn't succeed before he actually got a bulb to light up. It's important to understand that the nature of experimentation includes a good dose of frustration and constant "return to the drawing board."

It very well may have been in school that you learned that mistakes are bad, bad, bad. You were surrounded by same-aged peers just waiting for someone to stumble so they could have a good laugh. There is, however, a much more positive view of mistakes, as noted by nineteenth-century philosopher William James:

> Mistakes, obviously, show us what needs improving. Without mistakes, how would we know what we have to work on. . . . Mistakes are the portals of discovery.

Accept from the beginning that you will make mistakes within your homeschooling experiment; no one is promising you a rose garden. Undoubtedly you'll try a resource or learning method that just doesn't turn on the light of understanding for your child. Rather than immediately assume that one or both of you aren't cut out for homeschooling, use the failed portion of your experiment as the learning opportunity it represents.

> Accept from the beginning that you will make mistakes within your homeschooling experiment.

Because you'll be working so closely with your child, you will see failures quickly. No doubt there will be times that you feel like someone is shining one of Edison's lights upon it!

"I wish someone had told me that no matter how messed up your first year of homeschooling seems, it is the best growing experience you and your children will ever have," explains Florida's Terri Brennan upon completing her own first year. "We've gone from being formal to unschooling, unit studies to eclectic. [See chapter 5 for more on these approaches to homeschooling.] There were times I thought I had damaged my children permanently," says Terri, "but looking back, I see how much we learned from trial and error. I found out that I enjoy my children

WHAT I WISH SOMEONE HAD TOLD ME DURING MY FIRST YEAR OF HOMESCHOOLING

If someone had said, "What you do does not matter as much as the spirit in which you do it," I would have saved time and energy. Rather than trying to outschool the schools in my daughter's first-grade year, I would have spent more time laughing and playing with her, like we do now. My wish for other first-year homeschoolers is that they enjoy being with each other and learning together. To our family, that is the core of homeschooling.

—LYNNE LISA, OAKLAND, NEW JERSEY

much more when I let them tell me how they want to learn. My children have discovered that learning is fun and exciting."

Quick recognition leads to quick resolution. Learn the lesson, adjust your experiment, and, like Edison, try, try again.

3

HOMESCHOOLING NUTS AND

BOLTS FOR EVERY PARENT

"I wish someone had told me how to roll with the punches and use them to teach important lessons about life. In our first year of home-schooling, I would have hysterically squished the small snake that one day managed to find its way into our bathroom from the crawl space below. Now we gather it up in a bucket and research what kind of snake it is and what habitat is best. In our first year, if my son brought home a 'treasure' from the woods, I would throw it out as soon as I could get away with it, because it brought clutter and mess into the house. Now we sit down and really look at the treasure, sometimes taking all day to research and find out more about it."

—Cindy Riley, Norwalk, Ohio

*N*OW THAT YOU know the reasons homeschooling often appears a "scary" proposition and you are thinking about how you will fill the voids in schedule, organization, and planning, let's move on to the nuts and bolts of homeschooling so that you can get started on your homeschooling journey as soon as possible.

STEP NUMBER ONE: UNDERSTAND THERE IS NO STEP NUMBER ONE

NEW HOMESCHOOLING families read a book, attend a conference, or examine how a friend's family homeschools. They often then mistakenly assume that this is the way to homeschool—and only this way. If they stop here, in a very real sense these families are simply exchanging the externally imposed agenda of schooling for another externally imposed agenda, never experimenting or doing the work necessary to help homeschooling fill their own children's needs.

"I wish someone had told me not to be afraid to dream," says Jane Valencia, of Vashon, Washington. Jane has been homeschooling all along with her daughter, Amri, and they just completed their "official" kindergarten year.

"I wish I'd been told to imagine my ideal homeschooling situation and then to just go ahead and try to make it come true. I spent most of the year (or so it seems) imagining what I would do next year," Jane explains. "I figured I'd see if I could work out a co-op situation or friendships where Amri could be away part of the time. She was enrolled part-time in a small home-based kindergarten, and toward the end of our first year, I finally started getting to know local homeschoolers. Now I have more opportunities for co-ops and group learning than we dare take up. I realize that all I needed to do was speak up, to say, 'This is what I'm looking for—is anyone doing

WHAT I WISH SOMEONE HAD TOLD ME DURING MY FIRST YEAR OF HOMESCHOOLING

I get ideas from the Internet, cheap workbooks at Costco, and television shows like *Little Bear* and *The Magic Schoolbus*. I'm overwhelmed with excellent catalogs, curriculum fairs, newsletters, and support groups. I am welcomed into businesses and functions for field trips and have received unflagging support from my family and my husband's family. If I had known all of this a few years ago, my husband wouldn't have had to try so hard to talk me into homeschooling.

—JENNIFER L. YOAKUM, PROSSER, WASHINGTON

this already? If not, does anyone want to start this activity with me?' In other words, all I needed to do was be brave!"

There never has been and never will be one right way to homeschool. That there is no step number one may seem intimidating at first, but it's a key element of homeschooling success. The "step 1, step 2" approach that some families initially learned about may have worked wonderfully for the family that created it. Those families, however, may have turned to homeschooling for very different reasons than you did. Their children's needs may have been different than yours. Your family will be unique in some or many ways, and your homeschooling should be too.

> There never has been and never will be one right way to homeschool.

Margaret Simms, a homeschooling mom in Ontario, makes this notion clear when she says she wishes someone had told her—simply—"begin where you are." (More on this in chapter 5.)

WHAT I WISH SOMEONE HAD TOLD ME DURING MY FIRST YEAR OF HOMESCHOOLING

I sincerely wish that during our first year of homeschooling I possessed more insight about the act as a celebration of learning and bonding. I started out determined to be the "best" and to "stay focused" on scheduled academics. What we found was that this attitude only results in the same unnecessary stress that the public schools place on students and parents alike. When you take the time to focus on your child's individual needs and interests, it isn't necessary to be rigid. After all, you should be focused on enjoying your learning experiences together. Long lunch hours, chats, and even days off to go to the park or a local field trip should be an integral part of the process. I wish I had been told to "lighten up" rather than encouraged to teach and test mundanely."

—PATTI ANDERSON

"Focusing on the present, instead of worrying about the future, is so clearly the way to put one's talents to the best and fullest use," Margaret tells us. "Worrying never achieved anything and, unfortunately, it's contagious. If a child is already having difficulty learning something, worry only makes it harder."

So what's a new homeschooling parent to do? "Ban the word 'should' from your thoughts and words," Margaret advises. "This doesn't mean not having goals but, rather, disallowing the distractions of an artificial timetable and other people's opinions in your lives. I've found it more useful to reflect about how far we've come than to worry about how far we have to go. If I remember to live fully and happily in the present, the whole family is happier, and learning flows easily and naturally."

BECOME AN AUTODIDACT; OR, HOW TO BE YOUR OWN GUINEA PIG

ANY GRAND experiment needs a guinea pig, and at the starting gate of homeschooling, that's you! What better way to get a feel for independent education than for you to educate yourself about homeschooling? Call it your "immersion" experience, as you become an autodidact, or "a person who teaches herself."

Plan to get "enough" preliminary information without getting buried in and confused by it. This means reviewing enough sources so that you're not taking one person's point of view as the last word on homeschooling, but not so many that your kindergartner becomes a high school freshman before you feel you're ready to start. No matter whether you've made a last-minute decision not to send your angel off to kindergarten next week, or you're expecting your first baby at Christmas, or your teen is at risk of being expelled, here are three leads to get you to useful homeschooling information quickly.

The Internet and E-Mail

Many trend analysts predict that online learning programs will create another explosion in the number of families turning to homeschooling. (More on using your computer for academics in chapters 5 and 6.) They're probably right, but this gives short shrift to the many other ways in which homeschooling families are utilizing the power of the Internet.

Information sharing occurs at speeds unthinkable just a few short years ago. Today the Internet holds new and archived articles from every major newspaper in the world—and from many not-so-major papers as well. You'll find a wide array of magazine articles online, too, but there's also something much better: An untold number

LEARNING ACTIVITY

How Does Your Garden Grow?
(science/home economics; preschool and early years)

When I worried that my four-and-a-half-year-old kindergartner and two-and-a-half-year-old tag-along sister weren't covering any "formal" science, I realized how much they both learn by helping in the garden (by necessity, a very small one along with a few fruit trees). We learn about composting and life cycle of plants. We learn measurement and spacing. If you "dump" too many seeds in too little space, none grow. How many veggies can we squeeze into our small spot? Can we fudge on spacing? We learn about climate and zones. What varieties of seeds work best in our area? What birds and bugs come share our garden? It's almost endless.

—LORI KEPHART, LAS VEGAS, NEVADA

of Web sites providing information about homeschooling are created by the experts: homeschooling parents.

These Web sites wear many faces. Some showcase sophisticated businesses; others reveal cottage industries that involve the efforts of entire homeschooling families. Some hold general knowledge; others specialize in one aspect of homeschooling, such as conference announcements, book reviews, one homeschooling approach, or state-specific information. Some national sites, such as the National Home Education Network, spare no energy to present what you may need; others showcase one family's daily activities, travels, artwork, or musings.

Networking with other homeschoolers, too, is easier than ever. Looking to meet local friends with whom to share homeschooling?

Put out a call on a homeschooling e-mail list or bulletin board, and oftentimes another family within driving distance will pop in and say hello. Have questions unique to homeschooling parents who work full-time? Join the e-mail list focused on this aspect. Looking for a different math book? Ask others what they use. And where else would you go except to the e-mail list Unschooling-dotcom to see this sort of exchange:

> Hello, all. I'm unschooling three of my four boys. My youngest is five, so he isn't officially schooling yet. This was my first year and I loved it. I was wondering if anyone on this list lives near Youngstown, Ohio. I get my assessment tomorrow, and I am nervous about it because my children did more computer work and hands-on things. I now have a camera and video camera to use, so I guess this will help for next year. How does everyone keep track of all the projects and such? Thanks so much for answers to these questions.

> Hi. I'm from Ohio—about 40 miles east of Columbus. A lot of the people on this list will probably not know what you are talking about regarding assessments, as not every state makes people jump through hoops as we have to. I think it depends on who you have doing the assessment—ours have been done by a lady who is unschool friendly. All we really did was talk. She did look over some of the papers I brought along; mostly, I guess, they just sparked discussion of some of the things we had done over the year. I was really nervous about it the first time, and made the kids do worksheets and stuff so we would have something for the portfolio, but that was not needed. It turned out to be a really relaxed conversation with a nice lady who reassured me that yes, we are learning, we have made the right choice, I am doing enough. So, after that, I "deschooled" even more!   —Cathie

Your Local Library

I've always viewed libraries as our society's last bastion of free inquiry and, as such, our starting point in creating a learning vision that draws from and gives back to an entire community, young and old alike. The library is the "happenin' place" for homeschoolers. Where else can you find so much to learn about at such reasonable prices?

See what's on the shelves about homeschooling. Don't forget to check for magazines, then head for the vertical file, where a local or state support group may have donated introductory homeschooling information. Head over to the computer and see what the other libraries within your interlibrary loan program make available. Check out as much as you think you can read during the loan period.

If you don't have a computer at home through which to access the Internet and/or an e-mail account, your library can help. Most offer Internet access on public-use computers. If you open up a free e-mail account with services such as Yahoo, hotmail, or Juno, you can get your e-mail, too, during a trip to the library. (Double-check with your library before opening an e-mail account, though, as your library may have a policy forbidding such use of its computers.)

> No one can give you the lowdown on anticipating your relationship with your local school district faster than your most local homeschoolers.

Local Support Group

One thing you usually have in common with homeschoolers at the local level is the school district in which you reside (or at least people who know others in your school district). While laws and regulations about homeschooling originate at the state level (more about legalities coming up soon), an interesting quirk is how differently they may be interpreted at the school-district level. No one can give you the lowdown on anticipating your relationship with your local school district faster than your most local homeschoolers.

Among them you'll also find folks who will send you home with a bagful of resources so you may learn more than what a catalog description can share. Through local support groups you'll connect to

THE HOMESCHOOLING LAW'S "BUSYWORK"

The only problem we have—and it's not a problem, just an annoyance—is complying with the homeschooling laws. It amounts to a bunch of busywork for us that wastes our time and takes us away from real learning.

—MARJORIE LIESE, PITTSBURGH, PENNSYLVANIA

information about group activities, field trips, classes, speakers, camp-outs, socializing (for both you and your child), and more. That's where you will find the folks whom you can meet for a cup of tea to celebrate, commiserate, cry, rave, laugh, and share.

Start Putting Together an Educational Philosophy

What is it you hope your child's valuable time and learning will provide him with? This is your educational philosophy. If your child is old enough, make sure he, too, considers this. Thinking through an educational philosophy can shed valuable light on the best schedule, approach, and method for you. Indeed, formal or informal, on paper or in your head, an educational philosophy can be a beacon, especially during those times you feel you're lost.

Just two quick tips should help get your wheels turning:

✦ Begin with the end in mind. This was the theme of an Unschoolers Network conference a few years ago, and the idea has stuck. Knowing what you want your homeschooling to accomplish limits right off the bat the number of resources you'll have to consider, saving you time and money. More important, it can rapidly free you to jump beyond "how school is done" to "how you should go about education" to get to the end you have in mind.

✦ Remain open to change as you learn and grow. If you write down your educational philosophy, do so with a pencil. You do not know today everything you will know tomorrow. The best educational philosophy is one you revisit often and one fluid enough to incorporate all the wonderful things that you and your child will discover about learning—and yourselves.

Here's how LeAnn of St. Cloud, Florida, went about the process during her first year of homeschooling, learning a most valuable lesson at a time when others might have thrown in the homeschooling towel.

"What a year of growth for me!" LeAnn began when asked why her family is on the road it's on. "We started the year set up to do 'school at home,' because I didn't know any other way. Almost immediately, things seemed to drag. Work didn't get done, and the kids bickered with each other and competed for my attention," LeAnn explains.

Instead of quitting, LeAnn reviewed the reasons she wanted to homeschool. "I wanted the children to learn how to teach themselves, to lead to lifetime learning—and it wasn't happening," she says. "I started to think about how I learn things as an adult. If I have an educational need, I get a book and read what I need to know or get the needed materials and mess with them until I succeed." With this knowledge, LeAnn "stripped down my concept of a good education." She concluded that a well-educated person . . .

✦ can obtain information he requires (through knowing how to read well and knowing where and how to find needed information)

✦ can communicate effectively with others both orally and in writing

WHAT I WISH SOMEONE HAD TOLD ME DURING MY FIRST YEAR OF HOMESCHOOLING

I wish someone had told me you don't have to do everything all at once. When we first started homeschooling, I was so concerned that my children learn everything that they would learn in school so that they didn't "fall behind." After a few years of this, I realized they were learning an incredible number of things that were equipping them for adulthood, even though these things didn't fit under a subject heading that the state wanted us to cover. During the first year, we did every page of our purchased curriculum—and then some. The next few years, we used the curriculum as a rough guide, leaving out probably half of it while supplementing with other materials. Now, as teenagers, most of their learning is through reading.

—MARJORIE LIESE, PITTSBURGH, PENNSYLVANIA

✦ has a broad general knowledge base from which he can draw as needed

✦ possesses the math knowledge required for daily life, as well as an awareness, if not a working knowledge, of the intricate bonds between higher math and the workings of the universe

✦ has a love of learning that will facilitate education throughout the lifetime.

"With this," LeAnn concludes, "we've become eclectic homeschoolers. I have no doubt that my philosophy will continue to emerge over time, but I like what I see developing in my children. I really do believe that the final result will be well-educated, confident, happy, productive individuals."

Heard about the Laws in Your State?

Chances are that it's the legal nut and bolt—and the fears surrounding it—that will give you great impetus to start researching homeschooling. While it's ludicrous that in the twenty-first century an American could potentially go to jail or lose custody of her children for taking responsibility for their education, these extreme scenarios still play out on occasion.

Much closer to home for you as a beginner is to find out what regulations or laws your state sets forth for homeschoolers. You can accomplish this via any of the three avenues mentioned above—the Internet, a local support group, or your library. From one of these sources, get a copy of the law or regulation as written, not someone else's interpretation of it. Read it, then question experienced homeschoolers about it until you feel that you comfortably understand everything it says. There are three important reasons to take this step.

1. Only you can decide if you will comply with the law or not. In rare cases a law will have a requirement that you are unable to comply with. More often, noncompliance is a result of philosophical disagreement with requirements such as providing grades, administering standardized tests, submitting Individual Educational Programs for special-needs children, or similar issues.

2. If you plan to comply, the law lays out exactly what is expected of you. You can decide how you will go about gathering what you need, and stop worrying about those things you don't need to do.

3. Knowing the law prevents you from being coerced into providing any more information or paperwork than is expressly required. Don't put it past any school official to ask for more information than is legally permissible. If such a request is made of you, ask the district to send you a letter, and answer in kind. Keep this correspondence in writing to furnish proof of what has tran-

LEARNING ACTIVITY

Creek Offerings (across the curriculum; early years)

My five-year-old son, Mason, thrives on "creek time" when we pack a few snacks, magnifying glass, plain white paper, a few pens, and head for a nearby creek. On a recent trip I was struck by the desire to draw the berry bushes hanging over the creek and sketched. Mason watched how a leaf repeatedly cycled through a current which first pushed it down and away and then, at the surface, back toward the falling water that had pushed it down in the first place; picked up bugs to let them walk on his hand (which he would not have done even a month before); observed and wondered why water skeeters make shadows on the creek floor that barely show their bodies but do show a symmetrical pattern of circles; discovered a green bug that seemed metallic; touched a banana slug; navigated across the creek without falling in; watched Mom draw; tried to get as close as possible to birds. The experience included physics observation, pushing his own boundaries, physical education, observation of reflection, refraction, and shadow, patience and self-control. He remembered what he saw and did, asking questions in the moment and long after.

—ERIKA LEONARD HOLMES, RICHMOND, CALIFORNIA

spired in a way phone conversations can't. Ask the school personnel to cite the law that gives them the ability to request this. Chances are good you won't hear back, and you just may have inspired them to read the homeschooling law for the first time! If they persist, a local attorney who knows how to look up education law is usually all you need to resolve differences.

Providing too much information to school personnel sets a dangerous precedent: If given the information by one family, administrators become more inclined to ask it of others. New homeschoolers, proud and eager to share all their wonderful educational activities, are understandably prone to "overreporting." Control the urge and save your excitement for reporting to your mother-in-law.

> Knowing the law prevents you from being coerced into providing any more information or paperwork than is expressly required.

Many state laws sound worse than they are in practice, and a local support group can tell you how it plays out. "I wish that someone had told me not to take the first year so seriously," Vickie Heffner explains about laws. "Unfortunately we were in a state that required documentation, and I worried about doing enough or doing the right things. We are now in a state that requires minimum interference with homeschooling," says the Woodland Park, Colorado, resident, "and my second daughter is reaping the benefits of that, especially considering that she is a late reader and can't sit still very long. We were lucky enough to unschool her and not worry about state requirements."

ASSESSING YOUR CHILD'S PROGRESS

THERE ARE two reasons you might choose to administer standardized tests to your homeschooled children:

- ✦ to comply with a legal requirement to do so
- ✦ to satisfy your own curiosity about your child's yearly academic progress

If the former is your situation, your choice is to decide whether or not you will comply. If the latter is the case, you have a lot more wiggle room. Remember, standardized tests were conceived to apply to standardized education (and for businesses to make money, but

LEARNING ACTIVITY

Haiku Everywhere (language arts; middle years)

When I invited my son, Julian, to go to the beach and write poetry with me, he was so startled he accepted. I taught him about haiku because of several advantages. It doesn't require rhyming, which leads to much bad poetry because of its difficulty. Haiku is short, thus less intimidating. It has a precise structure, so even when written by beginners, it looks and sounds like poetry. We continued writing poetry in small cafes, outside, even at McDonald's. There seemed to be two keys: first, it was something we did together—we both wrote. Second, it wasn't sitting at the kitchen table, which was too much like school, or even in our house, which was too much like homework. Writing is still not his favorite thing to do, but it's among the activities he finds most rewarding.

—KATHRYN BAPTISTA, SALEM, MASSACHUSETTS

that's another story). They are tools for classrooms where knowledge of the children's abilities progressively dwindles as one moves through the ranks of the system, from teacher to administration to the state. How else, other than by giving the same test to all pupils in the same grade, can the state education department figure out how its schools are doing?

The scenario is different at home. You are watching (or helping to create) every learning opportunity in which your child engages. You are aware of every book read, every art project created, every word penned, every arithmetic problem solved. In other words, you observe progress on a daily, even minute-by-minute, basis. Under these circumstances it is wise to at least examine the need for a year-end assessment.

WEIRDEST HOMESCHOOLING LAWS

Here, in no particular order of weirdness, are some odd rules and regulations:

✦   Tennessee's kindergarten law. Compulsory-attendance ages are from six to seventeen, yet if you have entered your five-year-old into any public, private, or parochial school for more than six weeks, he or she, too, is subject to the compulsory-attendance laws.

✦   New Jersey is unique in requiring the subject sexual assault prevention.

✦   New York requires the subjects substance abuse and traffic safety.

✦   Three of Illinois' required subjects are honesty, justice, and kindness.

✦   Mississippi wants the social security numbers of all homeschooled children (a violation of the Federal Privacy Act of 1974).

✦   Colorado has the lowest "acceptable" standardized testing scores: 13th percentile. (Statistically you would score 23rd percentile by drawing pretty pictures with the fill-in-the-dots.)

✦   In Iowa, parents of special-education students must attend a lecture about the hazards of withdrawing their children from a special-education program.

✦   The only people in Nebraska who may legally homeschool are those for whom schooling violates a sincerely held religious belief or those who can't abide the degree to which schooling interferes with the decisions of the parents in directing their child's education.

✦   Colorado has mandatory standardized testing for eleventh graders, who are usually beyond the compulsory attendance age of 16.

✦   In Pennsylvania, parents must submit a notarized statement certifying that no adult in the home has been convicted of criminal homicide, aggravated assault, kidnapping, unlawful restraint, rape, statutory rape, involuntary deviate sexual intercourse, indecent assault, indecent exposure, concealing the death of a child born out of wedlock, endangering the welfare of children, dealing in infant children, prostitution and related offenses, a felony offense related to obscene and other sexual materials, corruption of minors, or sexual abuse of children—within the past five years.

+ Pennsylvania medical requirements are unique to the state:

all grades—annual height, weight, and vision screening

kindergarten—dental exam, medical exam, and TB test

first grade—hearing test

second grade—hearing test

third grade—hearing test and dental exam

sixth grade—medical exam (includes gynecological exam for girls) and scoliosis testing

seventh grade—hearing test, scoliosis testing, and dental exam

ninth grade—TB test

eleventh grade—medical exam (gynecological exam for girls) and hearing test

+ In South Dakota you may homeschool no more than twenty-two children.

+ Compulsory attendance in Montana ends with eighth-grade graduation.

+ Those who join certain homeschool support groups in South Carolina are exempt from state homeschool regulations.

+ Only those homeschooling under a religious organization may homeschool in Alabama.

+ In Massachusetts, "good behavior" is a required subject.

—KATHLEEN IUZZOLINO, COHOST, KALEIDOSCAPES
DISCUSSION BOARD FOR HOME EDUCATORS

Typical school assessment also includes those pop quizzes, chapter tests, and semester exams you can't forget. If you're using a purchased or online curriculum, and especially if you're using a provider's service to maintain an academic paper trail for your child (attendance, test scores, transcript), these activities are likely necessary. If you are using another homeschooling approach, however, choice exists.

> How else, other than by giving the same test to all pupils in the same grade, can the state education department figure out how its schools are doing?

There are some parents who, after careful consideration of assessment needs, determine that test results are necessary, if only for personal satisfaction, to silence a skeptical relative or even to prove academic success to the homeschooling child. Go for it if you feel compelled to. Just don't let tests become the focus of learning (your child could stay in school and do that). If testing ever becomes a point of contention between you and your child, remember you have options.

FINDING LEARNING MATERIALS

"I REALLY wish someone had told me not to invest so much money in curriculum our first year out," reports Stephanie Smith of Fort Worth, Texas, on the subject of learning materials. "I bought books, workbooks, and manipulatives for every subject. A few of the things I bought never even got used—what a waste of money!"

Many questionnaire respondents loudly bemoaned those typically large first-year investments in learning materials. You start out with good intentions, wanting nothing but the best for your children, only to discover that expensive doesn't necessarily mean best. It's akin to those who make a New Year resolution to lose fifty pounds, then go out and buy a zillion dollars' worth of exercise

WHAT I WISH SOMEONE HAD TOLD ME DURING MY FIRST YEAR OF HOMESCHOOLING

I wish someone had told me how much homeschooling information is available online. There are articles on starting out, different approaches, your state's requirements, types of curriculum, and Web sites devoted to swapping used curriculum. I went crazy buying anything and everything that fell within my child's age range, so I wish someone had warned me not to over-buy. Instead, take time to research what's out there, and try to examine things in person instead of ordering sight unseen. Once you've decided on a certain curriculum or program, try to buy things used. This can save tons of money. Find used stuff online, at garage sales, and at your support group's book sales.

—AMY KAGEY, TOLEDO, OHIO

equipment. As the exerciser discovers that a brisk walk in the fresh air contributes just as much to the desired outcome and costs nothing, you, too, may find that some of the best learning material is free—and makes a larger contribution to health and happiness.

You won't fall into the "break the bank with homeschooling" trap if you take the time to check out these free and low-cost materials sources, available no matter where you live:

- ✦ your library and its interlibrary loan participants
- ✦ nearby college and university libraries
- ✦ yard sales and library book sales
- ✦ online used-curriculum sales
- ✦ Internet-based materials for the cost of your connection

WHAT YOU NEED TO TEACH YOUR OWN CHILDREN

We can sum up very quickly what people need to teach their own children. First of all, they have to like them, enjoy their company, their physical presence, their energy, foolishness, and passion. They have to enjoy all their questions, and enjoy equally trying to answer those questions. They have to think of their children as friends, indeed very close friends, have to feel happier when near and miss them when they are away. They have to trust them as people, respect their fragile dignity, treat them with courtesy, take them seriously. They have to feel in their own hearts some of their children's wonder, curiosity, and excitement about the world. And they have to have enough confidence in themselves, skepticism about experts, and willingness to be different from most people, to take on themselves the responsibility for their children's learning. But that is about all the parents need. Perhaps only a minority of parents has these qualities. Certainly some have more than others. Many will gain more as they know their children better; most of the people who have been teaching their children at home say that it has made them like them more, not less. In any case, these are not qualities that can be taught or learned in school, or measured with a test, or certified with a piece of paper.

—JOHN HOLT, IN *TEACH YOUR OWN*

+ local support-group members whose children have outgrown or otherwise don't use materials anymore who will barter, trade, or sell cheaply

+ educational material requests for holiday and birthday gifts.

With three years of experience under her belt, Stephanie now purchases a good math text and uses a lot of unit studies to cover a wide range of topics. "I've discovered my librarian is my best friend," she adds. "We also found out that the Internet opens up whole new ways of learning and researching."

Author's note: Now that you've been encouraged to take it easy on first-year purchases, I can tell you that you'll find material sources in appendix A. We're about to discover more about ways of learning right now.

4

SEE, HEAR, TOUCH?
Catering to Your Child's Learning Style

In This Chapter

✦ First, a word about signs of readiness in little folks

✦ Gardner's theory of multiple intelligences

✦ The learning-style profile

✦ Developing your A-OK frame of heart

"My once-eager oldest son became a reluctant reader and writer in school. He was an experiential, hands-on learner and the school's methods were all mathematical/logical and linguistic. He did not excel enough to be in the more stimulating academically gifted activities, and he did not do poorly enough to qualify for re-mediation. I spent so much time doing 'enrichment' things with him after school that I finally decided it would be easier to do it myself and not have to work with him when he was so tired out from school."

—Jeanne Faulconer, Mooresville, North Carolina

*T*HE CLUES YOU are gathering about how your children learn best will guide many decisions related to getting started in homeschooling, including those related to schedule, organization, and method. As promised in chapter 2, you're about to look a little more closely at learning styles. Knowledge of the different ways in which human beings go about learning will help you put your clues to best use.

As books and magazine articles about learning styles hit the market, each categorizes learning traits in a slightly different way. All, however, repeatedly remind readers that no individual fits neatly into one category. Rather, we have tendencies toward one category or another, with doses of other categories in varying amounts thrown in for good measure. You'll soon see how the different ways in which families homeschool (coming up in the next chapter) honor these differences.

Don't let the lack of firm boundaries between styles confuse you. Look at them as confirmation that individuals learn in unique ways and that homeschooling can serve your child's distinctive preferences in a way that government schools can only dream about. Further study of learning styles is highly recommended.

FIRST, A WORD ABOUT SIGNS OF READINESS IN LITTLE FOLKS

AWARENESS OF your family's learning styles will help guide your homeschooling choices, no doubt. But as a parent of early-years children, often thought of as roughly three- to eight-year-olds, you also need to watch for signs of readiness. It's often pointed out within the homeschooling community that a little person grows in her abilities not only in her own way but at her own pace.

The simple truth that homeschoolers put to work for the benefit of their children is that not all children are ready to learn the same things at the same time. Some two- and three-year-olds—and four- and five-year-olds and even older children—aren't ready emotionally for frequent absences from the constant in their lives: family. Yes, many do get accustomed to it, but that doesn't make them any more ready for it.

Some of these children aren't ready to sit still for any length of time. Attention spans vary widely. Some are left brainers; others, right. There are introverts and extroverts. There are those who need to see, those who need to hear, those who need to touch. Some of them can't wait to dive into books independently, and some remain content just being read to.

> A little person grows in her abilities not only in her own way but at her own pace.

We don't honor this simple truth through the act of schooling. Instead, through schooling we lump together children according to age, do what's best for the adults involved, hope for the best, and continue throwing money at the resultant problems.

"In my first year of homeschooling, I wish I had known the concept of maturity," says Florida's Le Ann Burchfield. "In order for a child to learn certain things, something needs to be turned on neurologically. Each child has a built-in time clock for this to occur, and nothing can be done externally to turn it on any earlier. You can try to teach a three-month-old baby to walk," Le Ann explains, "but you will face only frustration until the baby is neurologically ready to walk. It works the same way with reading, writing, bike riding— just about any skill. Interestingly, the time clocks are completely independent of the child's relative intelligence and capacity to learn. I now realize that certain things cannot be rushed and have more patience and confidence to wait."

ADD, ADHD, Dyslexia, and Other Learning Disorders: Differences in Learning Styles, Perhaps?

When interviewing fifteen "grown" homeschoolers for my book *Homeschoolers' Success Stories* (Prima, 2000), I stumbled upon two who told me that perseverance in reading helped them overcome the

LEARNING ACTIVITY

Textbook Critiques
(critical analysis/subject content; middle and teen years)

When my twelve-year-old daughter came out of school, she was old enough to operate largely on her own, and she spends a great deal of time reading and writing. Sometimes I want to add a little overt math, science, or social studies to the mix, and I've found the best way to do it is to find something we can read to each other and discuss.

During the first year of homeschooling, we discovered it was great fun to read together and critique the life science book she would have been using in school that we borrowed from the district for the purpose. It had some interesting information, but there was a lot to criticize in it. We tore it apart from many points of view: logic, common sense, errors in grammar, extra padding, stupid activities, how suggested discussion topics would play out in a real classroom, etc. She got background in life science and good practice in critical analysis.

—LINDA JORDAN, NOTTINGHAM, NEW HAMPSHIRE

dyslexia label. When interviewing another twelve currently home-schooling youngsters and their parents for the same book, I was thrilled to learn of a young Canadian boy named Chris whose mom felt he had, through homeschooling, overcome undiagnosed autism. (Her reason for not seeking a diagnosis had to do with not welcoming the government assistance that accompanies such a diagnosis.)

A five-year homeschooling veteran, Mindy Tom, of Fitzwilliam, New Hampshire, is convinced that her middle daughter would have received a learning disability label had she ever entered government school. Mindy has utilized homeschooling time working on problems observed instead of "ignoring them with medication."

"Many times it's impossible to get her attention during the day," says Mindy. "She just has too many things she wants to do, or just cannot concentrate when the washing machine is running."

As their daughter moves about in the freedom of home education, the Tom family has discovered that "she is relaxed enough at nighttime and wants to be held and talked to," Mindy explains. "It's the time when everything on her agenda is completed and she is willing to listen and respond. It's the time when she needs us most—one-on-one—so we may be doing third-grade work at nine or ten P.M. After that she is worn-out and falls right to sleep. Before, it would take her up to three hours to fall asleep; not until the last light was out would she rest."

It's anecdotal as opposed to scientific evidence, but an awful lot of homeschooling parents tell of children given negative learning labels at school who thrive once they come home. Several families shared their stories in each book of the series *Homeschooling: The Early Years, Middle Years*, and *Teen Years*. Almost unanimously, the parents felt that their ability to shape learning in sometimes unorthodox ways made all the difference. Chris's mom, for example, figured out through trial and error that he best comprehended auditory material while jumping up and down on a trampoline!

Such stories lend credence to a growing argument that homeschooling accommodates the vast array of learning styles better than traditional schools. Parents who bring home so-called learning-disabled students—only to discover their children are indeed bright and eager learners—are leading others in asking whether schools are themselves suffering from a teaching disability. After all, the symptoms that elicit learning-disability labels disappear or lessen in a learning environment that honors the child's educational needs.

Other parents are turning to homeschooling to avoid or stop medications deemed necessary by classroom teachers. By 1999 the number of children receiving Ritalin—the most often prescribed psychoactive drug to counteract symptoms of attention deficit disorder, attention deficit hyperactivity disorder, and others—had skyrocketed

LEARNING ACTIVITY

Prize Bag Carnival (language arts/math; preschool, early years)

I set up carnival "games"; winning a game earns children a ticket. When they collect a given number of tickets, they choose from a prize bag filled with small things I have around the house anyway, such as old bandannas no longer used or trinkets or souvenirs that haven't been displayed since I got married. Some games are academic.

Once, we had a game where the kids shot my son's disk shooter down the hall. I had set up old Styrofoam produce trays with a letter written on each. When a disk landed on a letter, the child who could name a word that began with that letter won a ticket.

I wrote numbers in each compartment of a box that had once contained individually wrapped pears. The kids threw rolled socks into the compartments, and if they correctly added the numbers, they won a ticket.

There were also obstacle courses and mazes, less schoolish activities.

I don't do this often, but it's fun now and then, and I liked using my imagination to come up with games both fun and educational. Also, the games are easily adaptable to different ages and abilities. This helps the children learn that "fair" doesn't always mean treating everybody equally. It's appropriate to expect a seven-year-old to be able to do more than a five- or two-year-old.

—THYNE RUTROUGH, RICHMOND, KENTUCKY

to an estimated four million, 80 percent of whom are boys. Ritalin is a trade name for methylphenidate (MPH), a behavior-altering drug considered under the federal Controlled Substances Act to be a Schedule II drug, right alongside cocaine, opiates, and methamphetamines. The U.S. Department of Justice's Drug Enforcement Administration terms it "addictive and abusable."

According to a study reported in the *Journal of the American Medical Association,* about 1 percent of children ages two to four are currently using Ritalin or Ritalin-like drugs, even though Ritalin has not been approved by the FDA for use by children under age six. An additional 600,000 children take serotonin reuptake inhibitors, such as Prozac, now available in mint-flavored liquid for the little ones. Untold thousands more are prescribed lithium, formerly used only as an antipsychotic drug for assorted diagnoses—such as bipolar disorder, depression, and aggressive conduct disorder—and as a general mood stabilizer.

So that they may quietly tolerate the one way in which school "teaches," children's behavior is "toned down"—or, according to some, their spirits are broken—with drugs as readily as a wild stag's are with a rope and a fence. In a school setting, behavior is chemically altered when it is considered inappropriate, unacceptable, and/or disruptive to a highly inflexible system. As Vassar psychology professor Ken Livingston argued in *Public Interest* magazine, "In late twentieth-century America, when it is difficult or inconvenient to change the environment, we don't think twice about changing the brain of the person who has to live in it."

We parents can recognize and honor learning styles and readiness clues. Through homeschooling, families can change the learning environment. With this knowledge one could argue that at least a portion of those children whose behavior must be "altered" are the very same children who are not yet ready to sit still, who need to touch instead of hear, who are missing the still necessary security of family, who are the artists instead of the thinkers among us. Altering their behavior, simply because they learn differently, does them a great disservice. It ultimately brings great loss to society at large.

> In late twentieth-century America, when it is difficult or inconvenient to change the environment, we don't think twice about changing the brain of the person who has to live in it.
>
> —Ken Livingston, Vassar psychology professor

Here are two last pieces of food for thought regarding learning labels and subsequent drugging. "Many high school shootings have been linked to prescribed mind-altering drugs," according to a column in the June 2000 e-mail newsletter from the conservative *Eagle Forum*. "Oregon high school killer Kip Kinkel had been given Ritalin and Prozac. Columbine killer Eric Harris had taken another psychotropic drug. Georgia high school student T. J. Solomon had been on Ritalin prior to his alleged shooting spree. Oklahoma middle school student Seth Trickey was on two drugs described to have psychotic effects when he allegedly shot at four students." The effects on individual children of long-term exposure to stimulants have yet to be established.

To date, the law firm of Waters & Kraus, known for its work in cases regarding toxic exposure and cancer cases, filed class-action lawsuits in Texas, California, and New Jersey against Ritalin manufacturer Novartis Pharmaceuticals Corporation, Children and Adults with Attention Deficit/Hyperactivity Disorder (CHADD), and the American Psychiatric Association, charging fraud and conspiracy. Peter Breggin, M.D., author of *Talking Back to Ritalin*, updated in October 2000, serves as medical consultant for the suit.

After stating all of this—and before I yet again stand accused of painting too rosy a picture of homeschooling (and if I do, it's because I know it can help so many more kids today than it is currently helping!)—I'm not suggesting homeschooling is educational snake oil. I'm only recommending that homeschooling is worth looking into if your child has been labeled as having one of the multitude of educational sicknesses going around in epidemic proportion.

GARDNER'S THEORY OF MULTIPLE INTELLIGENCES

IN 1983 Harvard University psychologist Howard Gardner, Ph.D., wrote *Frames of Mind: The Theory of Multiple Intelligences* (Basic

Books) with mainstream psychologists as its intended readership. This theory suggests that we should employ a pluralistic view when measuring mental functioning. In other words, the theory sets forth a rationale for recognizing a variety of intelligent ways of thinking. Gardner refined his definition of intelligence in *Intelligence Reframed: Multiple Intelligences for the 21st Century* (Basic Books, 1999), calling it "a biopsychological potential to process information that can be activated in a cultural setting to solve problems or create products that are of value in a culture."

Frames of Mind listed seven types of intelligences to consider. (The first two are those almost exclusively valued in school systems.) By simply reviewing the traits of each intelligence, you will begin to understand how the majority of intelligences are underappreciated and how those in whom the other intelligences dominate can easily have problems in a school setting. In fact the odds appear better for trouble than they do for success.

+ Linguistic: think in words; possess good auditory skills; learn best by verbalizing or hearing and seeing words

+ Logical–Mathematical: think conceptually; enjoy patterns and experimenting

+ Bodily–Kinesthetic; process knowledge through bodily sensations; fine motor coordination; learn by moving or acting things out

+ Visual–Spatial: think in images and pictures; inventive and/or artistic

+ Musical: high appreciation of music or talent for creating, including singing; hear sounds that others don't; sensitive to nonverbal sounds

+ Interpersonal: good at organizing and communicating (or, negatively, manipulating); natural mediators; learn best by relating and cooperating

> ✦ Intrapersonal: possess deep awareness of inner feelings and ideas; deep sense of self; qualities of inner wisdom or intuition

In 1996 Gardner refined his theory by adding an eighth intelligence:

> ✦ Naturalist: skilled at observing, understanding, and organizing patterns in the natural environment; good classifier; analyzes minute differences, as in sounds of different engines or fingerprint variations.

Along came Thomas Armstrong, Ph.D., who in 1987 put a spin on Gardner's theory in *In Their Own Way: Discovering and Encouraging Your Child's Personal Learning Style* (Tarcher). Armstrong's work made the theory practical and accessible for parents and others who cared to use the information to customize education for individual children. After explaining how to use knowledge of learning styles, *In Their Own Way* provides a chapter on building support systems for your child's academic life, explains how to create positive beliefs in your child and yourself, speaks of honoring your child's individual learning rate, describes how to enhance your child's senses to improve learning, and even addresses providing a nurturing environment. Additionally, Armstrong took schools to task with chapter titles such as "Dysteachia: The Real Reason Your Child Isn't Thriving in School." In discussing ways to get the best education for your child, he suggested that parents "consider teaching your child at home."

Homeschooling families found a champion in Dr. Armstrong. *In Their Own Way* and subsequent books by Dr. Armstrong gave credence to all the wonderful ideas about learning that homeschooling families were discovering in their living rooms, backyards, and greater communities.

Gardner has continued to expand on his theory by connecting the wisdom of multiple intelligences to "individually configured education." (It's a nice synonym for homeschooling, don't you think?) In *Intelligence Reframed*—which, by the way, includes another "half" intelligence, existential—Gardner writes that "a moment's thought reveals the essential inequity in the uniform school," where the false assumption that all individuals are the same extends equally falsely to the idea that all students are being reached "equally and equitably."

Gardner is convinced that honoring children's varying intelligence strengths can work in all types of educational situations, including "uniform schools," despite arguments to the contrary from more traditional educators for whom application of this theory would present a logistical nightmare. This, he says, would require "learning about each student's background, strengths, interests, preferences, anxieties, experiences, and goals, not to stereotype or to preordain but rather to ensure that educational decisions are made on the basis of an up-to-date profile of the student." (Didn't I tell you that you are the expert here?) He continues: "Knowing the minds of students represents but the first step. Crucial, thereafter, is an effort to draw on this knowledge in making decisions about curriculum, pedagogy, and assessment." (And this is just what you'll be doing with the information with regard to schedule, organization, and method!)

> Dr. Armstrong gave credence to all the wonderful ideas about learning that home-schooling families were discovering in their living rooms, backyards, and greater communities.

Gardner's greatest hope for realizing within his lifetime his vision—of individually configured education based on his theory—is "smart" technology. "It can adjust on the bases of earlier learning experiences, ensuring that a student receives lessons that are optimally and individually crafted," he writes. "Once parents learn that there are indeed several ways to teach most topics and most subjects, affluent families will acquire the materials for home use." Despite Dr. Armstrong's assumption that a family needs to be affluent, homeschoolers have for years proved that a good education at home need not require large sums of money.

Looks like you're way ahead of the intelligences game with your growing knowledge of the benefits of homeschooling.

THE LEARNING-STYLE PROFILE

EDUCATORS MARIAEMMA Willis and Victoria Kindle Hodson feel that parents need to incorporate more background information about a child into their understanding of learning style. They wrote *Discover Your Child's Learning Style* (Prima, 1999), a workbook containing do-it-yourself assessments for learners ages six and up.

This approach has parent and child examine dispositions, talents, interests, modality, and environment in order to enhance the educational experience. A brief review of each aspect follows:

Dispositions

Performing

Prefers activities that are entertaining, relevant, challenging, and hands-on; learns best when teaching is short and to the point, allows movement, involves games, manipulatives, and audiovisuals.

Producing

Prefers structure and order, opportunity to organize; learns best when teaching is logical and sequential, allows planning, scheduling, and due dates.

Inventing

Prefers experimental activity and opportunity to question, design, and discover; learns best when teaching is direct and provides "intellectual" ideas, theories, models, and time for exploration.

Relating/Inspiring

Prefers social activity, incorporation of personal feelings, and opportunity to interact; learns best when teaching offers individualization, small groups, and cooperative interaction.

Thinking/Creative

Prefers activity that is creative and has artistic or philosophical aspects, provides artistic expression and opportunity to wonder, think, and dream; learns best when teaching allows for time alone and involves the creative process.

Talents

Note the similarities to what Gardner calls intelligences.
   Criteria to define talents are

+ activities that are done with ease

+ child is ahead of others in specific area without previous instruction

+ dormant if not developed, but not lost

+ have an underlying effect on other life aspects

Talents include music, math–logic reasoning, mechanical reasoning, word–language reasoning, spatial, body coordination, interactive–self, interactive–others, interactive–animals, interactive–nature, humor, and life enhancement.

Interests

The activities that your child chooses to pursue are valid expressions of your child's learning style, yet they

+ are often overlooked by parents

+ don't always support a child's talents

+ need to be observed

It helps if you assist child in prioritizing interests, especially insofar as recognizing short-term and long-term interests.

Modality

Modality refers to the senses through which information is taken in and processed. It takes into account the following:

Auditory

Learns through listening or through talking and discussing.

Visual

Learns through pictures (charts, graphs, maps, etc.) or through print (reading and writing).

Tactile–Kinesthetic

Learns through touch or through movement.

Environment

Do not ignore the understanding that we all learn best under different circumstances.

Sound

Preference for quiet or need for noise.

Body Position

Preference to sit, recline, or stand.

Interaction

Preference to be alone or with others, either quietly or interacting.

Lighting

Full-spectrum is better than fluorescent; dimmed lights have calming effect.

Temperature

Discomfort is created when environment is either too hot or too cold.

Food

Healthy food and drink, available as needed, help some children's learning efficiency.

Color

Affects mood, as some energize, soothe, or depress; favorite colors in environment contribute to positive thinking and motivation.

Time of Day

As discussed in chapter 2 as part of creating your own schedule.

DEVELOPING YOUR A-OK FRAME OF HEART

IT SEEMS the happiest humans sprinkled throughout mankind's history were those who found balance between head and heart, between intellect and emotion. (I think this is what the "do what you love, the money will follow" philosophy is doing for many people, but I digress.)

Yes, pay attention to frames of mind, and use this information to your child's benefit. But pay equal attention to your frame of heart so that you help create and maintain a healthy balance as you educate your child. This will develop joy and happiness in the life that will become your child's future. You can attend to your own frame of heart by remembering "A-OK": accept, observe, and know.

Accept

Whenever I think about acceptance, I'm reminded of the Serenity Prayer: God, grant me the serenity to accept the things I cannot change, the courage to change the things I can, and the wisdom to know the difference.

Much of what you'll learn about intelligence and learning styles will greatly aid the academic side of homeschooling, of course.

However, there's another benefit of possessing this knowledge that is of equal value. By uncovering those intelligences and learning styles unique to your child, you'll see how he is naturally inclined. In schooling, and even as parents, we sometimes choose to fight nature by trying to alter a child's natural inclination to fit someone else's picture of how this child should be. In so doing, we rob children of their uniqueness. (By default, we rob society too.) By knowing our child's intelligences and learning styles, we know what not to change; we know what to accept.

> By knowing our children's intelligences and learning styles, we know what not to change; we know what to accept.

You may right now be fantasizing about providing your daughter with the best education any future doctor could want. Are you prepared to find out that her uniqueness lies in a completely different province? Are you prepared to nurture her natural inclination toward a goal that may be dissimilar to everything you or your spouse or your mother-in-law ever hoped for?

Schooling—complete with the oft-repeated goal of getting into a good college in order to obtain a good-paying job—is a very narrow view of learning to set forth before a child, especially when you realize that this view is only one of many. Often a different educational goal would better honor the unique intelligence, disposition, and talents of an individual.

Once we acknowledge that it's best not to change something, it's easier for us to let nature take its course, to accept. Accepting, then, means giving up your own perceptions of what should be and allowing what *is* to blossom.

After we ask for the serenity to accept what we cannot change, the Serenity Prayer moves on to a request for courage to change the things we can. In this respect homeschooling is a courageous act, as we set about changing not the child but the thing we can change: the way in which he receives an education. By doing so, we choose differently than the vast majority of parents who are our friends, neigh-

WHAT I WISH SOMEONE HAD TOLD ME DURING MY FIRST YEAR OF HOMESCHOOLING

I wish I'd been told to try out all the different styles. I'm completely surprised that we ended up as relaxed as we are. I couldn't imagine how unschooling could work, but we tried it, and the kids really do direct their own learning. So don't put yourself in a box.

Sometimes the kids are so busy learning that I can't stop them to insist they do "school," and sometimes they need a lot of direction. We go with the flow on the first kind of day and use a few workbooks on the second. Both are valuable and fun. I would never have sent my children to school if I had known what a great education I'd get myself, and how much I would enjoy getting to know my kids!

—DEBORAH FERGUSON, THE DALLES, OREGON

bors, and relatives. By choosing differently, we are a minority who accept full responsibility for the outcome. By choosing differently, we fundamentally change the way in which our children spend the time known as childhood.

Going against the majority and accepting responsibility while others give it away take courage. While you line up your intellectual arguments for homeschooling with the head, the courage necessary to act upon them ultimately flows from love for the child, from the heart. Both acceptance of the unchangeable and courage to change what is changeable are served best by a strong frame of heart.

Finally, the Serenity Prayer leads us to request the wisdom to know the difference, the greatest challenge of all in life generally, and in educating our children most definitely. Your ability to discriminate between the changeable and the unchangeable about your child

WHY I CAME TO HOMESCHOOLING

I quit practicing law to become a full-time mother when Jane was thirteen months old. She is hearing-impaired, as I am.

Jane began speech therapy at two-and-a-half years old. About the same time, she began attending a local Montessori school two days a week, as well as a local school for the deaf two days a week. We moved when she was three years old, and she attended a local church preschool three days a week, as well as the school system's special-education preschool.

Although her hearing loss is mild–moderate, she continued to have severe articulation and language problems. So when she was four, we began a regimen of four weekly sessions of traditional speech therapy, as well as a hundred minutes per day, five days a week, of a computer-based auditory processing therapy program.

is ultimately more important than which curriculum you use, yet beginning homeschoolers put countless hours into fretting over the things of education instead of really getting to know who it is to be educated. Acceptance bestows remarkable peace on its bearer and on those who are accepted as they are. May you have the wisdom to know the difference.

Observe

In chapter 2 we reviewed observation as part of the grand experiment of homeschooling. Now it's time to add your frame of heart to the discussion, as this is the element that naturally separates the homeschooling parent from the impartial scientist, as well as brings balance to your educational endeavors.

As a homeschooling parent, your observation of your child is different from that which happened to you as a youngster in school.

I decided that preschool on top of all the speech therapy would be too much for both of us, so we did things at home—coloring, painting, playing in water and sand, listening to music, formal math and reading lessons, and reading, reading, and some more reading.

I was always interested in the possibility of homeschooling, but I'm not sure I would have had the courage to go through with it but for necessity. I tell people that we "stumbled" into homeschooling. I don't want to put her back in "regular" school even though her speech has improved tremendously and therapy sessions are drastically reduced. We're having too much fun.

This year Jane will be five. We'll be using second-grade readers and first-grade materials for other subjects. How many other children who were diagnosed with severe articulation, phonological, and auditory processing disorders at ages three and four have come so far so quickly?

—MARGARET SANDERS, HARTWELL, GEORGIA

There, the emphasis was on watching for what you might be doing wrong, whether shooting spitballs or talking to your neighbor. Your goal, of course, is not to catch your child doing something wrong in the interest of maintaining order in the classroom.

In contrast, you are watching for clues that will help you to help your child learn, and enjoy it. Ideally you will observe your child with a loving, open heart. Increasing your ability to accept the unchangeable will make this easier. A loving, open heart helps a parent to not just "look" but truly "see." In this way homeschooling parents learn many of their most important lessons, including, but not limited to, the following:

✦   Chances are good that your child's preferred learning style will be different from yours. Realize that just because you can pick up written directions in the blink of an eye, you can't assume your child does too.

THE CHILD YOU HOMESCHOOL IS NOT THE SAME ONE YOU SENT TO SCHOOL

Considered homeschooling before my youngest went to kindergarten, felt very unable to do it, didn't, and so he was in public school through second grade. He didn't want to do anything I wanted him to do, didn't want to be with me anymore, and was picking up bad habits.

While thinking about homeschooling, the thought occurred to me that the "easy" way out would be to not do it—push the kids out the door and have the day to myself. Wow! That is what I found myself even subconsciously doing. It was as if the kids weren't as much a part of my life anymore because they were separate from me so much of the day. It was almost an interruption when they came home. I don't know that I would have recognized it within myself if I hadn't overheard two mothers having a conversation at the store: "The kids are on break. . . .

+ Chances are good that if you have more than one child, you will be dealing with more than one learning style. Variety is the spice of life!

+ Life is filled with teachable moments. A natural part of observing your child learn is noting *when* it happens. You don't have to observe very long before this lesson becomes clear.

+ The child you homeschool is not the same one that you sent to school. Some of all that school "attitude" disappears with homeschooling, more slowly in some cases than others. Be patient; prepare for a lot of decompression time. (More on decompression in chapter 9.)

Many people mistakenly believe that homeschooling parents have some sort of corner on the patience market. Or are geniuses. Or have

I can't wait until they go back to school." I thought, How sad. Their children have become unpleasant to live around because of who they're around all day long in school. Coupled with lack of time with caring parents, and now they just want them out of their lives?

I knew that even though I had less of the push-them-out-the-door syndrome than they did, I had too much. I decided to do whatever it took to get my kids back.

I see a nice change in them, and must add that I have gotten part of the change I know I needed in myself for the sake of the children. It is scary that our children are mirror images of us. When we see something in our children that we don't like, it's often something in ourselves we're seeing. Talk about a course in self-enlightenment!

—DELAINE KEITH, STILLWATER, OKLAHOMA

genius kids. Perhaps what they are perceiving is not so much patience but more the result of blending observation and acceptance. Homeschooling parents and children really are ordinary people living a different lifestyle—or, as some see it, living extraordinary lives. (Don't think every day is a romp in the park. You'll get acquainted with all kinds of homeschooling challenges as you continue reading.)

Know

When you figure out your child's learning style, you know something about his intellectual aspect. That's good. The parent who keeps track of what his child is learning in school knows something about his child's intellectual aspect as well. But does knowledge of the child's intellectual aspect constitute "knowing" the child?

ACCEPTANCE

In my son Julian's last couple of months of public school third grade, as my partner and I looked forward to beginning homeschooling, we read book after book about it, and fantasized. We read *Better than School* (Holt, 1990), by Nancy Wallace, and were overjoyed at the thought of Julian, who was already musical, writing operas and becoming prodigious at the violin. (He had taken violin for a year at age four, then stopped. He would no doubt be anxious to begin again.) Julian and I would have long intellectual conversations with each other, and he would be so excited by learning that he would always know what he wanted to do next. My partner and I would be calm, patient providers of fascinating resources. Not that much patience would be necessary, because home life would be so serene.

It wasn't like that. Nancy Wallace's children might have enthusiastically thrown themselves into a life of unfettered creativity, but Julian wanted to read or play video games. If I suggested that he write something, he would cry. We never

Only partly. There are so many other aspects of our children that we need to understand in order to better "know" our children. Likely you remember your baby's first word, first food, where you were when first steps were taken, the theme of the third birthday party. That baby has grown. What makes today's child smile? Laugh? Cry? Think? Create? Get angry? What are the favorite book, color, cookie, song? Fears? Hopes? Political views? One could fill a book with just a list of things there are to learn about one's child.

There's really only one way to learn these things, and that's by spending time together talking. When you have time to talk, you did figure out how to use the Cuisenaire rods (colorful wooden or plastic rods used to teach elementary children basic math concepts).

But he was happy! He had as much time to read as he wanted, and on the first official day of "school," he read for eight hours. We didn't rush in the morning, we didn't fight about homework, and we had time to do things and get to know each other.

Remember how you read everything in anticipation of bearing your first child? Nothing could adequately describe the feelings of love, awe, and fear you experienced. Homeschooling is like that. There will be days of utter panic at what a terrible thing you've done to your child's life. There will be others when you are astounded at the enormous brilliance of your child.

Homeschooling is life, intensified. The fears come and go. Remember that success at homeschooling doesn't necessarily involve being the youngest child ever to perform with the Philharmonic. Sometimes it's just getting really good at staring at the cat.

—KATHRYN BAPTISTA, SALEM, MASSACHUSETTS

don't even have to ask about these things; the answers come out during the course of conversations. There is much to learn so that you may truly know your child. Homeschooling gives you the time necessary to do so.

5

IN A WAY THAT FITS YOUR FAMILY, BEGIN WHERE YOU ARE

In This Chapter

✦ Begin where you are

✦ Ways to homeschool that may
fit your family's lifestyle

"When I started homeschooling a fifth grader who had been in school up until that point, we rang the bell every morning at nine. (Literally . . . bought a bell just for that purpose!) We said the Pledge of Allegiance, studied each subject in a certain order every day, and even had recess! We burned out by October. The few other homeschoolers we knew used desks, globes, the flag, and a very stringent schedule. Until I started reading about how diverse home- schoolers are, I wasn't confident enough to homeschool in a way that fit our family."

—Mary Kenyon, Dyersville, Iowa

*Y*OU'VE LEARNED ABOUT different ways that different people go about learning, and even without this book's telling you to do so, I'm sure you read about them with your own children in mind. You are now "homeschooling," teaching yourself what you want to know. Your desire to do what you feel is best for your children propels you to learn more.

Now you are about to explore nine different homeschooling approaches. Please remember there are no brick walls separating these ways. Try to think of the different approaches merely as the places families land on a long continuum of places anyone who is homeschooling can land. Of course, as you read about the various approaches, I know you will keep in mind your child's learning style(s).

BEGIN WHERE YOU ARE

"WHERE DO I begin?" is a question I field repeatedly as the homeschool.com early-years advisor. As with any other life endeavor, isn't it best to begin with your strengths? The strength of every homeschooling parent is that she is the world's greatest expert not on children in general but on one or a few children in particular. In fact, when you begin to consider homeschooling as learning without school, you realize that all parents have been homeschooling their children since birth. Didn't you use "readiness cues," then employ homeschooling methods to encourage pat-a-cake, walking, talking, potty use, and more? If so, then you already have homeschooling experience under your belt.

> The strength of every homeschooling parent is that she is the world's greatest expert on one or a few children in particular.

If your child has been in school, you may feel as if you don't really know him very well anymore. As distanced as you feel, there's

WHAT I WISH SOMEONE HAD TOLD ME DURING MY FIRST YEAR OF HOMESCHOOLING

I wouldn't have believed what I wish someone had told me. I was so busy listening to the "experts" that I almost missed out on many learning experiences. I wish that someone had told me that I am the expert. I am the only person qualified to make the important judgments necessary to teach my son.

I had all of the "experts" in the school system telling me why homeschooling isn't the best thing for him. I had all of the "experts" in the family telling me how damaging this move was going to be for my son. I had all of the "experts" selling me expensive curricula. I have come to the realization that all of these people have their opinions, and none of them lives with my son daily. None of them has cried over the difficulty he had in school. None of them loves him as I do. There are no experts. Others can offer advice that might be helpful, but no one knows what I know about my own children.

—SUE CHRIS CARTY, CAPE CANAVERAL, FLORIDA

still no one else who got to know him better than you do, and you will use the time available in homeschooling to close the distance created by school attendance.

Begin with your strength as expert on your child and the only one with previous experience homeschooling him, and you will go into this extension of homeschooling with more confidence. The only logical place to begin, then, is right where you are.

If, as you conduct research to fill the "method" void created by your choice to homeschool, you torture yourself over finding the one perfect method, you'll spend a whole lot of energy revving your engine with your transmission in park, going nowhere fast. You've

WHAT I WISH SOMEONE HAD TOLD ME DURING MY FIRST YEAR OF HOMESCHOOLING

I wish someone had let me know how much fun homeschooling would be, and how much I would learn. My husband and I decided to use an umbrella school. We were disappointed it was not challenging enough, but it turned out to be a great learning experience. I took the curriculum and made it more interesting for my daughters. We also did a lot of learner-led exploring. Both daughters were fascinated by outer space, so we learned a lot about the planets and took imaginary trips to the moon. The great thing is that the whole family can learn a lot of new and interesting things together.

—LIZ JAWOREK, KENOSHA, WISCONSIN

got to put that transmission into drive in order to get onto the homeschooling continuum somewhere. Once in gear and moving, you'll have time to look around, take in the sights, and see what others are doing. Families move all over the homeschool continuum all the time, anyway, as their needs change with interests, ages, and family circumstances.

Homeschooling should always be comfortable, especially at the beginning, when you feel as if you have no idea of what you're doing. Where you are right now is the place where you'll be most comfortable. This means that if using textbooks makes you comfortable, buy textbooks. If textbooks make you cringe, don't buy textbooks. If family circumstances are such that you can sail around the Caribbean for a year, sail around the Caribbean for a year. If family circumstances are otherwise, don't sail around the Caribbean for a year. Being comfortable makes it a lot easier to tinker with homeschooling until it fits your family's lifestyle.

WAYS TO HOMESCHOOL THAT MAY FIT YOUR FAMILY'S LIFESTYLE

WITH AN educational approach as flexible as homeschooling, it was only a matter of time before simple categories helped define the varied approaches. Even before the diverse approaches were given names, though, the differences in style were noticeable, at least to those involved in homeschooling.

By presenting nine different approaches to learning at home, I hope that you can find one that seems comfortable enough to use only as a template from which you proceed to build your family's unique homeschooling journey.

Traditional School at Home

While this highly structured approach may only borrow a little from the schedule and organization of government schools, it typically utilizes its method; thus its name. The method can incorporate different educational philosophies, so you will find a governed approach available via curricula with labels such as Montessori, Waldorf, or Core Curriculum.

Traditional school at home is many a new homeschooler's starting point, and for good reason. Schooling is often the only model a parent knows, so it offers a relatively high comfort level when compared to methods with which we are unfamiliar. Because of this, we dive in and recreate our own experience for our children.

Within this homeschooling method, there's lots of wiggle room to modify your memory of school attendance. Just ask Lee Roversi, who homeschools on an organic family farm—with a bed and breakfast and whole-foods cooperative buying club on the side—in Kilauea, Hawaii.

After attending a private Waldorf school until they reached the sixth and highest grade, Lee's older children, Sky and Nell, came home to the Waldorf-based Oak Meadow School curriculum. Her

LEARNING ACTIVITY

Disappearing Wetlands (science; early years)

While learning about bird migration, we set up squares of vinyl all around the house from the front door to the back door. These represented rest and feeding areas in wetlands. The kids "flew south," stopping at their favorite wetlands. As they traveled, though, I slowly replaced wetlands with a mall, parking lot, or other structure. Eventually the flight south became too difficult with no place to stop and rest or eat. The kids had a blast trying to fly (jump) from one remaining wetland to another. I could see the effect of destroying wetlands written all over their faces.

—MARGARET SPONABLE, SCHENECTADY, NEW YORK

third child, nine-year-old Bay, came home in the middle of third grade to be with the rest of his family.

The older children learn with guidance and support from Oak Meadow teachers, a service offered by this and other curriculum providers, usually for an additional fee. The school encourages tweaking assignments to align with the children's interests. "The children send their work to the teachers every two weeks, and it's returned with comments (and grades, if the children want them)," says Lee. "Nell and Sky also keep in touch with their teachers via e-mail as they see fit—asking questions, telling a learning story, or just chatting. That leaves their dad and me the delightful experience of facilitating their process here at home."

All three children use the extra time available through home-schooling to contribute to the family's home businesses. Lee adds, "We're always reaching out for art and drama classes; there's junior lifeguard, sailing and scuba programs, and horseback riding lessons.

Sky interns at the local National Wildlife Refuge, and both Nell and Sky have radio programs on our local community radio station." Lee adds, "And we try to make time for just enjoying each other and this incredible place where we live."

Four years ago, after she'd spent much time volunteering in her children's classrooms—only to become convinced "there had to be something better"—Calina Clarkson and her family, of Sawyer, North Dakota, went through "a huge adjustment" to bring home their third and seventh grader. From their earth-berm home on 4.5 acres, they utilized a "hodgepodge" of curricula.

"I'd been told North Dakota has some of the strictest home-schooling laws, so I keep lots of records, taking pictures as 'proof,' and I'm working with the local school principal who monitored our first two years," Calina says. "I send him quarterly reports. We lesson plan and journal. The plans I make up on the Microsoft Excel computer program may look strict," she explains, "but they have afforded us a great freedom. The kids may do any subject, as long as they have six 'checkmarks' per day (only one blank per day allowed)." Calina continues, "I make up a yearly plan, usually copying the tables of contents of books. That way the superintendent, principal, children, and I know exactly what was covered." Still, Calina frequently incorporates changes, "according to our schedule, how fast or slow the kids are progressing, or if I get new books better suited to our needs."

Reasons respondents gave for choosing traditional school at home:

+ children will be at same academic level as age peers if they begin/return to public school

+ ready-made curriculum provides a starting point

+ keeps the family on track with regard to grade-level content if they alter the hours/days/months of the public school calendar

+ easy way to satisfy state legal requirements

+ allows the family to cover academics quickly and use free time in other directions

Classical Education

Another highly structured educational style, the classical method is based on a revival of the educational approach called the trivium, a three-part process of literally training a child's mind discussed by writer and theologian Dorothy Sayers (1893–1957) in her essay "The Lost Tools of Learning." In 1991, a Moscow, Idaho, pastor alleged that a biblical worldview was inherent in educational excellence, and since then he and other proponents have added their own worldviews and revived this method of learning.

Part one, for children roughly in kindergarten to fourth through sixth grade, is the grammar stage. During this stage, training consists of learning facts through memorization. According to the Classical Academy, a classical education charter school, this is a time called "Poll-Parrot," because "the students love to share what they have learned by reciting back, singing little songs and jingles, rhyming words, and playing with words, as with Doctor Seuss." The accumulation of facts during part one prepares a child for part two, the logic stage.

> The classical method is based on a revival of the educational approach called the trivium, a three-part process of literally training a child's mind.

Occurring during what are typically termed the middle school years, or approximately grades six through eight, the logic stage takes advantage of the child's growing ability to think analytically. Also known as the "Pert Stage," here "students dig deeper into subjects: what, who, where, how, why, of a subject," explains the Classical Academy. It is a time when abstract thought blossoms, so the goal of learning shifts from "the student will know and be able to answer" to "the student will understand and be able to explain."

Finally, in high school the student moves to the rhetoric, or Poetic, stage. Now that the child is possessed of knowledge and adept at employing rules of logic, the approach bears fruit as "students express themselves in polished, well-thought-out, grammatically correct spoken and written verse," explains the Classical Academy. "It is here," the academy continues, "that students are able and allowed to begin the process of specializing in subject matter of their interests," by pursuing either a math/science or a liberal arts specialization.

Three weeks before it was time for Regina Bourland's five-year-old son to attend kindergarten, she "dutifully trotted off to the school's parent orientation day." What she saw convinced her that the school didn't live up to its good reputation, so she immediately decided he wouldn't be going to school, and, since private school wasn't financially viable, contacted a friend for homeschooling information and advice.

Now in Little Rock, Arkansas, Regina began with a standard kindergarten curriculum, but "in first grade we began to branch out and away from the curriculum a bit, as my son struggled horribly with spelling. We needed to change our approach and materials," she says. "Each year I have become more comfortable with homeschooling and different styles of teaching. We now use a mix but seem to be moving toward the classical approach, with lots of supplements. I'm sure our approach will continue to expand and change as long as we continue our homeschooling journey."

When Mary Nunaley began homeschooling her two children four years ago, "we started out deschooling and using the traditional school-at-home approach." The Nunaley family experimented with several approaches until, entering their third year of homeschooling, "we switched to a classical-based umbrella program," Mary explains. "We joined a tutorial primarily for my daughter's math, science, and Latin. It's been great. She adds, "As she gets closer to college age, and aspiring to attend Purdue University, we're gearing up a classical set of studies to prepare her."

Reasons respondents gave for choosing classical education:

- ✦ preparation for college academics
- ✦ to study history in chronological order
- ✦ to use original source books in teaching
- ✦ to study the trivium

Charlotte Mason

British-born Charlotte Mason (1842–1923) espoused, taught, and continually refined her educational philosophy during her turn-of-the-century lifetime. Her method is experiencing a modern resurgence as homeschoolers and a growing number of private schools embrace it. All of Mason's writings—available as the six-volume Original Home Schooling Series—were printed in paperback in 1993. Mason offered up a liberal arts education, insofar as core subjects are accompanied by the fine arts, then refined that familiar idea. The trademarks of a Charlotte Mason approach include the following:

- ✦ use of "living books" (classical literature) in lieu of textbooks
- ✦ narrative summaries of learning in lieu of written tests and exams
- ✦ nature notebooks and sketching to develop observation skills
- ✦ creation of a "Century Book," which serves as a timeline and an organizational center where information gleaned from reading, field trips, and other sources is placed into "the big picture"
- ✦ copy work

Wisconsin's Kristi Schrampfer fell into this approach when it became clear that her son hated workbooks and performed poorly on tests due to stress. Pregnant with her fourth child at the time, Kristi latched on to her son's natural love of reading and his inclination to tell her about what he read. "I didn't refer to it as a Charlotte Mason approach, having never heard of her at that time," Kristi recalls.

Three years later, she says, "We're still using Charlotte's methods, supplementing with an occasional unit study, all based on the children's needs and current interests. We use the library extensively, and it's worked well for us."

Amy Cooper's embrace of Charlotte Mason's method is less formal. In her Kentucky home, she mixes and matches approaches based on her fascination with "intrinsic motivation" and aspires to become more like unschoolers. Still, "we've enjoyed reading about and implementing many of Mason's ideas," she says. "I want my children to love learning because they are doing the choosing."

Reasons respondents gave for choosing Charlotte Mason:

- ✦ child is an avid reader
- ✦ provides plenty of attention to fine arts, classical music, and literature
- ✦ promotes concentration
- ✦ focuses on what child knows, not on what the child doesn't know
- ✦ enriches parent's education at the same time

Unit Studies

The unit studies approach departs from the school's method in that it allows much more flexibility than the typical school structure. Rather than subjects being addressed individually, unit studies are theme- or topic-based and use as starting points anything from historical eras to good books, science topics to cultural exploration. Learning occurs within a framework provided by the topic, and study of the topic incorporates literature, science, social studies, art, music, and more. While it's also possible to weave math lessons into a unit study, especially in the lower grades, this method's proponents almost unanimously recommend some sort of math textbook to ensure sequential coverage of mathematical concepts.

For those who have an inclination toward addressing school subjects yet who are concerned about accommodating the learning needs of children of different ages, unit studies allow all to study the same topic but at individual ability levels. Prepared unit studies are available both for purchase and for free on the Internet. Although the method is relatively labor intensive, many families enjoy pulling together the resources for their own unit studies in order to accommodate their children's unique interests and for the creative satisfaction it provides, benefits unavailable from studies organized by others.

> Rather than subjects being addressed individually, unit studies are theme- or topic-based.

A typical unit study might incorporate fiction and nonfiction reading, independently and aloud together. More language arts are included through vocabulary lists culled from reading material, dictation for handwriting skills, and a child-created story, poem, play, or essay on the topic. Appropriate music and culinary arts from a time period or culture add to the mix.

Movies and plays supplement understanding. Related field trips to museums, historical sites, or commercial enterprises may be possible within your neighborhood or during family vacations. Murals, dioramas, sculptures, handmade books, and map drawing fulfill visual arts exploration.

Sarah Rose used unit studies for many years with her always homeschooled fifteen-year-old high school grad, Quinn, and twelve-year-old son, David. Sarah began each year by asking her sons in the summertime what they would like to study in the coming months. "I'd take their suggestions and add some of my own. They rarely (never?) said they wanted to study the United States Constitution or the Bill of Rights, so I'd combine what they wanted and what I thought was important," Sarah explains. "Everything was done in unit studies fashion, incorporating drama, music, art, math, science, history, literature, writing, field trips where possible, and even cooking, if I could figure out how to get it in."

Sarah calls it "a nice blend of mom-centered and student-centered learning." She adds, "Also, I had a lot of fun, and I think that was catching."

Rachel Rogg of Wichita, Kansas, has three boys, ages seven, nine, and ten, who have been homeschooling for six years. Their "Kings and Queens" unit study stands out as a family favorite.

"We spent several weeks studying the medieval age," Rachel remembers. "Then I learned that we had a Society for Anachronism in our city that held fencing and archery presentations as well as other activities. Through the society we met and visited a woman who built her own two-and-a-half-story castle in her backyard. She dressed in medieval garb and gave us a tour!"

Another society member let the boys try on medieval armor and gave the family some authentic recipes of the time. At the end of the unit, Rachel says, "Our family had a medieval feast, complete with a music program, jesters, poetry, and costumes borrowed from a local college drama program."

Reasons respondents gave for choosing unit studies:

✦ cuts down on lesson-preparation time when working with children of various ages

✦ allows time to study a topic in depth

✦ offers some guidelines without the rigidity of a curriculum

✦ easily blends child's and adult's learning interests

✦ often reveals "side learning trips" that the child might not have discovered otherwise

✦ good fill-in when life circumstances get crazy, such as a new baby, moving, or illness

Eclectic (or Relaxed)

Judging by our respondents' answers, "eclectic" best describes the majority of their homeschools. Indeed, the ability to look beyond school and recognize diverse educational methods and resources as what they really are—the world's largest buffet for the mind—can readily result in choosing a taste of this, a bunch of that, and a bit of those for added vitamins and flavor.

Through this approach families home in on studies personally important to them, in such a way as to make homeschooling fit their lifestyles, as opposed to having their lifestyles fit into a more traditional approach with regard to scheduling, testing, and more.

"I have high expectations for my children, and we do challenging work," explains Karen Linda B. Hall, homeschooling mom of four early-years children, including two who previously excelled in a public school in Easton, Maryland. "They are advanced readers and love it. We don't do the same thing at the same time each day, nor do we cover all subjects every day."

> Through the eclectic approach, families home in on studies personally important to them.

Karen continues: "I consider music, art, and movement to be critical parts of my children's education, and I'm happy to spend a whole morning or afternoon on a project in the arts anytime. I am not interested in scoring and grading. I focus on Friends' religious principles and on a sort of liberal arts curriculum, then provide the materials and opportunities and leave the children free to learn."

The Varley family, of Villanova, Pennsylvania, develops their own curriculum based in part on the interests of the two children and in part on the parents' idea of what a well-rounded education should be. Mom Kate remembers days filled with 4-H meetings and activities (one child is an aspiring veterinarian), music lessons, chess club, weekly ice-skating, and monthly Shakespearean readings.

"We also set educational goals of a more formal nature," Kate explains. "We read novels together daily, like *Journey to Welcome,* by Jo Christian Babich, and relate other activities to it. We study a predetermined period of history. We work at math, and we're working toward being able to write and speak French." Kate adds, "The children take classes outside the home at times. In addition to music lessons, they've taken art and cartooning classes, and our son participates in the public school band."

The Varleys and other local homeschooling families are currently considering arranging group classes taught by local college students in French and in specialized science topics.

Reasons respondents gave for choosing eclectic or relaxed:

+ offers flexible structure

+ didn't have a lot of money to spend on homeschooling

+ easy to incorporate the children's interests

+ frees one to do "real-life things of interest"

+ by accident after engaging in enjoyable activities in lieu of lessons

+ easy way to start homeschooling with early-years children

+ children seemed more enthusiastic about learning

+ helps children who had a difficult time in school

+ previously used purchased curriculum and didn't like paying for those components they didn't like or use

Interest-Initiated, or Unschooling

Homeschooling mom Sandy Keane shared her definition of unschooling when asked why she chose the approach she did. Here, from Sandy, is as interesting a definition as any I've read for this perhaps unfamiliar word:

"Unschooling: The process by which a person acquires specific and nonspecific skills and information as determined by the needs and interests of the person(s) doing the learning and by methods suited to, and chosen by, those doing the learning. A lot of this learning is intrinsic, and some of the learning is also accomplished by more traditional methods, but the what, how, when, where, and

WHAT I WISH SOMEONE HAD TOLD ME DURING MY FIRST YEAR OF HOMESCHOOLING

A good friend told me to trust the process, to trust my kids, that they will be learning even during those times when it seems like they're "just" playing. It was just too hard for me to accept or believe it until I'd experienced the joy and awe of watching my children learn in their own unique way. The more I let them take the lead, the better it gets. It's been easier to relax and let the process happen since I've found support through unschooling.com and *Growing Without Schooling* magazine. If I'd known of the "unschooling" label earlier, it would have helped me find some of the support resources earlier.

—THYNE RUTROUGH, RICHMOND, KENTUCKY

why are determined by the learner and his/her goals rather than by a curriculum designer who has never met the learner."

Unschooling is sometimes misunderstood as a "Lord of the Flies" upbringing in which children run amok with no limitations. That unschooling places the child's interests at the center of education is sometimes viewed as too much control placed in the hands of children who don't really know what they need to know. It is about as far away from learning accomplished through school means as your family can go.

"Here is my understanding of the reasoning behind unschooling," begins Thyne Rutrough, whose older child came to homeschooling after kindergarten, and who "enforced a school model of learning" but quickly relaxed.

"Children have a natural love of learning and desire to learn, which continue through life if encouraged," Thyne says. "Unschooling is unique, because it questions a lot of the assumptions that go along with schools and even curricula. Children do not need to be 'taught' at all. I think of myself as a facilitator who has lots of experience in figuring out how to learn something I want to know. I don't think of my children as students, either. This is a journey of learning we are all on together."

Thyne had discovered the term for what her family does—unschooling—just two weeks before sharing her take with us. "If the child is choosing, or at least has significant input into the choice, that's unschooling," she says. "For that reason, another and perhaps more positive label for unschooling is child-directed learning."

Thyne notes that her family recognizes no division between work and play or between school hours and play hours. When folks used to ask her what curriculum she used, she would say she'd created her own. This, she realized, was at best a half truth. "It would be more accurate to say that the children make up their own curriculum as they go along," she says, "with only two restrictions: We limit the amount of time spent watching TV and videos and the time they spend on the computer."

> Thyne notes her family recognizes no division between work and play, or between school hours and play hours.

Chris and Mike Gurniak, of Windsor, Ontario, are self-described hands-on do-it-yourselfers who thought their daughters, Jennifer (seven) and Jessie (five), would be too. Their unschooling approach started one day, Chris figures, when Mike, a self-taught woodworker, decided he could make the end tables the family needed.

"Encouraged, he continued to build things, learning primarily through trial and error," explains Chris. "The more he built, the better he got."

To learn about computers, Mike started pressing different keys to see what would happen. "Sometimes we had to go without the computer until our 'computer guy' arrived to install everything again," Chris remembers, "but he became quite competent. He's transferred this knowledge to his company and become responsible for maintaining and updating the company's computers, including the Web page he designed."

As she watched Mike, the lights came on for Chris. "I decided to try my hand at sewing," she says. "We had a quilt in need of repair, so in the spirit of the pioneers, I created a new quilt, using the old one as batting. It won't win any prizes, but considering I've never sewn before, I'm proud of it."

Chris observed her learning process. "I was aware of some of my mistakes while working on the quilt," she explains. "Others I figured out after it was done. As I worked through and around the mistakes, I discovered that I had great fun finding them, studying them, seeing why they were errors, and figuring out how to correct them. Once I understood what and why something was wrong, then I could prevent it from happening again."

How else did Mike and Chris learn? When a problem required more than they knew, they turned to friends, neighbors, or relatives who knew more about it than they did. As many homeschoolers discover, the Gurniaks found that most people are eager to share hobby and professional knowledge with a truly interested seeker.

Chris knows that this learning approach is readily acceptable as a way to teach oneself a hobby, but extending it to academics is often considered unsuitable. She strongly disagrees: "A passion for a hobby will inspire you to learn all you can about it. Academics are picked up along the way on an as-needed basis. For instance, Jennifer wants to write and illustrate books. Does it matter if she learns to draw before learning to write? When she's ready to add words to her drawings, she will learn to write with the same passion with which she draws."

For the Gurniaks, then, learning "is about sharing thoughts and ideas with each other, quietly observing the world, and questioning everything. It's an ongoing, personal, and creative process that requires lots of time to think, do, explore, and wonder."

Reasons respondents gave for choosing interest-initiated, or unschooling:

- ✦ it's an extension of parenting their children as honorable and joyful, full-time work

- ✦ it mirrors the way many adults go about learning something they want to know

- ✦ can nurture both learning styles and interests at the same time

- ✦ allows for the most efficient, accurate learning in all arenas

- ✦ had previously observed how much their children were learning simply by asking questions and receiving answers

School-Sponsored Homeschooling Programs

As if there weren't enough choices in homeschooling styles, in recent years we've seen a new entrant to the list. Government schools—sometimes in the form of charter schools but also as an extension of their own offerings—are arranging programs specifically geared to their perceptions of homeschoolers' needs. The programs wear many faces.

The idea isn't totally new. To accommodate children living far off the school bus routes in Alaska, for example, the state has for years offered correspondence courses, resources, and teachers' assistance to families. In some Canadian provinces, homeschoolers can find school boards willing to provide, in exchange for reports on progress, funding and resources that include computers and software.

Through such programs, school districts are rapidly blurring the line between homeschooling and government school attendance. In part, this is because school districts almost always receive at least some state and/or federal funding when they can count homeschoolers among attending bodies. He who pays the bills must be accountable for the money he's spending, thus the need for some sort of report from the homeschooler who is the beneficiary of said funds. You become accountable to him who gives you money.

Charter schools are popping up all over the country, and these, too, are sometimes created for homeschoolers, sometimes *by* homeschoolers. These schools receive funding from the same sources as traditional school districts but are free from some of the regulations normally attached to the funds. Feverishly debated by proponents and opponents alike, it won't be long before we begin hearing more reports as to their relative merits (from proponents) and their relative shortcomings (from opponents).

> Through such programs, school districts are rapidly blurring the line between homeschooling and government school attendance.

Laurie Meyerpeter helped found a California homeschooling cooperative nearly a decade ago, and her family still participates in it today. She explains that the Meyerpeters are eclectic homeschoolers and that her children recently began participating in a public school–sponsored homeschooling program through a charter school too.

"This past year I have taken a more active role in the school," Laurie says of the charter school, begun and run by parents. "My children have taken several classes offered on Fridays, including photography, writing, and art. It feels similar to our co-op, except that there is a lot of paperwork."

California is breaking ground in charter schools, so it's no surprise we learn that Dar Quinlan, of Alameda, California, and her seven-year-old daughter are also utilizing a public charter school while unschooling. "It's important to note that the two aren't mutually exclusive," Dar explains. "The charter school we use asks that we list activities we've done each month according to 'subject area,' but since most subject areas are artificially segregated parts of life, this isn't a problem."

When unschooling Dar and daughter read the book *Julie of the Wolves,* then, it covered reading, science, and social studies. A visit to

Uncle John in Hawaii "is great social studies. My daughter learned about earthquakes from a Donald Duck cartoon," Dar adds. "It all counts!"

Reasons respondents gave for choosing school-sponsored homeschooling programs:

+ has similarities to homeschool co-ops

+ potentially makes it easier to receive needed special education assistance

+ accountability levels are currently low

+ attending classes fills socialization needs

+ ability to pick and choose what to learn at home and what to learn at school

+ to fill in perceived gaps in education due to personal constraints on time, ability, or other life circumstances

Independent Cooperative Learning Situations

Learning cooperatives can resemble parent-led charter schools—with a notable exception. These are independent of government regulation, free to be whatever those who create and utilize them want them to be.

Independent learning cooperatives have grown right along with the number of homeschoolers, aided by a growing trend to see value in a "free market" approach to education. (For more information on this concept, please see the book *Creating Learning Communities,* a project of the Coalition for Self Learning [Foundation for Educational Renewal, 2000]. It is available for downloading at http://www.creatinglearningcommunities.org.)

> Independent learning cooperatives are free of government regulation, free to be whatever those who create and utilize them want them to be.

"My children would probably say that their favorite part of homeschooling is the twenty days we spend each semester together with fifty or more families at our local homeschool co-op," says Laureen, a coordinator of the co-op, which is now five years old. "They've taken a wide variety of classes: machine sewing, American Girl classes, Spanish, and sign language."

The co-op has a waiting list backed up six months to a year, due to space limitations in their rented building. "At the end of the year, we have a closing program where the children display their work or, through performance, share what they've learned," adds Laureen. "They develop great public-speaking skills for this night."

Self-described unschoolers, the Norell family came home after the older of their two children had attended Montessori, private, and public schools by the middle of second grade. Today they enjoy much of their learning through travel. When in their Orlando, Florida, home, however, the Norell children are among the hundred homeschooled youngsters who comprise the Champion Kids Club (http://www.championhomeschool.org). They meet each Monday for three classes, then are "taken by hired school bus to a sports complex for tennis, swimming, or ice-skating lessons," mom Robin explains. "This fall they're starting an integrated program where they will all study 'A Day in the Colonies' while incorporating all of the disciplines."

Reasons respondents gave for choosing independent cooperative learning situations:

+ interaction with other children

+ combining funds to reduce costs of lessons to individual families

+ offers choice of classes that might be unavailable otherwise

+ parents have learned how to come together and blend their different approaches to learning

Online Learning

As Internet-capable computer prices fell and the number of "connected" households skyrocketed, marketers quickly realized they had

> ## WHAT I WISH SOMEONE HAD TOLD ME DURING MY FIRST YEAR OF HOMESCHOOLING
>
> We're convinced that a prepackaged curriculum is the easiest way to start homeschooling. It provides a structural basis that you would otherwise have to develop yourself or piece together from the work of others. Thus a curriculum removes many of the challenges of the first year and simplifies your initial homeschooling. Later, you can either stick with the structure or modify to your heart's content, but you at least have that basis to look to.
>
> —JIM HENDERSON

a ready-made sales tool sitting in homes across the country. Coupled with the Internet's ability to rapidly and cheaply share information, it wasn't long before trend analysts predicted that education would become a major Internet growth industry.

"Free marketers" didn't disappoint. For-profit education companies quickly formed, offering services for everyone from kindergartners to college-bound teens and adults. A November 2000 policy analysis from Cato Institute, a nonpartisan public-policy research foundation, stated that for-profit education, "which constitutes approximately 10 percent of the $740 billion education market, demonstrates that private enterprises, even when competing against a monopolistic system, can deliver a wide range of affordable high-quality educational services." Indeed, today it is possible to receive a complete curriculum-driven education, from learning how to read to obtaining a master's degree, in your living room, and complete it in your pajamas if you so desire.

Many families new to homeschooling state that this revolutionary approach is their first stepping-stone into learning at home.

LEARNING ACTIVITY

Not-Back-to-School Camp-Out (nature studies; all ages)

We decided to celebrate every year of no school by taking a camping trip in late September. Our first annual "not back to school" trip was glorious on the coast of the Strait of Juan de Fuca (Washington) to explore the tide pools. The kids found crabs, barnacles, and limpets. They set up a habitat in a Rubbermaid bowl, watched them all day, and released them in the evening. They collected rocks, and three years later we finally got a rock tumbler to polish them. We brought quick-drying plaster with us and made sandy footprints of each of the kids, which hang on my wall along with a picture of them with their dad on the shore at low tide. We met a retired couple who had been kayaking who shared their knowledge and experience with us, telling us about the otters they encountered in the strait and explaining the Native American uses for kelp. We roasted marshmallows and hot dogs, took hikes, played ball, and told stories by the fire. On rainy days we colored marine-life pages I'd brought along. Now we know life is educational, and with eyes open to learning opportunities, we find them everywhere.

—JENNIFER MILLER, PUYALLUP, WASHINGTON

Programs vary widely in price, substance, and quality. As a buyer, you should beware and research the many options thoroughly in light of your own financial commitment and time commitment and each program's compatibility with your child's needs and learning style. Remember, too, that the free-market approach allows you to pick and choose the most useful elements of different programs or choose to use online learning for just a portion of study.

While there's no doubt that online learning is creating new millionaires, the volume of information available for free on the

Internet also provides you with the opportunity to create your own low- or no-cost learning experience. While many homeschoolers enroll in complete Internet programs, the number pales in comparison to the number who confidently put to work other information free for the taking, based on their understanding of education as a buffet for the mind.

Lillian Jones's eighteen-year-old son, Ethan, began learning in their Sebastopol, California, home when in first grade. "In no time it became clear that he was his own best teacher," says Lillian, "and, regardless of periodic anxiety attacks that come with the homeschooling territory, he has continued to be his own best teacher."

In keeping with this philosophy, Ethan's online learning consists of researching topics as he encounters them through reading, movies, conversation, or the news. Recently, when Ethan visited a college's used-book store, Lillian was surprised that he didn't want to purchase books on topics she knew he was interested in. "I can find better information on the Internet," Ethan told her.

"I'm continually surprised by how much he knows about things I didn't even realize he was researching on his own," says Lillian. "One doesn't need to hook up with an online curriculum provider to get an interesting education online—Ethan is his own online provider!" She adds, "It's the same principle as using the library. We've never gone in and asked a librarian to plan and direct a reading program for us, either."

Reasons respondents gave for choosing online learning:

+ child's ability to research any subject of interest
+ information available at all times, day and night
+ availability of wide range of opinions/approaches on topics
+ child enjoys using computer
+ programs are convenient, as they can cover an entire curriculum

With your educational philosophy before you as a guiding light, you, too, will step onto the homeschool continuum. Likely, you will combine the educational approaches described above, taking what you like and discarding the rest, until you create a comfortable and unique approach for your family.

Now that you've read descriptions of a variety of ways to homeschool, we'll get a feel for how these approaches play out by peeking at some weekly learning journals.

6

A WEEK IN

THE LIFE

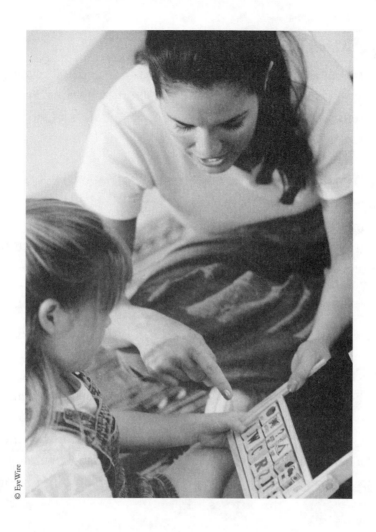

© EyeWire

"The biggest lesson I've learned through trying all of these
approaches has been that if it doesn't work, change!"

—Laraine O'Donnell, Alexandria, Ohio

CHAPTER 5 GAVE you a taste of the endless mixing-and-matching, changing or abandoning, of homeschooling approaches that occurs depending on a child's needs or a family's situation at any given time. Now we've been invited to visit the homes of families as they put each of those approaches into action.

You'll glimpse a week in the life of each family so that a sense of the daily rhythms becomes clear. This peek will help you see why every homeschool is as unique as a fingerprint, as well as spark ideas for your own family's adventure as you set about to define your own schedule, organization, and method.

TRADITIONAL SCHOOL AT HOME

DONNA WATTS and her husband, Phillip, make Wimberley, Texas, their home along with sons Jake (thirteen years old) and Luke (eleven). The boys began homeschooling in 1999, after stints in Montessori kindergarten followed by public school attendance. Donna and Phillip, the boys' stepfather, own Retail Technology Inc., which specializes in data communication for chain stores.

Jake enjoys team sports (soccer is a favorite) when he's not reading *Harry Potter* or G. A. Henty's boy heroes or involved in outdoor activities. Luke enjoys inventing, experimenting, studying insects, and making pies. Each young man cares for his own dog, cat, and guinea pig.

> This peek will help you see why every homeschool is as unique as a fingerprint.

Sunday

After Sunday school, we all go to the Blue Hole, on Cypress Creek, to swim and picnic. Jake and Luke snorkel, inspecting various "caves," bugs, fish, turtles, and (from afar) water moccasins. We can't answer all of the questions that arise but make plans to find the answers. The boys swing on ropes out over the water and splash into the deep pools. We jokingly call this P.E. (physical education).

Monday

We set up a practice test for the algebra I correspondence course Jake and Luke are taking from Texas Tech University (TTU). Because last week we mailed in the last of ten lessons in the course, this Friday the boys will take the comprehensive end-of-course exam. We try to copy the seating, timing, and overall atmosphere that the boys will experience when they take the final exam, proctored by TTU in Austin. They must pass the test in order to receive credit for the course, and the exam counts as 50 percent of their grade, so today is rather tense.

Later, while playing Frisbee, another form of P.E., Luke finds an almost perfect fossil, which he carefully puts with our collection, some of which we have been able to identify after a field trip to the University of Texas–Austin museum earlier this year.

Tuesday

Jake and Luke work on the review problems we have chosen for them based on the results of the practice tests they took yesterday. Jake prefers to work outside on the porch, while Luke works at the kitchen table. Both ask their computer programmer dad for help whenever they have questions. After working on his review, Luke uses the Internet to research prices on a CD he is "saving up for." Then on his computer he pulls up the new Encore Math 2000 software that he will use next semester. He uses a tutorial and completes a quiz that allows him to play a game he has been looking forward to playing. Meanwhile, Jake has finished working on his review and is now reading an Anne McCaffrey dragon book.

LEARNING ACTIVITY

Reenactments (history; all ages)

Our family participated in Civil War reenactments for five years, dressing in period attire, preparing and eating 1860s-style food, sleeping in canvas military tents, listening to music of the era, and living briefly as our forefathers did. We answered questions from the public, set up and took down camp, and helped with crowd control. Even the youngest children had important jobs to do. My daughter developed a business making and selling hardtack to "soldiers," usually sold out before we left. The children enjoyed these activities because adults were involved and they were respected as legitimate reenactors and expected to be knowledgeable about the time period. They took the task seriously, researching the time period intensely between reenactments.

—LAURIE MEYERPETER, LINCOLN, CALIFORNIA

Wednesday

The boys are bug hunting today and caught another of the nearly indestructible "red-butted" bugs. We don't know what they really are but have discovered many unusual characteristics. Along with the "tough bug," the boys' insect examination jar contains a mother scorpion with about twenty babies on her back. Jake and Luke carefully examine the insects, using special tweezers and other equipment they have assembled. Afterward, the boys' pet ant lion (a winged insect) is fed one fire ant at a time, because it was discovered that if more than one or two ants were put in at once, the ant lion ended up being bitten by the fire ants. Both boys work again on algebra reviews. Then we go to the Blue Hole again for P.E.—Texas is hot in the summer!

Thursday

Field trip to the water park in New Braunfels, Schlitterbaughn, for aqua lab. This is homeschool week for the park, on the Guadelupe River. We received workbooks containing information beforehand— exercises on water speed and volume, ride construction, numbers of participants, and new-ride proposals. Everyone comes home worn-out. We have to leave early tomorrow morning for the hour-long drive into Austin for the boys' test.

> We have to leave early tomorrow morning for the hour-long drive into Austin for the boys' test.

Friday

After completing the final, we go to the convention center and watch the Olympic fencing trials for a while, then go to the yearly Homeschool Book Fair at Palmer Auditorium. There the boys discover a juggling instruction book with three Hacky Sacks to learn with. We'll add them to our P.E. equipment. Jake and Luke spend two hours reading pieces of textbooks, novels, and other homeschool materials. They choose G. A. Henty's boys' adventure books, written before 1900 and historically accurate, in addition to being fun to read. Jake and Luke also chose a book on braille, and two Peterson's field guides (insects and fossils), while Mom finds a wonderful new geography book.

Saturday

Luke and Jake help install more bookcases in the "school" area of the breakfast room. Luke installs Encore's Science 2000 software on his computer and begins to peruse the various subjects. This is the program that he will use to direct most of his structured science learning next year. Because Luke prefers to work alone, he will complete units and print out the records that the program keeps and give them to his parents. Jake will continue with the TTU courses, so today he completes an experiment for the biology course that he has nearly halfway completed. Then he goes to his computer and starts the virtual lab for the biology course and works with its experiments and journal.

CLASSICAL

TERI AND Bob Nine's daughter, Jessica, attended public school kindergarten, came home for first and second grades, and went back to public school for third and half of fourth grades before coming home again. Jessica's little brother, Jonathan, attended public school kindergarten before homeschooling. Both children love to read and to play with educational software.

Bob handles Web sites/eBusiness for Fortune 1000 companies in Dallas but enjoys Saturday field trips and "teachable moments." Teri plans lessons a week at a time and provides the children with one notebook per subject, in which they will keep single-subject-related papers for four years to serve as a portfolio.

Sunday

Day of rest. Go to church, come home, hang out!

Monday

Start off day with breakfast, then daily and weekly chores. Pledge of Allegiance. Jessica works independently in A Beka math and language books. Spelling and vocabulary exercises are followed by reading Henry Wadsworth Longfellow's poem "The Village Blacksmith" and preparing to memorize it. I work with Jonathan on A Beka math and English before we take a thirty-minute break to stretch and do laundry. Together we work on social skills for about fifteen minutes before going on to oral exercises, then reading for fun. (Jessica: *Great Expectations;* Jonathan: the early learn-to-read Bob Books.)

After lunch it's world history with Usborne's *History of the World,* learning about archeology and ancient writing. Jessica writes three paragraphs about what we read, and Jonathan dictates one paragraph on what he remembers. Both draw a picture of their favorite thing we just read about (Jessica shows a man digging for "finds"; Jonathan draws the Rosetta Stone). I make mental note of their interests to get library books later on. We exercise (calisthenics) before Jessica copies three sentences of dictation, using spelling words. Jonathan plays, then copies one sentence three times (same sentence for one week), while Jessica plays before piano practice and Latin study. Bob takes Jonathan to tae-kwon-do; Teri takes Jessica to theater class. Family time, during which we read or discuss scripture, pray, or watch a scripture video, is followed by checking schoolwork and reviewing the next day's work after children go to bed.

Tuesday

Social skills review is first, then oral exercises and reading handbook. I review yesterday's work with Jessica, and she corrects circled problems while Jonathan plays.

For another hour Jessica drills with multiplication flash cards and completes a page of math. Jonathan and I use manipulatives before he does a math page. On her own, Jessica does English, spelling, poetry, dictation, and continues memorizing a poem while Jonathan and I cover English and he does copy work. Today we use the Barbie exercise video for physical education before lunch.

Science is next, and both children sketch a cell and label its parts. Enjoyment reading time is followed by reading the book *Mouse Paint.* We look at Renoir's *Dance at Bougival* online, then discuss how primary colors draw the viewer's attention. We paint in free expression with yarn and tempera primary colors. Latin and piano practice for Jessica; Jonathan off to tae-kwon-do.

Wednesday

Journal writing, social skills, oral exercises, and reading handbook. Jonathan reads Bob Books, while Jessica and I review yesterday's work. Jessica works independently on math while I help Jonathan with manipulatives and one math page. Both work on language arts before lunch. In world history we study the Sumerians and Mesopotamia, the Ziggurat of Ur. Jessica writes three paragraphs; Jonathan dictates three or four sentences on the same thing. Both find the location on the globe and a map and draw an illustration of Ziggurat of Ur. We drive to park and walk for exercise. Jessica reads, practices piano, and studies Latin. Jonathan to tae-kwon-do.

Thursday

A lot to do before Jessica's family birthday celebration tonight . . . trash school plans! Shop, run errands, bake/decorate cake. (Three of Jessica's friends stop by unannounced. Kids play while I make cake.)

I teach them about color mixing and decorating. Send them home when errand time arrives. (Jessica usually has piano class from 5:00 to 5:30 P.M. each Thursday.) Family arrives, and we celebrate birthday, open gifts, eat cake/ice cream, chat. Family leaves. Family time and ready for bed.

Friday

Just daily chores followed by oral exercises, reading handbook, social-skills review. Jessica completes dictation while Jonathan plays. He completes copy work while Jessica corrects Wednesday's work. Math is followed by reading time while I get household chores done. We start a cell experiment, using potatoes. Both children begin their cell reports at age-appropriate levels. Set experiment aside for tomorrow and eat lunch. Language arts exercises precede physical exercises, then Jessica practices piano and, with a Latin review, is ready to start the textbook on Monday. I plan next week's lessons, record in my journal how this week's went, clean up school room, and file away papers in the children's notebooks. Jonathan has T-ball practice before dinner and family time. Now I'm a day behind; I hate that! The thought comes that next week we'll have school just on Thursday, to do this week's Thursday's work, and take a vacation the rest of the week! (I only wish!)

> Math is followed by reading time while I get household chores done. We start a cell experiment, using potatoes.

Saturday

Lazy family day. We attend Jonathan's T-ball game and check the cell experiment—it really works! The kids finish their reports and make drawings of what happened to the potatoes. Mom files them away.

CHARLOTTE MASON

APPLETON, WISCONSIN, is home to Kristi Schrampfer and her husband of seventeen years, Kurt. Kurt teaches math at a local technical college while working on his MBA. Although they began homeschooling in 1996, Kristi is enjoying the first year with all four children (Paul, twelve; Kate, ten; Marie, seven; and David, three) at home. "I stumbled into Charlotte Mason's method partly because of my interest in children's literature," says Kristi, who holds a B.A. in English and worked for two legal firms prior to becoming a stay-at-home mom when her oldest was ten months old. "It was after I read *For the Children's Sake,* by Susan Schaeffer Macaulay, that I began utilizing her methods in our homeschooling."

Kurt is a Star Trek fanatic, Kristi a collector of children's books. Paul enjoys Legos and computer games; the girls like soccer, dance, and basketball. The three oldest take piano lessons, and all are avid readers.

Sunday

Our day for church, rest, and recreation. I start thinking about lesson plans for the upcoming week, and later I write up a brief outline summarizing these plans. If we happen to be starting a new unit study, I write up a book list, using at-home references such as E. D. Hirsch's *Books to Build On* or my personal book list. I also access our library's catalog via the Internet and search for books by subject, adding them to the list if they seem appropriate. I try to include nonfiction, biographies, historical fiction, experiment and/or craft books, poetry—anything that we can relate to our study.

Monday

We start with a trip to the library after breakfast and morning chores. The older children search for books on our topic on the computer catalog, or find them directly on the shelves. I encourage them to make their own choices, offering some guidance based on my prepared book list. Back at home, I work with them individually in their respective math texts. They are allowed time for journaling or a writing assignment based on our unit topic. While studying Ancient Greece, they pretended to be archeologists who find a Greek artifact. They describe it and tell how it could help us understand life during that historic period. After lunch and play time, the rest of each day is theirs to complete assignments, read, practice the piano, and play.

Tuesday

We meet to discuss our topic as a group. The children often have questions about their reading or want to share something interesting they have learned. This is what Charlotte Mason called "narration." I encourage them by asking specific questions about the readings. Sometimes I read aloud. For Ancient Greece, I read many myths and Aesop's fables to them, and these generated very interesting discussions. Even Mom learns a lot when she listens to the insights of her young children! The rest of our morning is spent on math and other individual needs, such as spelling and phonics for my first grader. After lunch, when the toddler is napping, we perform any science experiments related to our study.

Wednesday

Today begins with a meeting for discussion. In a science study, we perform more experiments, like the ones for buoyancy, displacement, and capillary action we did with our water unit. Depending on their ability level, the children either write up or orally narrate the experiment: What was done, what we expected to happen, what actually happened, etc. Then they spend more time reading their chosen books and narrating portions of interest aloud to Mom. They each keep a list of unfamiliar vocabulary words used throughout the week for spelling and/or dictionary practice. Sometimes I use the computer and make word puzzles for related vocabulary study. I work individually on math with each child, and the afternoon is spent completing assignments.

> Sometimes I use the computer and make word puzzles for related vocabulary study.

Thursday

On any given day of the week, there may be music or dance lessons or soccer or basketball practice for one or more of the children. This is our day for visiting or having friends over in the afternoon, so we try to have our schoolwork out of the way first. I work on math one-on-one with each child and assign any writing or spelling that may be needed, then they read silently from their unit books. Each one narrates a portion of interest from the books read, and we keep an ongoing list of books read for the year.

Friday

We continue with reading, narration, and individual work. On Fridays we do crafts and projects related to current study. For our study of Ancient Greece, my youngest colors several pictures from an Ancient Greece coloring book. The older children construct a model of the Trojan horse, and my oldest traces, colors, and labels a map of Ancient Greece. For quiet afternoon time, we listen to story tapes related to our study, or perhaps some music appreciation. We listen to Handel's *Water Music* during our unit study on water.

Saturday

Saturdays are days off, schoolwork having been completed for the week, but there are children's sports events to attend. Room cleaning and other household chores are completed before playtime, and the rest of the day is free for children (and Mom!) to pursue their own interests. I correct and look over the children's work that I haven't gotten to previously. Dad fixes supper, and he enlists the help of the children. After evening chores and playtime, we read before retiring for the night.

UNIT STUDIES

OUR UNIT studies family, the O'Donnells, lives in Alexandria, Ohio. Continuing in sales as a profession, dad David has just started a new job, selling newspaper advertising. David and Laraine have been married for twenty years. Laraine worked as a secretary/administrative assistant for a variety of companies before becoming a mom, and began thinking about homeschooling when her first daughter, Leslie, was four years old. However, due to the oppressive legal environment in the state in which they lived, Leslie attended public school for two years, then attended two more years after the family moved to Ohio and into what they were told was the best school district in the state.

After problems with academics (math), and physical and emotional health issues related to school attendance, now eleven-year-old Leslie is healthy, studies algebra, is an avid reader, and has dreams of marine biology or veterinary medicine in her future. Her sister, Melissa (seven), a homeschooler from the beginning, taught herself to read, print, and write cursive. Science is Melissa's current favorite, and the sisters enjoy swimming and skating. Laraine runs the homeschooling Girl Scout troop her daughters participate in, coordinates a unit study co-op, assists a 4-H club, and has a small proofreading business at home.

Sunday

All of life seems to tie together for us. What do the kids learn about at church today? Ephesians 6:1—Children, obey your parents in the Lord.

Monday

After Bible lesson, we read chapters 18 and 19 in *Prairie Primer* unit study, Little House series. The town-and-country parties are fascinating to the girls. They don't know it yet, but we will have our own party later this week. Looking at Ma's attitude as she taught the girls is wonderful. We look up what vanity is and talk about kindness, forgiveness, and attitude of heart when we make choices as Laura did (or not as Laura did) when tricking Nellie into the water, where the crab lived. We study leeches as well—lots of groans! Complete math in about an hour and spend half an hour on the week's spelling words. We do a pretest, and later this week the girls will be tested only on the words they missed. If they know them right off the bat, there is no reason to review to death—so many other fun things to do. Speaking of fun things, we're off to Girl Scouts for the afternoon—on the way, the girls complete their pages for the day in their *Comprehensive Curriculum* books. Math is done when we get home.

> We study leeches as well—lots of groans!

Tuesday

For Bible study we look up the word "vanity" in the concordance and read the verses it's found in. We compare what we find there to the dictionary definition. Work on mathematics and spend some time on silent reading and *Comprehensive Curriculum* workbooks. Geography workbooks cover latitude and longitude—a bit tough for the six-year-old, but the ten-year-old laps it up. On U.S. maps, we chart the Ingallses' last move into Walnut Grove. The girls complete review of the next three U.S. states in chronological order of their coming into the Union. Friendship books done today—we discover that vanity is not good for a friendship in any way.

Wednesday

Old Testament story for Bible. We read the next two chapters in *Little House* and continue reading about the Transcontinental Railroad—the Golden Spike (left over from last week). It always amazes me how the girls will groan, then grow enthralled as we read. The rivalry between the two railroads mirrors the vanity subject we've encountered throughout this unit. Math, *Comprehensive Curriculum,* and grammar as usual. Weekly chores—hamster pens, cat boxes, etc., cleaned. Organizational projects—in their rooms and helping others (cleaning the bathrooms with Mom and helping with laundry). Read some of the book *Julie* just for fun.

Thursday

Older daughter volunteers for library story time. Younger daughter works on phonics with Mom and does math. Older daughter does math later. Off to the ice rink for fellowship and physical education. Once home, I let it slip that tomorrow we will make the vanity cakes that Laura served at her party in the Little House—but little do they know they get to go to their own party! We write formal invitations to a party and "send" them to one another in make-believe mail-boxes. They make a formal reply.

Friday

Mom's big day! After another Old Testament Bible story, we make the dough for the vanity cakes. We deep-fry them, watching them roll over on their own in the oil. Some of them need a little nudge (math for the day—measurements and temperatures). The girls sprinkle the cakes with powdered sugar and go to their rooms to dress up for a party. When they enter the living room, they greet me at the door with proper introductions and yesterday's invitations in hand. Got to make that etiquette training live! But with my best efforts it is still pretty hokey—oh, well, at least they have been introduced to it. I usher them to their living room seats and serve lemonade and vanity cakes! Yes, the cakes did turn over on their own (for the most part) and are hollow inside, just like the science project in the *Prairie Primer* says. The ones that needed help turning over are not as hollow inside but are more like donuts—hmm, what happened there? We include another *Prairie Primer* activity—watching the *Beauty and the Beast* video while munching vanity cakes (all hollow inside, just like some of the *Beauty and the Beast* characters). I will never view that video the same again! The vanity from start to finish is incredible—the prince, the beast, Belle, Gaston, the asylum keeper, the animated clock and candle—yikes! Why had we never seen this before? We decide that being vain isn't the road we want to take.

Saturday

Bible story and off to run errands. Never got to that spelling test this week, so did it in the car as we ran errands. Spend time on 4-H projects and prepare for the *Prairie Primer* co-op group on Monday—we will be working on covered-wagon transportation.

ECLECTIC

AFTER OBTAINING a master's degree in teaching, New York state's Donna Ruppel taught briefly, then went back to college to become a registered nurse. Her per diem nursing position allows her great flexibility in her work schedule. She and husband Kurt, whose work for an agricultural company keeps him on the road for two to four days each week, brought their daughter, Alix (ten years old), home from public school at the end of second grade. Alix has two older stepsiblings, one of whom currently lives in the family's Greenwich home. After having her public school education supplemented at home, Alix has now enjoyed two years of homeschooling and appreciates the freedom to pursue her interests in pets, karate, ice hockey, and reading.

Sunday

Alix surprises us all this morning by making pancakes from scratch, a rewarding family tradition. They were delicious. Afternoon and evening fill with ice hockey, as Alix had a game and then we watched a friend play. Although we often travel thirty to sixty minutes to take Alix to hockey practices and games, we make the most of our time in the car. We hold discussions or listen to books on tape or foreign-language tapes. Today we review different types of word analogies, then discuss how stock purchases help both investors and companies.

Monday

We begin by watching a show on elements and compounds while eating breakfast. Next we practice paragraph organization, but I didn't tell Alix. (I have learned that how we approach or begin things makes a huge difference in their outcome.) Instead I ask Alix to write a "newspaper story" about my athletic pursuits, interests, and accomplishments. I also do the writing exercise with her, using her as my subject. Alix enjoys the entire project, especially reading my review of her. My participation in a project increases her desire to be involved. After lunch we read about nuclear power and vegetarianism. Driving to the library, we listen and sing to a French-language tape. Alix collects a couple of vegetarian cookbooks from the library, then we head to the grocery store. We select some new soy-based foods to try and do a price-per-pound comparison on several different items. The day ends at 9:00 P.M., after Alix's ice hockey practice.

Tuesday

Alix takes piano lessons, then teaches me—I am homeschooled also! I start practicing some songs and find myself "kicked off" the keyboard, and Alix practices. We finish by playing songs together. I ask Alix to write and type a letter to the Colorado Chamber of Commerce requesting information. Later we revise it together. I read aloud while Alix snacks. We learn about Clara Barton, and author Jean Fritz holds our attention in *Where Was Patrick Henry on the 29th of May?* At 6:00 P.M. we drive ten minutes to Alix's half-hour piano lesson. At 9:00 P.M. we drive forty-five minutes to my hockey practice, listening to *Dominic,* by William Steig. During practice, Alix watches other younger children while their moms practice, and she also serves as our team assistant. We return home at 12:30 A.M.

> Alix takes piano lessons, then teaches me—I am home-schooled also!

Wednesday

We sleep in until 10:00 A.M., then walk our four dogs. Three of them are retired racing greyhounds, and caring for them is a volunteer activity in which Alix participates. Next we clean and feed our rats and mice, then weigh them on a gram scale to track their health and to chart, format, and analyze the data in an Excel spreadsheet, an excellent ongoing math/computer project with real data on live critters. Alix loves her pet rats, and we have read mountains of information on their history, health, and care. Next we search for presidential nominee candidates' biographies on the Internet and read them. We cut out newspaper articles of them also and paste them into a journal. Alix and I have a one-hour hockey-skills lesson in the evening. Again we listen to *Dominic* during the car trip.

Thursday

A review in French and some piano practice start our day. Then we combine art and science by painting large-scale atoms of different elements, using different colors for the neutrons, protons, and electrons. Information is included about each element at the bottom of their portraits. Each element is studied before and after the painting session. My husband, Kurt, also reads aloud a newspaper article on platinum regarding its price and numerous uses. Alix spends half an hour on an interactive/animated Web site involving atoms and electricity.

Friday

I taste-test two new recipes that Alix tried from her vegetarian cookbooks. She then reads *Harriet's Hare,* by Dick King-Smith, and later begs me to read aloud from *Thomas Edison: Young Inventor,* by Sue Guthridge. During lunch we watch a stock market report and then research some companies and their stocks on the Internet. We review mean, median, and mode from her earlier rat weights and hockey statistics. Alix watches a video on Galileo and writes letters to two pen pals. While I plan for the next few days, Alix works for almost three hours on her homemade cookbook. Two weeks ago, she sent letters to friends and family requesting their favorite recipes for her personal cookbook. Now she organizes and prepares artwork for each section.

Saturday

I work the day shift at the hospital while Kurt and Alix complete some chores. Alix also cares for her pets, practices piano, reads *Journey Through the Northern Rainforest,* by Karen Pandell, and watches *Henry Ford,* a History for Kids video. When I arrive home, we all go to watch Alix play ice hockey. At bedtime I read through some of *National Geographic World* magazine with Alix.

INTEREST-INITIATED, OR UNSCHOOLING

MEET NEW Jersey's Pamm Kerr, who heard of homeschooling in 1977 and clung to the idea for seven years, until the birth of her first child, NcKinsey. Her second child, JaQuinley, joined the household in 1988. (*Note:* Pamm's descriptions of her children are purposely gender neutral.) Pamm is a single mom who works from home as a counselor specializing in issues of domestic violence, incest, and forms of stress reduction.

As the Kerr children have grown, Pamm has watched her role as homeschooling parent evolve from organizer and presenter to facilitator, magician (finding brilliant mentors to support her children's interests), and chauffeur. NcKinsey spent ninth grade in a private school, then came back home to add college courses to a busy life. JaQuinley foresees a career of professional singing and enjoys varied physical activities and strong friendships.

Sunday

After brunch with my parents, JaQuinley decides to walk the 1.5 miles home. Finds butterflies and bugs along the way, then works on math, reading projects, and karate practice at home. NcKinsey and I spend the afternoon networking with the gallery owner at a benefit art sale. NcKinsey has three paintings on display. (No paintings sold. NcKinsey has to be satisfied with having sold two paintings earlier this year.) After we gather for dinner with a friend, the kids cycle the 1.5 miles back into town and rent videos. NcKinsey chooses war history and art films; JaQuinley, one with rock music. No surprises there.

> Pamm has watched her role as home-schooling parent evolve from organizer and presenter to facilitator, magician, and chauffeur.

Monday

JaQuinley and I finish a 1,000-piece jigsaw puzzle. NcKinsey checks the business news and personal stocks and bonds online. JaQuinley and I bake a pie. NcKinsey reads some of *The War for America, 1775–1783, Great Expectations, A Clockwork Orange,* and *Catch-22.* JaQuinley is slowly reading *The Magician's Nephew.* NcKinsey walks five miles to my parents' house to chat with my ailing father and help out my mother. JaQuinley picks up Beanie Babies at a store en route to karate. I fill out forms for JaQuinley's upcoming youth black belt test. JaQuinley completes a brilliant 360-degree spinning leap in class. Go to a family dinner. Russian, Spanish, French, and German are spoken. JaQuinley stays overnight with cousins. NcKinsey, permit in pocket, drives home.

Tuesday

Drive NcKinsey to work (dishwasher at a cafe) due to rain. Pick up JaQuinley to drive to voice lesson (show tunes and arias). NcKinsey walks/runs 2.5 miles home from work. Pick up a cousin en route to

Quin's gymnastics class. Set up private lessons for next month (no summer classes). After gymnastics, take cousin to piano lesson via a record store and a quick stop for supper. Discuss teaching styles, what works, what doesn't, and music concepts. JaQuinley does a minor sewing repair. Everyone reads. We all discuss ethics. JaQuinley asks to take jazz dance and fencing classes in the fall. NcKinsey still plans to take classical Greek III, introduction to logic and Italian I in college in the fall.

Wednesday

Drop off Quin and friend for another friend's ninth birthday (causing Quin to miss science/math lessons with a Ph.D. chemist friend) after JaQuinley takes care of changing the litter for our two cats. Their overnight stay includes swimming, setting up a fort, and working on their communal Indian lore project. Talk to NcKinsey about reading, which now includes the book *Panzer Battles*. NcKinsey plays computer games (Civilization and Capitalism) and chats online with friends about designing boats and alternative societies. NcKinsey and I cook and set table for dinner with NcKinsey's art mentor/friend and her grandchild. Afterward, we watch *Law and Order*, talk about justice and procedures.

Thursday

Meet with other homeschoolers at roller rink. JaQuinley and friends, ages five to fourteen, skate together. NcKinsey skates with other teens. Discuss musical preferences, fashion, politics. NcKinsey helps make lunch. JaQuinley and I discuss psychological issues. Discuss opera before driving to meet with other homeschoolers for a preparatory lecture and to see a dress rehearsal of *Carmen*. NcKinsey talks with a friend about a theater workshop they'll take in the fall. Bring fourteen-year-old back to stay overnight. Discuss domestic violence, how Bizet portrayed it well and poorly.

Friday

Pick up friend for Spanish class. Drop off other friend. Discuss local geography and geology while driving. Stay after class to play with classmates. Make cotton candy. Explore plants. NcKinsey rides bike to work and back. Spend time on computer and reading afterward. Rework two paintings. JaQuinley and friend work on Indian project at home, then JaQuinley and I watch a French video at home. During the day, we talk about legal issues, math concepts, and the books we are reading. NcKinsey is invited to a staff party. Instead of bringing a significant other, NcKinsey asks me to come along.

Saturday

Early-morning discussion about future planning of possible tutors and special events. JaQuinley spends morning with a fifteen-year-old friend before friend leaves for a trip to Romania. JaQuinley sings while friend plays jazz piano. JaQuinley is practicing projection for a play performance next month. NcKinsey's voice teacher comes over for lesson. NcKinsey walks to work and gets driven home by chef/ owner. JaQuinley and I go swimming and walking with friends, then to an art opening at a nearby gallery. We discuss various styles of painting. JaQuinley does more math work; asks for me to review. NcKinsey asks for my opinion on a political issue. We talk about morality, truth, and obligation. NcKinsey learns new German words. I am working on "petit conversations" in French with JaQuinley.

INDEPENDENT COOPERATIVE LEARNING SITUATIONS

THE CO-OP approach comes to us courtesy of Colleen Bauman and her family: husband Dana and daughter Willa (nine), of Eugene, Oregon. A secular family choosing to homeschool as an extension of their home-based approach to life, they also work together in Dana's Cheescake, a home-based bakery business that has for twenty years offered its delights at the Eugene Saturday Market and local festivals.

"Our academic co-op is a group of nine homeschool families with children ranging in age from seven to eleven," Colleen explains. "We formed our group to experience group process, to share talents and resources, as well as to provide mutual support."

This week the co-op participants are busy winding up an eight-week unit study on the Middle Ages. "Many of the ideas for our medieval unit came from the Core Knowledge Web site," Colleen says.

Sunday

A day off from lessons. Willa helps some with the market dishes, but it is really a day to play. She is passionate about modeling clay. Today she finishes a model of a medieval knight from the 1100s. She will present this clay figure along with two drawings showing how armor changed over two hundred years.

Monday

After morning lessons, Willa makes her shield and sword. She draws an eagle design inspired by a library book on the Middle Ages. Before gluing the white paper onto her red shield, she uses it as a pattern and cuts out the shape in white felt for her red tunic. She's decided to go as Sir William. She studies helmets and picks the style she likes best. While making a helmet out of papier-mâché, we decide to make a hog's head for the feast table. Now both the unfinished helmet and the hog's head live on the dining room table.

Tuesday

Co-op day. The kids are excited about the coming feast night. Several projects are presented. The children earn points toward moving themselves up the "social ladder" for the feast. One of the other moms knights Willa and presents her with a certificate of knighthood. The best part, according to Willa, is that Kelly used a real sword! Laurie, Dion's mom, arranges for a special guest today, a fight choreographer. He demonstrates his craft, teaches some mock fight moves, and describes a day in the life of a serf. At lunch we eat like serfs; the only utensils we use are knives and picks. We are entertained by Haley dressed as a jester, performing acrobatics and riddles.

> At lunch we eat like serfs; the only utensils we use are knives and picks.

Wednesday

The hog's head still graces the table. The helmet is almost dry. Sir William has big plans about jousting at the feast. Math lesson is cut short this morning so Willa can have time to finish her projects. She's been working on an illustrated dictionary, to be ready by feast night. She copied a medieval alphabet from a library book and has been coloring the letters with metallic gel pens. She has searched hard to find a word for every letter of the alphabet and was thrilled to find that Urban II became pope in 1088! That took care of the letter U.

Thursday

Most of the same kids in co-op are also in our homeschool campfire group, led by Kelly. Both before and after the meeting, the kids play "Middle Ages." They use their knowledge of the time in their play.

Friday

Feast day! We go to the Internet for medieval recipes and find feta honey cheesecake. While the cake is baking, Willa covers the helmet in tinfoil. The painted hog's head looks more like a wolf. I'm relieved to get it off the table. It will look better with an apple in its mouth. I must admit Sir William looks pretty impressive wielding that sword around in the kitchen. I did want her to wear the dress I made, but she insists that the men had more fun back then, and she wasn't about to sit demurely at the feast while the boys had all the fun. Several of us arrive early to decorate the Grand Hall. The tables are set, complete with golden candlesticks, and garlands overhead. We hang up around the hall life-sized knights the children made by tracing one another. Medieval music is playing when the rest of the co-op arrives. All are in costumes befitting the stations they achieved by earning points with projects. There are tables filled with projects. A particularly amazing one is a mock newspaper of the time, complete with articles about fire-breathing dragons and help-wanted ads. There are sculptures, posters, book reports, and poems. The parents are mostly serfs, the children kings, knights, and ladies.

As we enjoy our feast, Daniel, an accomplished young minstrel, entertains us with medieval music on his recorder. After we have our fill, Jesse and Kira (sister and brother) teach two games using authentic toys they made. The children burn off some energy jousting outside. The evening closes with some circle dances Laurie taught us during the unit. On the way home, Willa says she doesn't want the Middle Ages to end. We all feel the same way, but we've got this exciting oceanography unit planned that includes a campout at the Oregon Coast and two days of labs at the Mark Hatfield Marine Center.

Saturday

A good market day. We have regular customers that often ask Willa what she is studying. She enjoys sharing details about last night's feast. It's been a good week.

SCHOOL-SPONSORED HOME-SCHOOLING PROGRAMS

ON ANY given evening, Ruth and George Dunnavan, along with children Beatrice (nine) and Lee (eight), might be found in their Moultonborough, New Hampshire, home enjoying musical comedy recordings while cleaning up the kitchen. Homeschoolers for three years, they use the Calvert curriculum combined with public school classes and activities. Lee has been jump-rope champ for his grade at school for three years. Beatrice most enjoys chorus and carries a book wherever she goes.

George, a retired naval officer, works as a consulting meteorologist. Ruth was also in the navy and once worked as a secretary for Congress and in the Philippines as a teacher of refugees. Now she loves the life of a stay-at-home, homeschooling mom.

Sunday

A lazy Sunday. Lee spends time on the computer, on his bike, with his video game, and, between almost every activity, he goes out into the driveway to shoot baskets. Beatrice curls up in a corner of her room with a book for much of the day. She breaks off to play with a buddy who stops by.

Monday

We start schoolwork about eight A.M. I dictate sentences to Lee, using his spelling words, then start him on his formal curriculum. I drill math facts with Beatrice, then we buckle down to her curriculum. Around ten A.M. I turn on the classical music station, and the kids get a break. Back to work about 10:15 A.M. We hit the road about 11:30 A.M. to get Lee to lunch/recess [at school] at 11:50 A.M. After recess Lee stays with his class for recreational reading from 12:50 P.M. to

1:10 P.M. At 1:10 P.M. he goes to music with that class. Back from music at 1:55 P.M., and he stays with the class until 2:10 P.M., when he goes to P.E. with a different second-grade class. He arrives back at his original class at 2:40 P.M. and follows their end-of-the-day routine until he takes the bus home at 3:05 P.M. After Lee goes to lunch, Beatrice stays with me until 12:30 P.M. Beatrice and I go to the school media center and shelve books for the librarian. At 12:30 P.M. Beatrice goes to lunch and recess with her third-grade class. From 1:25 to 1:55 P.M. she stays with her assigned class for Spanish. At 2:00 P.M. she joins another third grade for art. At 2:50 P.M. she returns to her class for their end-of-the-day routine and then joins her brother on the school bus. We eat dinner at 4:30 P.M. today, because at 5:00 P.M. I drive Beatrice and two friends to a ballet/modern dance class.

Tuesday

We do our homeschool as usual, then go to the school. Beatrice has a loaded afternoon: P.E. at 11:55 A.M. with her assigned class, then lunch, then third- and fourth-grade chorus, then twenty minutes back with the assigned class, then music with another third grade, then a little more time in the assigned classroom for the end-of-the-day routine, and finally art club after school. Tuesdays are always nice for Beatrice, because her homeschooled friend joins her for chorus and music. Lee has lunch and recess, and I get a free hour to read in the car. Lee and I go home after that. I get some housework done, and Lee reads a video game magazine. Lee and I go back to the school for an after-school grade-2 gymnastics club. I get another hour to read before I pick up both children at 4:00 P.M.

Wednesday

We rush out the door at 7:40 A.M. today to get to jump-rope club, which is a before-school activity. We get home about 9:00 A.M. and go right to work on a "no-frills" homeschool session—no drill or review. George doesn't have to work today, so he does the children's math lessons. Today is lunch/recess and art for Lee at the school, and lunch/recess and Spanish for Beatrice. They both finish at 2:00 P.M., so we go to the town library for an hour. We return to school at 3:00 P.M. to pop Lee on the school bus for home and deliver Beatrice to her after-school gymnastics club.

Thursday

Our homeschool morning is pretty normal, but I spend a lot of time supervising Beatrice and Lee at the school this afternoon. First I drop off Lee for lunch/recess and wait with Beatrice in the media center. Then I drop off Beatrice for lunch/recess and read in the car for fifteen minutes. At 12:50 P.M. I pick up Lee and supervise him at the media center, where he uses the computers. At 1:20 P.M. Beatrice joins us in the media center, and at 1:40 P.M. Lee rejoins his class for P.E. At 2:15 P.M. Beatrice rejoins her class for P.E., I pick up Lee, and we finally drive home. Beatrice rides the bus home. This is Brownies night for Beatrice, so we eat early, and Beatrice and I leave at 5:30 P.M. I stay for the meeting as a parent helper.

> Our homeschool morning is pretty normal, but I spend a lot of time supervising Beatrice and Lee at the school this afternoon.

Friday

We do our usual morning curriculum, then go to the school for lunch/recess for Lee and lunch/recess and Spanish for Beatrice. Lee gets to play kickball on the playground, which is always a hit with him. I get another of my fifteen-minute reads out in the car, then pick up Lee and supervise him at the media center while waiting for Beatrice.

Saturday

Today is a basketball day. Beatrice's team plays at 8:15 A.M. and Lee's at 10:00 A.M. It's an underwhelming program set up by the town recreation department, but the children love it. The children pal around with friends from the neighborhood this afternoon.

ONLINE LEARNING

KATE AND James Montanio met and married in Waco, Texas, before moving to Austin fourteen years ago. James has always worked in the computer field and has done so as a LAN administrator for the state for ten years. Kate sold her decade-old real estate management business to become a homeschooling mom at the time the couple's oldest child, AJ (thirteen), entered middle school. When second child Blake (eleven) found out that AJ was coming home, he wanted this also. Indeed, he asked to come home back when he was in second grade, and Kate laments, "Do we wish we had listened better!" Baby sister Elena (now six) stayed in preschool but wanted to be home for kindergarten.

"We jumped off the cliff, away from the crowd, and hoped we wouldn't crash," says Kate. "We didn't. We're still floating down gently, seeing the world like few others and loving every minute of it."

Sunday

I go online to pull out the next week's plans from our online unit study. We've done a unit study through Online Class (http://www.onlineclass.com) every semester since we began homeschooling, with classes "attended" by both public schoolers and homeschoolers. We've explored the oceans with famous seamen, tracked weather in Antarctica, learned Greek mythology, and traveled the trail with

Lewis and Clark. This semester it's dinosaurs. I spend about three hours reviewing teacher's notes and pulling together related material. I find the greatest word puzzles based on dinosaur vocabulary while following links from a Web search. At night we watch *Who Wants to Be a Millionaire* and play along interactively on the computer. It's a great test of knowledge—tonight AJ outsmarts us all on the $64,000 question!

Monday

The boys log on to Online Class to read background material for the week. Elena completes her math lesson, then trades places with the boys to play a math game on the computer while the boys and I talk about what they read online. After discussion they do some research on the dinosaur that they will be reporting on. They'll search the Internet, using online encyclopedias, university libraries, and various search engines to gather what information they can. They hope to find some pictures of dilophosaurus they can download. Later we work on piecing the boys' information into a report to send in to Online Class. Elena works on computer reading activities, then we all play Scrabble.

Tuesday

The kids do special handwriting exercises in a journal of famous quotes that come from a collection that I printed off the Internet. We read some great books about dinosaurs and fossils and begin a fossil-making experiment we found online. I leave Elena and Blake to read some more. AJ and I discuss his desire for a "real" diploma. He thinks distance learning is what he wants. He is impressed that he can "go" to college, and he is most interested in the University of Texas program. I do a general Web search of schools offering high school programs. As we look over the sites, we find that they offer pretty much the same things, but the costs are not all the same. The

LEARNING ACTIVITY

Let It Snow (science/arts and crafts; early years)

Both of my children were sick when my two-and-a-half-year-old looked out the window and yelled, "Snow, Mommy, snow!" We couldn't go out and enjoy it, so I did an Internet search on "winter crafts and activities." Soon we were building snow sculptures from toothpicks and marshmallows. We put out bowls to collect snow for indoor snow cones. We folded paper and I cut intricate designs, then my son unfolded the paper snowflakes and hung them on our windows. We talked all the while about the difference between hot and cold, winter and summer, and changing seasons. This activity helped foster a desire to learn, setting a backdrop for years to come. As we built snow sculptures, we fostered hand–eye coordination and learned a bit about how to engineer a structure to stand. As we unfolded the geometric design snowflakes, we learned how each snowflake is unique, just like us. As we talked about the winter season, my son's eyes were round with eagerness to understand all about the activities we were doing.

—CAROL NELSON, DERWOOD, MARYLAND

University of Texas has a distance-learning office not far from our house—big plus. Our broad search even yields information about schools that are not affiliated with universities but that are much less expensive.

Wednesday

We watch a Nova video on a dinosaur excavation that caused a serious lawsuit. The online site for Nova has correlating lesson plans and discussion questions. (Many TV stations offer this type of resource, and we use them often.) Since the video is a few years old, we search the Internet for news items that reveal how the case was finally resolved. We volunteer at the food bank with our homeschool teen group. When we return home, Blake e-mails to Online Class the report he and AJ completed. Elena has a play date at a friend's house. She and her friend sew stuffed animals, I mean dinosaurs, a pink icthyosaurus to be exact!

Thursday

Our package from Art to Go arrives. (For the cost of return postage only, we borrow things from the Museum of Fine Arts in Houston to use in our studies.) From the online list I select a video on drawing and some prints of ancient cave drawings depicting dinosaurs. Our discussions have been about how and when dinosaurs became extinct, and AJ's thoughts are fueled by the drawings, made thousands of years after the supposed extinction of the animals. AJ works at the library this afternoon. When we pick him up, we stay for a few minutes, and Elena has her reading program log reviewed by the youth librarian. Blake looks for a book to read this week from a list I created by merging every children's reading list I could find online into one comprehensive list. I pick up the books I ordered through the library's online catalog. Many come from libraries all over town.

Friday

It's weekly park day with our small support group! The boys complete a math lesson at SBG Math, which has interactive online math lessons—practical-use lessons. Today's is about calculating calories, building menus, and other dietary calculations. It's all done online, then printed out to show their work. It's more fun than the everyday lessons they do and reinforces skills they have mastered. Today they get a good workout in fractions and percentages. We do some more reading.

Saturday

Between loads of laundry and grocery shopping, I help the boys plan our next camping trip. We're trying to visit all the state parks and historical areas in Texas. They look at the Parks and Wildlife's Web site and determine where we need to go next. They check what other places of interest might be nearby, plan the driving route, schedule menus and supply lists. When we get it all figured out, AJ makes our reservations online. While planning, we look at the city of Austin's Web site for fun and interesting places to go around town. The boys volunteer to schedule the homeschool teens' club calendar for the next month.

> We're trying to visit all the state parks and historical areas in Texas.

7

HALF A DOZEN

HOMESCHOOLING MYTHS

In This Chapter

✦ Myth #1: Your child will become a social prune

✦ Myth #2: You, too, can be Supermom with a "perfect" homeschooling family

✦ Myth #3: Homeschooling is a one-way, all-expense-paid ticket to Harvard

✦ Myth #4: You need teacher training, dearie!

✦ Myth #5: Homeschooling is for a rare few who have nothing but time, money, patience, and devotion for their children's education

✦ Myth #6: Homeschooling is undemocratic and hurts the government school system

"We are now finishing up our first year of homeschooling, and I find myself thinking of a job I once had. It was hard work, long hours, but excellent pay, and I stayed for as long as I could. It wasn't until I was away from that job that I felt the greatest rush of relief! I find myself feeling this way about the public school system. It was okay while we were there, but the longer we're away, the more I realize what it was taking from us. I'm hoping that we can continue to homeschool."

—Allison Dodrill, a remote Air Force station in Italy

*T*HE LESS AN existing society understands something, the bigger the myths that surround it. While understanding of homeschooling fortunately is on the rise as more families participate—and therefore more people know homeschooling families—some of the associated myths refuse to die.

Understand that in part this is due to the many whose paychecks depend on perpetuating compulsory school attendance. It is not in their best interest to let these myths die. The media deserve their share of blame, too, as sloppily researched stories and editorial opinions pass as fact.

Some myths are intended to frighten you away from your decision to homeschool. Myths are an excellent way to accomplish this, because they play on all of your parental fears. They gently lead you to feel underqualified, too poor, too impatient, too "outside the law," even un-American.

> Some myths are intended to frighten you away from your decision to homeschool.

Other myths come from within the homeschooling circle itself. Some of the greediest among us allow a quest for money, prestige, and political power to justify presenting a false picture of homeschooling to the media. Studies touting astronomical standardized-test scores, kitchen-table classrooms, photos of nine perfectly coifed, identically dressed, smiling siblings and their parents on magazine covers all lead to a Lake Wobegone vision of homeschooling—i.e., all homeschooled kids are beautiful, strong, and superintelligent. This image is just as damaging to the confidence of the new homeschooler as the negative extreme.

At this point you've done too much thinking and learning to fall for myths from either extreme. Let what you've discovered so far help you see the frequently repeated myths as the smoke screens that they are.

MYTH #1: YOUR CHILD WILL BECOME A SOCIAL PRUNE

IF I had to choose any single myth about homeschooling that really gets my goat, it's this one. For starters, it is a blatant lie. Even if there exists a parent who would not make plans to incorporate socialization opportunities into her homeschooling, the activities of a functioning household would provide some. There are trips to the grocery store, bank, post office, hardware store, gas station, library, pizza parlor, and dentist's office. Most families, at least on occasion, visit the ice cream store, movie theater, church, beach, museum, parade, park, and skating rink. Don't forget the homes of neighbors, friends, grandparents, cousins, and support group hostesses, or the many activities that even homeschooled children's schooled peers participate in: Scouts, 4-H, swim classes, summer camp, sports, music lessons, and, as they get older, paying jobs.

While engaging in these common and necessary activities, homeschooled children meet and converse with real people doing real work in the real world. Not only does this present socialization opportunities with people who aren't going to call the children foul names or extort their lunch money; it also provides lessons in practical life skills that they will use throughout their entire adult lives.

Prevent this myth from paralyzing your homeschooling efforts by taking a closer look at the school version of socialization so highly touted by homeschooling critics whose primary argument always comes out sounding something like this: "School is not just about academics. It's about learning to work with others and being exposed to those who think differently. It's about learning how to handle conflict. I fear for these [homeschooled] children who won't understand America's diversity or be able to handle the real world when they're grown." (I don't know how, but they always say this with a straight face too.)

Schools by their very nature are institutions. Socialization that occurs within their walls centers around the institution and its functions with the major goal of keeping the institution running as smoothly as possible. How "real" is life within this institution?

For starters, the school is filled with residents from a very small geographic area, oftentimes from a single neighborhood. Such narrow parameters don't typically offer a huge amount of socioeconomic diversity. Next, these single-neighborhood residents are sorted according to age, effectively separating siblings (unless they are twins, and even then a lot of schools try to put them in separate classes). During his time in the institution, then, a six-year-old receives the majority of his social clues from . . . other six-year-olds! I think most of us would agree the vast majority of six-year olds are too weak in the social graces to serve as the ideal models of behavior for one another. In this way a mass pecking order based on age is also established.

> School socialization is controlled as readily and intently as the timing of the bell that signals the end of the day.

School socialization also sets up the "us vs. them" perspective held by so many students regarding teachers and, by extension, other adult authority figures. Within the institution, children's socialization is accepted only insofar as authority allows it. School socialization is controlled as readily and intently as the timing of the bell that signals the end of the day. Does this train children to purposely test the limits and to look upon the person stopping the natural flow of socialization as the enemy?

Now compare these circumstances to "real" life once a child leaves school. Is the world set up so that he associates only with people who live near him? Will he work with only people born in the same year? When he meets a pretty girl, will a boss keep him after work for talking to her? Institutional socialization is about as artificial as socialization can get.

The truth is that the vast majority of homeschooling parents *do* make plans to incorporate greater socialization opportunities into homeschooling. The truth is that *The Kiplinger Newsletter* of August 25, 2000, called an increase in the number of homeschooled youths entering the workforce "good news for employers. Those taught at home often score higher on standardized tests. . . . More colleges are recruiting them because of their good track records. Usually taught to be independent thinkers, hardworking, self-motivated." As hard as I searched, I couldn't find any similar comments about those spending lots of time in the artificial socialization of schools.

MYTH #2: YOU, TOO, CAN BE SUPERMOM WITH A "PERFECT" HOMESCHOOLING FAMILY

SWALLOW THIS myth, and you're setting yourself up for a fall — fast and hard. Trouble is, many homeschooling moms start out with this unrealistic goal in mind.

Ask Litchfield, New Hampshire, homeschooling mom Hallie Pentheny. "First-year homeschoolers tend to be extremely crazed," she explains. "They lean toward overcompensation for taking their kids out of school. They feel the need to become supermoms with superkids to prove to everyone who has either objected to or scorned the idea of homeschooling that homeschooling is better."

How do newly homeschooling moms go about this?

"They overextend themselves, sign up for too many activities, and purchase too much curriculum—sometimes way too much curriculum," says Hallie. "Would new homeschoolers believe you if you told them this? *I* wouldn't have listened. It may just be a necessary stage for us to go through. But at least you could put down that this is a normal stage and that the new homeschooler will get over it. Then explain about all the online resources for selling off that stuff

WHAT I WISH SOMEONE HAD TOLD ME DURING MY FIRST YEAR OF HOMESCHOOLING

I wish someone had told me not to expect perfection the first year, that there would be a lot of trial and error after bringing home a second-grade boy from public school. I wish someone had told me not to judge my homeschool success by his feelings and that continually asking if he liked homeschool or public school best would keep him confused and unsettled.

—DEANN UTLEY, HOT SPRINGS, ARKANSAS

you thought you wanted but never got to." (These are in the resource section, Hallie!)

Certainly the desire to impress those who doubt us is a strong motivation to go overboard. I think another reason perfectly normal parents turn into first-year zealots stems from deeply rooted, maybe even subconscious, self-doubt. In other words, we also need to prove to ourselves that we can do this, especially after a lifetime of believing that educating children is the province of professionals.

I can't count how many e-mail messages I've received through homeschool.com from new-to-homeschooling parents that list every book and subject imaginable that they plan to use, then ask me if they've left out anything. "Whoa, relax," I tell them. "Does your child really need to learn about rocket science this year? He's only four years old!"

As for the perfect homeschooling family, well, I've met a lot of homeschooling families, and while I love them all, I wouldn't call any of them perfect, including my own. Homeschooling doesn't turn little ones into Stepford children. Instead, it allows you enough time with your child to get to know each other, understand each other, trust each other. This leads to happiness, if not perfection. Since we are all fallible human beings, happiness is more attainable than perfection, equally worthy of your efforts, and, in the long run, much less likely to produce the need for therapy.

It's more important to reduce self-doubt than to prove to your mother-in-law that your three-year-old can speak five languages. Here is some insider knowledge to help you:

+   You are accomplishing more in an hour of attention to your child's education than a school accomplishes in a day.

+   You are observing your child's growth on a daily basis. Do you really think any major deficiencies are going to escape you?

+   Neither you nor your child is perfect—make your mistakes and move on.

+   Has any teacher ever told you she loves your children?

"When I blow it or make a mistake, I can quickly go to my children and admit I was wrong and ask for their forgiveness," explains Ritzya Mitchell, a Herndon, Virginia, homeschooling mom. "They learn that I'm not perfect. More important, they learn that they're not perfect and that I love them unconditionally."

Who needs to become Supermom with a perfect family anyway, when becoming Available Mom with a happy family is so much more fun?

MYTH #3: HOMESCHOOLING IS A ONE-WAY, ALL-EXPENSE-PAID TICKET TO HARVARD

OF COURSE, if homeschooling children are sweeping the Scripps Howard National Spelling Bee, winning the National Geography

Bee, and tromping the competition in everything from robotics to filmmaking, your child is guaranteed a free trip through Harvard if you homeschool, right? (And, boy, wouldn't your mother-in-law have to eat her words after this accomplishment!)

A free ride at Harvard or another prestigious university is certainly a possibility. Along with a traditional love of high SAT scores, Stanford University's admission personnel echo a new and growing appreciation for the homeschooling experience. When asked to offer comments on my book *Homeschoolers' Success Stories: 15 Adults and 12 Young People Share the Impact That Homeschooling Has Made on Their Lives,* Jon Reider, Stanford's former senior associate director of admissions, noted how the profiled homeschoolers have led "an examined life" and further stated that "in the face of enormous cultural pressure, they learned to find their own ways, through trial and error more than through ideology."

This appreciation and understanding is beginning to translate into a relatively high college acceptance rate compared to the general college-age population. (See Karl Bunday's site at http://learninfreedom.org/colleges-4-hmsc.html for a list of 1,000 colleges and universities that have accepted homeschooled students.)

Rebecca Winters, writing for the September 11, 2000, issue of *Time,* reports that 26 percent of thirty-five homeschooled applicants had been accepted into Stanford University's 2000–2001 freshman class, "nearly double the overall acceptance rate." The twenty-three homeschooled freshman entering Wheaton College in September 2000 had submitted SAT scores an average "58 points higher than those of the overall class." Just as with other children, though, a scholarship at a highly esteemed college or university is not guaranteed for homeschoolers. Thorough academic preparation and hard work are prerequisites for all. If this is a goal of your homeschooling, let it guide your choices throughout your child's time at home.

That said, when starting homeschooling it's important to remember that college attendance is but one of many avenues open to

LEARNING ACTIVITY

Getting to Know the Bard
(language arts; middle and teen years)

A retired actor advertised that he wanted to get together with others to do readings of Shakespeare plays. Our children—nine and eleven years old—were the only kids in the group of actors; the others were adults just interested in Shakespeare. We started with *The Taming of the Shrew*, and the children got a feeling for what goes into creating a character, how blocking is done, how an actor uses voice, and more. Two years later, they have read five performances of Shakespeare and watched films of three others. They have no idea that some people are afraid of Shakespeare. Since we moved from the area and our Shakespeare group, we've started one of our own in our new area.

—KATE VARLEY, VILLANOVA, PENNSYLVANIA

a homeschooled child, and I sure wouldn't wish Ivy League attendance on a child who may be ill-suited for or disinterested in this type of schooling. This is a point of contention because our culture inculcates in us the belief that the only way to become a successful adult and productive citizen is to have obtained a college degree in something or other. While this belief has for years steadily driven up the price of degrees, consider this:

More than three out of every ten college freshmen don't make it into sophomore year. Three out of every four students (75 percent!) who do continue still don't have a degree five years later, according to the National Center for Education Statistics. There are obviously an awful lot of ill-suited or disinterested students in our college classrooms, but your child doesn't have to be one of them.

Some homeschoolers choose to utilize their time together as a family emphasizing aspects of life other than academics. They, too, use knowledge of their personal educational philosophy to guide their choices.

> It's important to remember college attendance is but one of many avenues open to a homeschooled child.

"I wish someone had told me that my child doesn't have to be a genius in order to validate our decision to homeschool," says Becky Jackson, of Hatfield, Arkansas. "My daughter doesn't even have to keep up with or be ahead of schooled kids, because she lives and learns in an entirely different world. Standardized tests or stars on a chart that validate only cognitive learning cannot accurately measure her knowledge, skills, feelings, attitude, and experiences."

Let me note that working on a fast academic track and working on other life aspects are not mutually exclusive. Whether or not your child winds up in Harvard with a scholarship depends on your child's learning style, interests, and future career plans. It shouldn't depend on an externally driven desire for what is often a degree that leaves its bearer in debt and is a poor substitute for real-life learning if that degree isn't essential to desired life's work.

MYTH #4: YOU NEED TEACHER TRAINING, DEARIE!

SPEAKING OF high-priced schooling . . . what about those teaching degrees? Don't people go to college for four years —or longer— to become professional teachers? Mustn't learning the skill of teaching be learning the secrets of how to light fires within youngsters' minds, setting them on a course to appreciate and pursue learning for a lifetime?

Not according to many reports, including one from the Council for Basic Education (CBE), a membership organization based in

LEARNING ACTIVITY

Ticket to Grammar (language arts; early years)

This activity is courtesy of *Poemcrazy*, by Susan Wooldridge. Cut out words from magazines, catalogs, junk mail, etc., and paste them on to tickets, which you can keep in a box to play with. I bought a huge roll of raffle tickets at an office-supply store for a few dollars. The kids enjoyed the cutting and pasting, then using the tickets just like magnetic poetry. They arrange them into poems and silly sentences or sometimes just pull out a few words and play with them to spark their writing imaginations.

—DEB BAKER, BELLEVUE, WASHINGTON

Washington, D.C. that advocates for high academic standards in K–12 education, titled "What Teachers Have to Say about Teacher Education" (located on the Web at http://www.c-b-e.org/articles /drperspt.htm). This is information any parent should have, but especially parents who may right now be stressing out over their own ability to teach.

Noting that teachers are rarely asked to critique teacher education and their preparation for the job even though it's a cornerstone of many cries for educational reform, in 1995 the CBE sent surveys to 1,650 teachers, mostly award winners, in addition to all of those teachers certified by the National Board of Professional Teaching Standards. More than six hundred teachers responded, 503 who had taught for more than ten years. The respondents taught in high, middle, and elementary schools.

The CBE report states, "We were expecting (and received) far more negative responses about their preparation for teaching than positive comments. Even the most devoted teacher educator admits

WHAT I WISH SOMEONE HAD TOLD ME DURING MY FIRST YEAR OF HOMESCHOOLING

I wish that someone had told me how much fun having my children with me would be. I wish they had reminded me of the inherit joy in mothering and the small but delightful experiences we could share together. I was a cautious new homeschooler worried about possible "gaps" in my child's education. I went with school-in-a-box curriculum, which my son and I endured while I got over my fears by talking with homeschoolers on the Internet. They expanded my horizons, I overcame my fears, and I learned that the biggest part of homeschooling is the fun—the small joys, the sudden hilarity—those family moments we couldn't hope to reproduce or explain to someone else.

—ELIZABETH DAVIS, COLORADO SPRINGS, COLORADO

to serious flaws in teacher education, and the teachers were eager to suggest major improvements."

A previous report from the National Commission on Teaching & America's Future, called "What Matters Most: Teaching for America's Future," listed five major problems of teacher education (apply what you've been learning about homeschooling to this list for an interesting exercise):

+ inadequate time (a four-year undergraduate program is not enough)

+ fragmentation (course work is separated from practice, and education school and arts and sciences faculties are insulated from one another)

+ uninspired teaching methods

+ superficial curriculum

+ traditional views of schooling.

To this list, the teachers surveyed added:

+ inadequate and unsupervised school-based experience

+ poor quality of many teacher candidates

+ university faculty inexperienced in the schools.

There's more. In November 1999, the Thomas B. Fordham Foundation, in its report "The Quest for Better Teachers," graded the United States on how it is doing "when it comes to putting policies into place that will improve teacher quality."

In its foreword the report states, "The news is not very good. Overall, the states earn a 'D+' for their teacher quality policies. *The grades would have been even lower had we not engaged in grade inflation.*" [Emphasis added.] Two states, Texas and Florida, received A's.

Feel better?

Good. Now realize that when it comes to homeschooling, none of this need apply to you anyway! The school's method is such that it requires a teacher in the classroom, it requires that teacher to manage a roomful of twenty to thirty children, and it requires materials that fill up the teacher so that she may "pour" out a lesson to a group of children.

> The news is not very good. Overall, the states earn a 'D+' for their teacher quality policies. The grades would have been even lower had we not engaged in grade inflation.
>
> —Thomas B. Fordham Foundation report

This is not necessarily your job at home. "Everyone is nervous about this choice during the first year, because we've been taught that we can't do it unless we have a degree in teaching," says Cynthia McDaniel, of Springfield, Virginia. "The nervousness about doing it causes many parents to recreate school at home."

So what do you have to take the place of a D+ teacher training (after cheating, previously called grade inflation)? "I found that if you

WHAT I WISH SOMEONE HAD TOLD ME DURING MY FIRST YEAR OF HOMESCHOOLING

I wish someone had told me that it was okay to start the year with a list of about a thousand interesting homeschooling plans and ideas and to 1) start some of them, but not finish them because everyone loses interest in the subject, 2) never start some of them because the kids think the projects are stupid, 3) never start some of them because you realize they are just too much work, 4) lose interest in topics everyone thought were so fascinating only months before, and 5) run out of time before you make another list of a thousand things to do next year.

—LARISSA LEE, EAST BRUNSWICK, NEW JERSEY

can read, are willing to learn, and are willing to help your children, you can do this," Cynthia reports. "Learning to love learning again, through trips in the woods, alone or with a book about nature or with a specialist (ranger, scout leader), is an excellent way to proceed."

Over the years you've developed many characteristics as a parent that transfer well and can help in your new role as homeschooling parent. Instead of being trained teachers, successful and happy homeschooling parents, by and large, are . . .

+ delighted to spend time with children whose company they appreciate

+ possessed of basic literacy and math skills and ready to learn more, if necessary

+ aware that they will be criticized—sometimes by those closest to them—and sufficiently convinced that they are doing the right thing to withstand criticism

✦   open to learning from mistakes and to change based on what they've learned

✦   working on becoming more observant and accepting of their children, warts and all

✦   possessed of wonderful senses of humor, leading to the ability to laugh at themselves

✦   giving and receiving support from like-minded friends

As you can see from the above, you are a lot more likely to have what it takes to homeschool than what the myth of needing teacher training reveals. By using and constantly honing the parental qualities you already enjoy, you are much closer to learning the secrets of lighting fires within youngsters' minds, setting them on a course to appreciate and pursue learning for a lifetime, than many, if not most, trained teachers.

MYTH #5: HOMESCHOOLING IS FOR A RARE FEW WHO HAVE NOTHING BUT TIME, MONEY, PATIENCE, AND DEVOTION FOR THEIR CHILDREN'S EDUCATION

SOUNDS LIKE you'd have to be a saint to consider homeschooling, doesn't it? Homeschooling critics, while telling the press (in not so many words) that parents aren't capable of educating their own children, often add this myth for good measure. Just in case you have the nerve to think you're competent enough to homeschool, perhaps you'll believe that you don't have enough _____ (fill in the blank with any of the above).

If it's any consolation, I've homeschooled three children, and I'm no saint. None—I repeat, none—of the homeschoolers I've met are

LEARNING ACTIVITY

Puddle Play (science; all ages)

There's a huge puddle on one of our walks. Though often ignored, when it was covered with a thin layer of ice, it served as a model of Jupiter's moon Io. We hurled "meteorites" onto it that skittered across the surface, broke through the ice, or embedded themselves in the surface, depending on angle and velocity. It's been a testing ground for the effect of wind on makeshift rafts of various shapes and materials that happened to be lying near the puddle. When a disturbance stirs up mud from the bottom, it provides a visual model of the complex, chaotic currents. It always serves as a reminder that the biology of dogs, as exemplified by our dog, prefers dirty water to clean.

—JOYCE FETTEROLL, MEDFIELD, MASSACHUSETTS

saints, either. They're simply families who for one or more of many reasons figured they could do a better job of educating their children at home than by sending them to school.

For good measure, the myth is sometimes further backed up by a mention of how many two-income families live in our nation, so a large percentage of potential homeschoolers are immediately discounted by critics. They don't have the time.

Then there's the cost of homeschooling, a financial burden you carry on top of paying your school tax bill. Surely in order to homeschool, two-income families will have to drop down to one income, and educating children is expensive, don't you know. (Take another look at your school tax bill to see just how expensive government control has made it.) If families don't have lots of extra money, they, too, are shuffled aside, because they couldn't possibly financially afford to homeschool.

How overwhelming it must seem for a two-income family driven by the government school schedule to possibly possess the patience and devotion required to "sacrifice it all" for their children's education. Surely Americans are stressed-out workers with stressed-out children returning home from school each day, and this state of affairs ensures that even if they think they can pull it off financially, they don't have what it takes emotionally.

The truth is, more and more two-income families are making homeschooling work. Sure, it usually takes some really good time-management skills—but, hey, you're a homeschooler; go get a book and learn about time management. You'll likely discover you've been experiencing a whole lot of wasted life moments, and regain some of that time too.

Maybe you've been molding your work schedule to the school's more overwhelming one. Now you get to change the overwhelming schedule to one that fits better. You'll probably find that the freedom this affords you will provide you with even more time to live and learn together than you might at first glance have thought you had.

Perhaps instead of working full-time, you could make the same amount of money part-time from home. Or you might figure out you could live with less and switch to part-time work, or no work at all—maybe for your spouse, if not you. Maybe you can add up all your work-related bills, deduct them from your pay, and discover that your time isn't nearly as valuable in dollar bills as you thought it was.

That brings us to money and how in the world, at a time when you are cutting back on everything else, you'll afford the additional cost of education.

The fact that it costs your local school district an average of $6,200 per child to get and keep children in school doesn't set the price tag of education. Home education can be, and most often is, much cheaper. Since you're the one setting it up, you control the price tag.

Anything you lack in greenbacks can be compensated for with creativity. There are several useful books about stretching your homeschooling dollars. Borrow one from your library, and let your imagination go. As you begin to live a learning lifestyle that you might not be able to imagine quite yet, you'll grow accustomed to seizing the educational opportunities of any of life's moments. Money need not be an object.

It's a rare homeschooling parent who hasn't wondered if she has what it takes emotionally. This consideration tugs at our heartstrings whenever we hear another mom or dad express doubt about parental patience or devotion. Both are virtues parents possess, but when living with the school's schedule, organization, and method, how much time is really available to give these virtues regular workouts?

> Anything you lack in greenbacks can be compensated for with creativity.

Homeschooling provides you with time to do just that—regularly exercise patience and devotion—and they grow stronger and brighter in the process. Parents of children who previously attended school especially marvel at the feelings of cooperation and partnership that spring out of homeschooling. I believe this happens because the children's patience and devotion grow at the same time.

Again, it may be hard to believe at the beginning of your first year, but the child you will be homeschooling will be a different child after a year than the one you brought home from school. Thanks to discussions and activities together, you'll know each other better. Because she'll be away from constant peer influence, you'll relate to each other in a different way. After both of you have learned "outside the box" for a year, both of you will think differently. Even if you can't see yourself possessing patience for the child before you today, homeschool for just a little while. You and your child will change.

You may not have all the time, money, patience, and devotion in the world, but then you don't need it all; you merely need enough.

MYTH #6: HOMESCHOOLING IS UNDEMOCRATIC AND HURTS THE GOVERNMENT SCHOOL SYSTEM

THIS MYTH assumes that compulsory school attendance is as old as the Rockies and, for good measure, incorporates a dash of the lack of exposure to cultural diversity.

Critics who circulate this myth need to go back to the American history books to discover that compulsory school attendance made its way into all existing United States a mere 150 years or so ago. (Whoops. They may not find that in textbooks—much history is missing from them.)

Perhaps they could go to a dictionary instead and look up "democratic." (You could also argue that the United States of America was founded as a republic, not a democracy, but let's not split hairs.) The American Heritage Dictionary of the English Language defines democratic as "pertaining to, encompassing, or promoting the interests of the people."

Is homeschooling undemocratic according to this definition? Of course not. A parent who researches educational options and concludes home education is the best route for his children is "promoting the interests of the people," the people being the children for whom he is responsible.

In return, one might question if it "promotes the interests of the people" to compel all children, regardless of ability or interest, to take part in one-size-fits-all schooling. The definition of compel is "to force." Does imposing legal penalties on parents who choose differently—including the loss of liberty through prison—"promote the interest of the people?"

Those who believe that the state has a compelling interest in the education of children would argue that the individual's needs must be set aside for the sake of the whole. This sounds more like socialism than democracy. On the other hand, those who believe that ultimate responsibility for education lies with the parents and not the state trust that those parents, because of their intimate knowledge of their own families, can best "promote the interests" of their children.

One who argues that homeschooling is undemocratic, then, must believe that the state's interest supersedes that of the parents. It's an argument that arose when the first soldiers escorted Massachusetts' children to school at gunpoint almost two hundred years ago, and it continues today. It's a belief that allows home-schooling critics to feel that something critical is taken away from a child who doesn't experience the "socialization" of government schooling. Is it really socialization that they are worried about, or might they be worried about something else that homeschooled children don't receive at home?

> When any viable choice, especially one recognized as bene-ficial to a growing number of citizens' in-dividual interests, is la-beled undemocratic, it's time to worry about the labelers.

The belief that the state's interest supersedes parents' interest in children's education naturally results in concrete and abstract school lessons that serve the state's interest first. These lessons ebb and flow according to whatever is currently "po-litically correct" but always infiltrate every aspect of the curriculum, class discussions, and test questions. In this way children are molded to be-come the society that current powers-that-be wish it to be. You can decide whether to call this education—or conditioning.

The truth is that homeschooling is a choice available to all fami-lies. When any viable choice is labeled undemocratic, especially one recognized as beneficial to the individual interests of a growing num-ber of citizens, it's time to worry about the labelers.

8

WHAT TO EXPECT WHEN STARTING AT THE BEGINNING

© EyeWire

"A common first-year experience that particularly bothered my husband was when the children would invariably be questioned about why they weren't in school. They felt uncomfortable when questioned about this or about what school they attended. We tried to be honest and tell people that the children were homeschooled, but that occasionally led to confrontation. Mostly we learned to avoid these conversations or I would deftly change the subject. I rarely am asked this anymore, perhaps because homeschooling has grown more common."

—Laurie Meyerpeter, Lincoln, California

173

*T*HIS CHAPTER HIGHLIGHTS the challenges unique to starting homeschooling with children who have never been to school. The next chapter will do the same for challenges more frequently faced by those for whom homeschooling is a transition from more traditional schooling. Please note, however, that many challenges don't recognize strict boundaries between the two different starting places, as the opening paragraph reveals. Many more respondents shared experiences that can be claimed by both groups than noted specifics for one group or another.

Since at least one of the following typical first-year experiences will likely touch you no matter what the age of your child, we'll first briefly review these more common experiences before we move on to specifics.

WHAT ALL BEGINNING HOME-SCHOOLERS MIGHT EXPECT

Lest you believe that the experienced homeschooling moms surrounding you are saints or that you're the only parent grappling with a gnawing feeling in the middle of the night, read on.

Panic Attacks

Homeschool panic attacks look different from those discussed in psychology journals. Instead of shortness of breath and dizziness, your mind is gripped by an overwhelming certainty that every single child sitting in a classroom is learning four times as much as your child is at home—at least. Are you studying the right things? Are you doing enough? Pushing too hard? Not hard enough?

The triggers of panic attacks vary with individuals and range from thoughts planted in you by others to thoughts going on nowhere but inside your own head. No matter the trigger, there is readily available relief for homeschooling panic attacks.

"For me, panic days are usually precipitated by comments from relatives or friends expressing doubts, or maybe by realizing that my young nephew, who is in private-school kindergarten, is reading better than my seven-months-older son," says Le Ann Burchfield. "The best way I have found to combat these days is to dig out my homeschooling books and read. It helps to review the same literature that made me realize not only that homeschooling was 'doable' but that it has advantages that cannot be found in any other method of education."

> Your mind is gripped by an overwhelming certainty that every single child sitting in a classroom is learning four times as much as your child is at home— at least.

Desire to Throw In the Towel

A town near our home always sponsors a winter carnival during the subzero temperatures of February. The goal of an entire week's worth of activities is a much-needed break from the "cabin fever" that grips the human soul during some of the shortest, coldest days of the year.

Interestingly, February is often a make-or-break homeschooling point, a time of year when new homeschoolers might consider throwing in the towel. In February, the initial thrill of home-schooling has likely mellowed into a routine, the hectic holidays have come and gone, and—in the colder parts of the country, at least—childhood energy isn't finding release through daily outdoor activity. Cabin fever sets in.

"I can remember telling my children, 'I am going to stop the first school bus and put you on it. I don't even care what school it is going to!'" Amy Cooper remembers. "They knew I was kidding because I was laughing when I said it, but believe me, sometimes I would have liked that freedom."

WHAT I WISH SOMEONE HAD TOLD ME DURING MY FIRST YEAR OF HOMESCHOOLING

No one ever told us that February is typically a very difficult month for home-schoolers. We were stunned when our old doubts resurfaced during the coldest, most dismal month of the year. How could this be? We were sure we were doing well; we were almost finished with our kindergarten curriculum. What did she mean she wanted to go to "real school"? Why did I want to put her on that shiny yellow bus?

Thanks to a wonderful support group, we made it through this period. I got on the phone with some of the more experienced homeschoolers and found out this is a typical phenomenon; in fact some of them were experiencing it. We have spoken to public school teachers who admit that February is their toughest month of the year too. Boy, that sure would have been a nice thing to know!

—EMILY MCGRINDER, MARIETTA, GEORGIA

Amy notes that during her first February of homeschooling, she requested applications from three private schools. "In our second February, I called only one school," she continues. "Since then, we just take off a week in February! I now know that sending the boys to school would infringe on our freedom as a family."

Forewarned is forearmed. If you think about remedies before-hand, your family's cabin fever shouldn't reach epidemic proportion.

We're Going to Homeschool Just Like They Did in That Book!

In the early years of our homeschooling, one of the few first-person accounts of homeschooling I read was the Colfaxes' *Homeschooling for Excellence* (Warner, 1988). While I may have been uncertain about exactly how and what I was doing, I now knew at least one thing I wouldn't do: pack up and head for California to raise goats.

Perhaps my children were lucky that the only story I read included a lifestyle that I couldn't imagine for us, for I may have done what many new homeschoolers do: try to duplicate another family's homeschooling and claim it as our own.

Today first-person accounts of homeschooling abound, so I imagine it's much easier to relate to an experienced family's circumstances and to emulate it. While it is likely that a minority of the authors of these books desire to show you the way to homeschool (their way), many more want their work to showcase the educational diversity available in homeschooling's freedom. They want to spark the readers' creativity, and they hope that an idea or two may be helpful in your own homeschooling adventure.

This is as it should be—each family finding its unique educational fit. Besides, trying to be just like another family usually yields less-than-desirable results.

"Before we began homeschooling, I read *A Patchwork of Days,* by Nancy Lande, in which a number of families describe one day," says Kate Varley, a Villanova, Pennsylvania, mom of two. "I wanted to capture what those families had done, like making different kinds of muffins every week and snuggling happily with my children as we read together."

Simple enough, right? But "my children only like one kind of muffin, and we usually didn't get around to making them anyway. We read together a lot, but reading about chemicals used in mummification didn't make for good snuggling," Kate says. "And besides, my daughter didn't want to snuggle, because she was too big for that. My son would sit close but often seemed to be trying to climb behind me. We were not going to have a re-creation of someone else's homeschooling."

Kate and her family worked in the direction of their own kind of homeschooling instead. "As time goes on, my memory of the families

WHAT I WISH SOMEONE HAD TOLD ME DURING MY FIRST YEAR OF HOMESCHOOLING

If I could go back and give myself some advice during the first year, I would tell myself not to second-guess all of the choices I made about curriculum. I got all panicky when my girlfriend said that she was teaching her son about the Vikings. Yikes! I hadn't covered that with my son. Should I drop everything and do that? There is so much pressure to "do it all" and to "prove" yourself. If the curriculum I chose was working well for my son, then there was no need to reconsider it at that time.

—JOY HAYDEN, STERLING, VIRGINIA

in Lande's book fades, but I can say with reasonable certainty that our homeschooling didn't turn out like any of them," she concludes. "It did turn out to meet our needs, our talents, our energies, our values, and our evolving ideas of education; and homeschooling does that better than anything."

Choosing the Most Structured Approach You Will Ever Use

"We never actually ordered curriculum or planned to do school at home," says Deb Baker, "but I have found it hard from time to time to resist the urge to sit my son down and teach him something I think he should know, even when I know that he generally doesn't respond well to that sort of approach. It seems pretty common that folks find unschooling a little uncomfortable at first. Some people seem to come to it more easily, but I don't know anyone who has never struggled with letting go."

Although letting go and loosening up are understandable struggles for many, anecdotal evidence has always indicated that homeschoolers tend to do just that. I decided to check into this a little more closely while writing *Homeschooling: The Early Years* (Prima, 1999). When I asked sixty-six homeschooling families to compare the amount of structure in their homeschooling when they began to where they are now, 59 percent had moved toward less structure. When Shari Henry surveyed sixty-one more families for *Homeschooling: The Middle Years*, 64 percent had also become less structured in their approach.

> This tendency reveals that many home-schoolers eventually allow trust in themselves and their children to replace structure.

This tendency reveals that many home-schoolers eventually allow trust in themselves and their children to replace structure. It also shows that just as with any endeavor, it takes some time and experience to relax enough to feel comfortable doing something new.

Inability to Trust That Children Will Learn Even When You Don't Teach

This common first-year experience is the province of the more eclectic and interest-led homeschoolers, as they are the first to begin to try this. The inability to trust that anyone—most especially children—can learn without someone's teaching is routine in a society raised on compulsory school attendance.

It's hard to go against societal expectations, even when you're totally convinced they are wrong. "It was tough to trust the unschooling process unless I saw the kids doing 'schoolish' things or making great strides in some area," explains Thyne Rutrough. "But I'm slowly beginning to trust that those times when they aren't apparently learning anything are essential to their learning—they're processing and putting together bits and pieces of old and new knowledge from here and there. Later, it pops up unexpectedly in the most fascinating combinations."

LEARNING ACTIVITY

Colorful Reading (reading/art; early years)

Our favorite learning activity right now is for the children to color while I read aloud from chapter books. I have purchased several Dover coloring books and have a large box of colored pencils, put away until reading time. This works especially well for my wiggly four- and six-year-old boys, who might not get much out of the reading if they had to sit still on the couch and just listen.

—KATHY FLY, DERBY, KANSAS

Again, time and experience help, as does your growing parental ability to pay more attention to what is happening than to what isn't happening. "Try to relax," adds Thyne, "let the learning happen, and join in as much you can."

So Many Questions!

Funny, but a child out and about in the real world during school hours might just as well be wearing a sign that says, "Ask my mom or me why I'm not in school today!"

Most often inquisitors are friendly, curious folks who would also ask why you are wearing a fur hat in July if you chose to do that. Even so, new homeschoolers sometimes find the situation uncomfortable if they must define or at times defend their choice. This is even truer for the children themselves.

You are never under an obligation to give a stranger your life story, but you'll probably want to think about the answer you'll give (and the education you'll provide!) when the inevitable questions occur.

"We took a lot of time to read and educate ourselves so that we could meet interrogations calmly and strongly," says Nina Sutcliffe, Middletown, California. "I made a point of responding with confidence, not attacking their choices, and not getting in the least defensive. In most cases this diffused the bomb, and we are now respected for our choice. I think that the constant questioning makes us better homeschoolers, more attentive to our children's needs."

WHAT TO EXPECT IN YOUR FIRST YEAR WHEN YOU'RE STARTING AT THE BEGINNING

MORE AND more families are choosing homeschooling for the preschool years as well as for kindergarten. The youngest among us, filled with an enviable energy that they naturally use for learning, make this a memorably fun time to learn together as a family. Help these little folks use their energy positively, and together you'll rise above any challenges created by the following common experiences.

Getting Schooling Out of the System

It's obvious that families who bring children home from school face a major educational transition, as their children have spent time entrenched in the school's schedule, organization, and method. Families who begin homeschooling with children who have never been to school think that they will escape these repercussions. But as if to show us how deeply ingrained in our collective cultural consciousness the idea of schooling truly is, even the youngest, nonschooled children often need a chance to get "school" out of their systems.

"My children were kindergarten- and preschool-aged when we began homeschooling, but they had seen their friends go to school

WHAT I WISH SOMEONE HAD TOLD ME DURING MY FIRST YEAR OF HOMESCHOOLING

I wish someone had told me when homeschooling starts! When does the first year start? We'd been doing stuff and learning stuff way before we got to the official have-to-file-an-R4-form age (one of California's options to make homeschooling "legal"), so I couldn't tell if we were now homeschooling or if we'd been homeschooling all along. I'd been telling people we were going to homeschool before we filed our form—omigosh! Does that mean that all the learning that we did before we filed the form didn't count? And when does the first year end? When the school year ends? Or when another year has passed? Or on my kids' birthdays? My birthday?

—NINA SUTCLIFFE, MIDDLETOWN, CALIFORNIA

on the big yellow bus and come home again with backpacks overflowing with phonics workbook papers, all crinkly and sporting happy faces drawn in red ink at the tops," remembers Kellye Just, of Alpharetta, Georgia. "School took on a sort of mystique that fascinated my younger. One day he wanted us to set up school at home."

> Even the youngest, nonschooled children often need a chance to get "school" out of their systems.

Kellye's son requested a desk and his own pencils and papers. He wanted workbooks, erasers, and a chair that was his size. "The school district happened to be selling old children's desks and chairs for one and two dollars apiece that week," says Kelley. "We purchased two for the kids, hauled them home in the van, and cleaned them up."

TIPS FOR COPING WITH KINDERGARTNERS WHO WANT TO GO TO SCHOOL

✦ Get your adult mind settled that homeschooling is best for your family so that you may answer questioners solidly as a parent making the best decision for your young children, rather than being wishy-washy about it.

✦ Determine what about the idea of "school" appeals to your child, and try to meet that need at home (it might only be "recess").

✦ Pretend "school" every once in a while. Sit at desks, sit still, be quiet, raise hands with questions, do worksheets, etc.

✦ Talk about the aspects of school that don't fit with your family's values or priorities, and the aspects of homeschooling that do fit.

✦ While doing something fun and interesting, point out that if your child was in school, s/he wouldn't be able to be doing it.

—SUSAN HOREIN, MADISON, WISCONSIN

The Just family living room became a new school site. The children arranged their new desks in a row, filled them with supplies, and sat down to work in phonics and math workbooks. "When my son had completed his work, he crinkled his paper a bit, like the ones he'd seen in his friends' backpacks, and brought it to me," Kelley says. "I scanned it carefully, nodded my approval, and, playing the role of 'teacher,' commented that he had done an excellent job. I welcomed him to go out to 'recess.' He hesitated.

"Where's my A?" he wanted to know.

"Oh, how thoughtless of me!" Kelley answered. She found a red pen, marked a large A at the top of his work, and, for good measure, drew a happy face before returning his paper.

He frowned. "What'd you do that for? You messed it up!"

Kellye admits she didn't know what he meant or wanted at this point. Her son sighed, then headed for the school-supply cupboard. Out came construction paper, pencils, clear packaging tape, and scissors, and he set to work until he completed a large red A, laminated with the packaging tape.

"Now this," he proclaimed proudly, "is an A!"

The little boy knew exactly what he wanted—a real letter A to hold, to save, to show to his friends. He didn't want Kellye marking up his careful work with silly red scrawls.

"After that, we made a whole bowlful of A's to hand out for 'school,'" says Kellye. "We got creative, with flowers and glitter and fancy colors. Some were really big and some minuscule. Some were magnetic and could be affixed to the refrigerator. All were highly prized."

Due to a love for the letter A, the Justs' school-at-home phase lasted about four to six months. After a while, the appeal of going to school for letter grades faded, as did the curiosity about the bus, the special desks, and classroom accoutrements. "All of those school aspects that fascinated my children were addressed in alternative ways—rides on several kinds of buses when opportunities arose, school boxes with papers, pencils, and erasers, lunch boxes packed with sandwiches and apples," Kellye says. "My kids' 'school,' having satisfied their need to know, eventually returned to the kitchen table and the great outdoors. The letter grades lived in the windows or swung gaily for a long time from the ceiling in brightly threaded mobiles. When their colors eventually faded, the A's were respectfully laid to rest—as was the whole idea of 'school'—in the trash can."

Mom Gone Overboard!

Advertisers' back-to-school hype begins in the middle of summer and continues relentlessly until a community's first school bell rings. Those

LEARNING ACTIVITY

Grocery Store Learning Center
(math, marketing, more; early years)

The grocery store has something to entertain each of my children—seven, five, and three years old and eight months old. My seven-year-old loves selecting and bagging the produce, then guessing what it weighs. We challenge each other to see who gets closer to the correct weight. She is learning how to choose the best pieces.

I'm also showing her how to interpret the price signs. Some are per unit and some are per pound. We have done lots of addition and division, and she even asked me to show her how to round numbers in order to add in her head.

The five- and three-year-olds love to count out the fruit and veggies as we put them into the bag. We discuss the different colors and names of the large variety of produce. We've tasted blood oranges and touched the hairy coconuts and discussed where they grow. An added benefit is that they meet all kinds of people and chat with them at the grocery store. By turning grocery shopping into a learning activity, it's now enjoyable instead of a dreaded weekly responsibility.

—MIMI DEMPSEY, FREDERICKSBURG, VIRGINIA

who choose homeschooling for little ones aren't necessarily immune to the hoopla, as Lynn Foster of Smithville, Indiana, mom to four-year-old Nicholas and five-month-old Adrian, recently discovered.

"During the summer before our first 'official' day of school, I began plotting out a schedule and gathering supplies," says Lynn. "I went school shopping and bought all of the essentials. Copies were made, pencils sharpened, lessons waited in our makeshift schoolroom, the kitchen. I was ready."

The first day began with a bang. "We went against our natural tendencies to sleep and arose early," Lynn says. "We were like soldiers racing into battle: 'Grab those play clothes! Brush your teeth! Faster, faster! We've got to start school by eight o'clock. Eat your cereal. Don't get off track!'"

Lynn calls herself the captain of a little army in her home, one who cracked the whip and barked out commands. She deemed that first day, which included poring over workbooks for hours, a success.

Success lasted exactly twenty-four hours. "I was in the last trimester of pregnancy and not sleeping well. Before long I was a walking zombie in the early morning, and my son was the same way," says Lynn. "I decided we could sleep a bit longer and start school a bit later than most people, and this worked well." She adds, "Only trouble is it left me riddled with guilt."

No sooner had Lynn and Nicholas adjusted to the new schedule than Lynn gave birth to Adrian. She had decided to take off six weeks to recuperate, then jump back into "school." After all, she reasoned, how could Nicholas stay up to par without her daily drills and all those workbooks?

"God must have been trying to teach me to slow down when He gave us Adrian!" Lynn continues. "He slept little and abhorred sitting still. So much for more than five minutes of worksheets!"

Adrian now at five months, the family's homeschooling looks much different. "Nicholas now learns more through actual life experiences," explains Lynn. "He learned how to count while helping me microwave dinner on hectic evenings. He learned how to recognize letters by searching for them on billboards during car trips. We read on the couch while I'm nursing the baby. To those who don't know us well, it may not seem as though we could possibly be 'having school.' It was hard for me to get used to also! New homeschooling parents should realize that learning takes place in many ways, in different locations, and may not clearly follow a daily schedule. You'll know if your child is learning or not, so don't feel guilty if your lifestyle doesn't fit the mold."

Speaking of the Effect of Infants and Toddlers

Families that start homeschooling at the beginning often include members who are future homeschoolers—infants and toddlers. Infants and toddlers have needs that are immediate, and they have a way of spoiling even the best-laid plans.

Homeschooling: The Early Years and *Homeschooling: The Middle Years* include tips from experienced homeschooling parents on "inclusion and diversion tactics" for the littlest ones. You're sure to find ideas you can implement with your own even as you learn to bend homeschooling to make sure the needs of all of your children are met.

With two children four years apart, Susan had a younger child who was easily held, nursed, or asleep when they began their homeschooling journey. As the baby grew into a toddler, "he was restless and curious rather than the sort who would sit quietly and play while I worked with his big sister," Susan explains.

To keep everyone happy, Susan developed a temporary "field-trip curriculum."

"Three or more times each week, we went on a trip somewhere to learn," says Susan. "It served us well that year, since it entertained my restless curious young one while introducing my older child to lots of new and interesting things. As the baby grew and eventually was able to occupy himself quietly for periods of time, we modified our approach to include more at-home, quiet time together."

Your Children Will Remain Children Longer than Their Peers

Homeschooling proponents often point to young homeschooled children's social skills, which include the abilities to comfortably converse with a wide age range of people, to participate in meaningful community service, and to generally seem mature beyond their years. The critics' charges that children can't possibly become well-socialized in a home setting sound ludicrous when held up against this reality. The problem may be that neither proponents nor critics take into account the very real difference between this social maturity and popular cultural maturity. The distinction, however, is important to understand, especially for new homeschooling families.

Popular cultural maturity has nothing to do with the ability to communicate/work/get along with others. It is instead an understanding of the thoughts, mores, and attitudes that permeate our culture through every medium available—schools, television, newspapers, magazines, Internet sites, movies, and computer games—and accompanying advertisement for same. Questioning the suitability of many of these thoughts, mores, and attitudes for young children, a homeschooling parent may choose to exercise her right and responsibility to minimize their impact on her children's lives.

> Popular cultural maturity has nothing to do with the ability to communicate/work/get along with others.

When critics charge that they see (or sense) a social immaturity in homeschooling children, I believe that they are misnaming relative cultural immaturity. When critics charge that homeschooled children are isolated, I believe that they are misnaming homeschoolers' ability to protect young children from cultural conditioning.

Choosing to minimize the impact of popular culture on their children's sensibilities often places homeschoolers at odds with today's "hurry up and grow up" mentality. Often homeschooling families put off the cultural-conditioning influences that create more knowledge of the world than a child is emotionally or psychologically able to handle in a healthy manner, waiting for a time more suitable to the individual child. To put it succinctly, they choose to allow their children to enjoy a childhood.

It's inevitable that eventually popular culture will catch up to your children no matter what you do. In the meantime, there's a lot of enjoyment to be had with little ones who can enjoy your company, don't beg for hundred-dollar sneakers, and still think that "gay" means happy.

WHAT I WISH SOMEONE HAD TOLD ME DURING MY FIRST YEAR OF HOMESCHOOLING

I wish someone had told me that when the day's work is done, you are done. My son and I hated homeschooling the fifth week through the fifth month! We would work from 9:00 A.M. until 3:00 P.M.—those were regular school hours, after all. We were both in tears and wishing we'd never tried homeschooling.

Thankfully, a friend told me that when we completed the lessons for the day, we were done, even if we got it all done by noon. What a difference! We immediately started enjoying the lessons. My son learned quickly how to manage his time and not dawdle at his work. He soon had his work done before lunch, and we both loved having the quiet afternoons to ourselves to read. Homeschooling became a joy. We are now in our fifth year of homeschooling and holding strong.

—TAMMY CUTSHAW, INDIANAPOLIS, INDIANA

"A child is no different from a tender shoot of a new plant," explains Teri Nine. "One must protect it until it is strong enough to stand on its own. In that way, it will not fall when the thunder and rains come. Protect and shelter your children during these early, formative years. Remember, we are preparing our children to make it in the 'real world' on their own two feet not by the time they are ten years old but by the time they are eighteen, so take your time!"

Tossin' and Turnin' to Get Comfortable

Since you are starting homeschooling during the preschool or kindergarten year, chances are good you'll be homeschooling for quite some time. The longer you homeschool, the more you will learn. You'll likely find yourself dabbling in educational theories, learning styles, the reading wars (phonics vs. whole language), Goals 2000, and heaven knows where else your interests will take you. The more you learn, the more opportunity and/or need you will have to rethink and adjust your homeschooling.

We've already discussed that it's a good idea to begin homeschooling wherever you feel most comfortable, secure in the knowledge that change comes easily. But like trying to get comfortable in a strange bed, new homeschoolers find they sometimes do a lot of tossing and turning before they get there.

After "tons" of research in her Las Vegas library, about education in general and homeschooling in particular, homeschooling mom of three Lori Kephart thought she knew something about education—until it came time to face the immense choices in curriculum.

After deciding the cost of "complete" curriculum was too high, Lori chose to piece one together from materials available at the local teacher-supply store. "Guess which way actually cost more," Lori says, noting that she made far too many trips to the store.

She then tossed some money at different publishers to sample their wares, and discovered some good materials, some bad. Next she turned to the local homeschooling support group, which sponsors a "show and tell and swap."

"We meet monthly, pick a subject, and bring anything we've used (liked or not) and explain what's good or bad about it," Lori says. "This has probably saved me a small fortune. Frequently these items are available for sale or loan so that your children can try them out."

Lori then cast her attention to her computer and online shopping for used curriculum. "Beware," she warns new homeschoolers. "This is very addictive! I've learned to keep a list of things we actually need. I've learned that I won't go near those Internet boards, where wonderful resources are for sale, unless I'm prepared to buy new if need be. I suspect curriculum fairs are just as bad, but I haven't had the opportunity to attend one." (I've been to a lot of them for quite a few years now. I think about how much money attendees are spending, and I find it difficult to keep my jaw off the floor.)

Lori and many homeschoolers have come to the conclusion that "there is no perfect curriculum." While right now you may be disappointed with this news, Lori adds, "that in itself is a relief. I'll probably change what we use many times as the kids get older and their interests change. I really liked Ruth Beechick's phrase 'Teach the child, not the curriculum.' I don't think I'd ever spend a lot of money on any one single item or curriculum. That would create too much pressure to 'make' it work."

You Will Learn to Let Even the Youngest Children Help Figure It All Out

Most of us spent our formative years silently and obediently following someone else's notion of what our own educational experiences should look like. The notion that children can help map out their educational journeys is, for many, a shocking idea and another area in which homeschooling parents find themselves bucking popular cultural notions.

Still, even within the homeschooling community, debate rages about just how much say the children should have. One side argues that young children have no idea as to what it is important to know. The other side asserts that no one, regardless of age, will truly learn anything until he is interested.

> The notion that children can help map out their educational journeys is, for many, a shocking idea.

As you've probably figured out, different homeschooling approaches allow more or less leeway for children's (or parents') input. Yet even if you choose the most structured of approaches, homeschooling allows room for children to help chart their educational course. The reward, homeschoolers find, is children who grow into young adults accustomed to examining what is important to them.

LEARNING ACTIVITY

Vicarious Travel (social studies; early and middle years)

We decided to "visit" and learn about each of the fifty states. Because we couldn't actually go to all of them, we relied on various sources for information: books, Web sites, games, maps, etc. We hung a four-feet-by-five-feet outline map on the wall and colored in each state as we learned about it. We joined a home-school postcard exchange to collect a postcard from a homeschooler in all fifty states.

My seven-year-old daughter doesn't like to write, so she dictated a note, which we printed and affixed to each postcard we sent. Each day she'd eagerly go through the mail, looking for a postcard from one of the states we'd sent to. To see her face light up when she got a card, to see her rush into the house to hang the card near its state on the map, to know a family of strangers was willing to add to our enjoyment of learning in this way, was a true joy to me. With the exception of North Dakota, we obtained a card from each state and even some from around the world.

—CAROL MOXLEY, FORT WORTH, TEXAS

Accepting and sensibly dealing with the responsibility of one's own education also leads to an appreciation of the benefits of learning as well as increased responsibility in other life aspects.

"I tried very hard in our first year to make homeschooling as much like 'real school' as possible," remembers Lisa Smith, a Villa Rica, Georgia, homeschooling mom who began homeschooling with the oldest of her three girls. Lisa's daughter flew through the first- and second-grade curricula within one year, but "I found it too stressful and realized that my daughter reacted in a typical way that public school children react; her love of learning was declining," says Lisa.

Over the summer, the Smith family took a break, joined a local support group, and watched their daughter enjoy independent study on topics of personal interest. More important, Lisa had "a nice heart-to-heart talk with her, and we came to some agreed-upon standards so that we would both be happy and she would still get the education I wanted her to get."

Together mom and seven-year-old daughter decided to drop the set time to start schoolwork and maintain a looser weekly schedule. Now they join their homeschool group on Monday and use the Calvert curriculum on Tuesday and Thursday. They spend the rest of the week reading other books and focusing on a topic of interest.

"It seems to be working out well," concludes Lisa, "and her attitude is much better."

In Hudson, New Hampshire, Merilyn "officially" began homeschooling when her daughter was two-and-one-half years old. To answer her self-imposed question "How do I do this on a day-to-day basis," Merilyn turned to her bookstore. She liked what she read about real people's experiences in *The Homeschooling Book of Answers* (Prima, 1998). From there she went to the Internet in search of the right curriculum, only to wind up frustrated.

"I then tried to set up my own curriculum and a daily schedule," says Merilyn, "and got frustrated with that. Finally, I just listened to my daughter and continued doing with her what she likes best." This includes lots of reading, a favorite activity since birth, supplemented by concepts, introduced from time to time, that Merilyn wants her to learn. "If she's ready to learn something new, then she's very interested; otherwise she'll let me know right away," Merilyn explains. When it's important to her daughter to learn something, "I'll find other ways to teach her, which include my husband, computer software, video, manipulatives, and field trips."

9

WHAT TO EXPECT WHEN
BRINGING A CHILD
HOME FROM SCHOOL

In This Chapter

✦ Your child doesn't know as much as
you thought she knew

✦ Missing friends

✦ Serious students have their own worries

✦ "Decompression" time facilitates a
smooth transition

"Boredom can be a good thing. It forces children to be creative in coming up with ideas on what to do with their time. We wouldn't have life-sized dinosaurs all over our basement walls, complete with the country of origin and period in which they lived and died, if the kids weren't 'bored' some of the time."

—Ellen Stukel, Naperville, Illinois

*F*OLKS WHO ENTERED their first year of homeschooling by bringing children home from school note more first-year challenges than the parents who started at the beginning. As you'd expect, these unique challenges typically arise due to the transition away from the school's schedule, organization, method, and socialization toward autonomy.

In my own home, our oldest child was the only who attended school, half-day kindergarten. With the effect it had on him, I can only imagine what it's like for a child to come home after an even longer or more intense school experience. Between my firsthand knowledge and stories I've heard, though, the transition reminds me of a newborn baby's.

Accustomed to the coziness of the womb and subsequent swaddling, the newborn at first flails at her freedom. All that space is a shock to a nervous system unfamiliar with it. The baby must adjust to an environment that now includes physical freedom, learning where she fits into this larger world.

If you are bringing a child home from school, realize that he, too, is making a huge adjustment. He has been "swaddled" intellectually and socially by schooling, and he may flail around in newly provided intellectual and social space. We guide our infants gently into their new physical freedom, knowing that with enough experience they'll soon enough settle down and enjoy and experiment with the greater freedom. We should take our cue and do the same as our older children acclimate to intellectual and social freedom.

YOUR CHILD DOESN'T KNOW AS MUCH AS YOU THOUGHT SHE KNEW

THIS SCENARIO plays out in a frightening number of instances when parents bring their children home to learn. The circumstances are always similar.

Parent believes child is doing very well in public or private school. After all, child is on the honor roll, receiving straight A's on report cards, is liked by teachers, and is producing copious amounts of homework.

Here's how this scenario played out in the St. Charles, Missouri, Swanson household when Stephanie, the oldest of four children, came home from public school in fourth grade because private school wasn't financially possible.

> That children often flail around in newly provided intellectual and social space is to be expected.

With too little confidence in her own abilities, mom Jenny bought a curriculum she calls "idiot proof" and began homeschooling by reviewing what her oldest child knew. "She was not as educated as I thought," remembers Jenny. "She had major trouble with reading and spelling, and she had no learning skills whatsoever. How did she make it to fourth grade on honor roll like this?" Jenny wondered.

Coming home was a wake-up call for Stephanie, too, as she realized her former A's and B's, awarded for speeding through lessons while learning little, were meaningless. "I gave her smaller assignments and helped her concentrate harder on them," says Jenny. "I tossed out the grading system, and we just didn't move on until she knew the material. At the same time we switched to a different style of curriculum so we could stay away from the 'school' formula. She loves to read, so we do a lot of reading and projects."

The results? Within a year Stephanie acquired better study skills and could once again move quickly through lessons. "She enjoys learning much more now," Jenny says, "and comes away with more knowledge."

Mary Nunaley's sixth grader was on the honor roll during her stint in a Tennessee private school. Imagine Mary's surprise upon discovering that her daughter didn't know the times tables and her reading was "horrid."

Math became a homeschooling nightmare. At the end of the first year, Mary's then-three-year-old son learned to run screaming out of

TEACHING VS. LEARNING

I began homeschooling with the notion that I actually had the power to teach my son things, even if he thought he didn't want to learn them. The peculiar focus of this insanity for me was math. Sam is a voracious reader, so I figured that most other "school" topics would be addressed in his reading, but what about fractions? Probability? What if I completely forgot to teach him geometry?

I brought home workbooks, textbooks, software—everything I could find to make this subject he had learned to despise in school more appealing. I asked for one page of math per day. No, make that thirty minutes of the latest math-based computer game.

One day, while sitting at the dining room table with Sam and the math book, I experienced a revelation. We were reviewing some topic that he'd completed in public school the previous year, yet he was not demonstrating any command

the room in anticipation of conflict whenever Mom mentioned math or Saxon (a math textbook series).

"Three years later," says a proud Mary, who hung in there with lots of repetition and alternative math activities, "not only is she breezing through math and enjoying it; she is also partway through the algebra 2 book as an eighth grader. I never would have believed it if I hadn't seen it myself."

MISSING FRIENDS

RARE IS the homeschooling household—no matter at what point it begins—that hasn't considered the issue of missing friends or, more specifically, missing the sense of common experience home-of it whatsoever. In frustration I fumed, "You know this stuff! You learned it last year!"

His matter-of-fact response was "Yes, I did it last year but no, I didn't learn it. And if I didn't learn it then, what makes you think I'll learn it now?" I was so stunned by the simplicity of his reply that I couldn't answer at first. Of course! I was never going to make him learn anything. After a minute I said, "You know, you're absolutely right," and closed the book. Permanently.

Do I worry that he's never going to be able to calculate the area under a curve? Yes. Do I still experience lack-of-math anxiety occasionally? Definitely. But I am coming to trust that if he ever needs to determine the unknown variable in an equation, he will be motivated *by that need* to find out how it's done. And that's the kind of learning that sticks.

—MICHELLE YAUGER, TUCSON, ARIZONA

schooled children don't share with their peers. Some children readily feel it. Parents readily understand it. It's an issue that may have drawn as many teens back into school as the desire to participate in team sports, if not more.

So that we may discuss how you can handle this if it occurs in your home, we'll have to set aside a deeper discussion of what can only be called government school's social monopoly. Suffice it to say that if telephone company, banking, or software monopolies bother you, a social monopoly should scare the pants off of you.

One might think that the longer a child has been in school, the greater the challenge of missing friends would be, but this doesn't seem to be the case. Even young elementary school children know that they are a minority not stepping on that yellow bus each morning and that they are indeed living a different lifestyle.

LEARNING ACTIVITY

Geography Notebook (geography; all ages)

I put an atlas in front of a notebook, then gathered my large stash of *Smithsonian* and *National Geographic* magazines (very cheap to purchase at used-book sales). The children cut out pictures of scenery, animals, cities, people—anything that caught their interest. We glued the pictures on notebook pages and I identified the state or country at the top. At the bottom, I asked questions. For example, on a picture of piranhas from Brazil and Venezuela, I asked them to find the countries on the map of South America. What is the largest river in that area? Is this area likely hot or cold? We divided the countries by continent. State pages are alphabetical in another notebook. Although the children are four and six years old, they know more geography than older students, because the pictures are so interesting. They are learning physical geography, the difference between continents, countries, states, and cities, and where many places are on the map. The project is also very low cost.

—MICHELLE DUKER, OTTUMWA, IOWA

Growing from the Loss

Kimberly Wilkinson came home after just half a year in kindergarten in the country environment of Big Sandy, Texas, and has been home for five months. Few other children live nearby. Having been close to her friends, Kimberly still talks about them, and mom Julie notes that it's been difficult to help a child this age understand the changes, especially after a summer full of contact with friends that abruptly ended for the start of school.

"I try to keep Kimberly busy with lessons and trips to the park and zoo," says mom Julie, "but even now, she still talks about her friends and has even dreamed about them." Julie recently discovered a support group nearby and hopes this will help. "We are going back to our old church now, too, and Kimberly is really happy to see her old buddies."

The quantity-vs.-quality issue of friendship sometimes moves to the forefront in homeschooling families' considerations too. Since age-mates are conveniently gathered in one place at school, it's relatively easy to meet quantity. The desire to be "popular," to call a wide array of classmates "friends," often overshadows the depth of such friendships. Opportunities to converse at length in order to get to really know each other—a staple of true friendship—are rare in school, and large homework loads and extracurricular activities fill up nonschool time. It may be difficult for children coming home from school to accept and cope with a sudden drop in the number of friends. However, the experience can leave them with a better understanding and appreciation of quality friendships that will serve them well in future life relationships, as well as help them to be true friends to others, instead of mere acquaintances.

> The quantity-vs.-quality issue of friendship sometimes moves to the forefront in home-schooling families' considerations.

A year ago, Kelly Ford's fifth-grade daughter, Kendall, came home to learn in the company of two much younger brothers in Fredericksburg, Virginia. "Kendall commented often about how she missed her friends," says Kelly, "so, to remedy the situation, I told her she could have two sleepovers per month with her school friends. She has never taken me up on this."

Kelly continues: "She has called friends, but many calls go unreturned. We also have three girls in the neighborhood, two very pleasant ones right next door. The third, one of Kendall's best friends, seems to be making known some familial viewpoints about homeschooling, which is changing the friend situation somewhat."

Kendall also plays soccer with school friends, some of whom have told her that she is going to be dumb because of homeschooling.

Kelly still has to engage in "extra deprogramming" each time Kendall comes home from practice or a game. She is grateful that Kendall lets her know what's going on.

"I believe she is now seeing that these 'friends' may not truly be friends," says Kelly. "She's learning how to better judge character and what friendship really is. This is also helping to change the situation." She is quick to point out that even while attending school, Kendall never had the friends over except for birthday parties, and Kelly is confident that at some level her daughter is beginning to put everything into perspective.

"We also participate in a homeschool group, and we're fortunate in that there are several girls around her age," Kelly adds. "Not only that, but they are all so nice—immediately friendly and not carrying the same attitudes as the public school friends. I think you probably know what I mean—the cruel, let's-gang-up-on-this-one-or-that-one attitude, the intense sarcasm, cliques, criticism due to what clothes one wears. Kendall's attitude changes when she's been around her public school friends. She is very snappy with us when she comes home. I would never have believed the attitude thing until I witnessed it firsthand."

Only an Empty Cup Can Be Filled

For other children, spending every weekday with many children in a school setting is a nonissue. They readily accept that they are moving into a different lifestyle, one that doesn't necessarily include daily contact with former schoolmates (although homeschooling certainly doesn't *have* to preclude this, either). They may be the ones who see that the social environment one encounters in school is neither all that positive nor all that it's cracked up to be. With that environment out of the way, the "empty cup" may be filled with something else that often is more nourishing.

Sixth grader Kirk and Derek, a high schooler, came home to unschool in Lynda Dionno's Eureka, California, home, and neither has missed day-to-day school interactions.

WHICH IS MORE WORK?

When people ask me, "Isn't homeschooling a lot of work for you?" I always say, "Not nearly as much as when she was in school." Oddly enough, every parent I've said this to has had an instant flash of recognition: how much work it takes to keep a child moving through the school year. Now we have no daily scramble to get ready to catch the bus by 7:00 A.M.; no sorting out after-school activities and schedules; no sudden projects requiring trips to the store to get unavailable supplies; no PTA activities or fund-raisers; no lunch money; no homework headaches; no bus hassles; no teacher conferences; no bad-teacher years; no jockeying for a better teacher for next year; no calls to the principal to try to sort out episodes of harassment, bullying, and peer violence. We had a lot more hurdles when Zoe was in school.

—LINDA JORDAN, NOTTINGHAM, NEW HAMPSHIRE

"They seemed to immediately fall into a habit of doing what they wanted during the school hours," says Lynda, "and then the beeper and phone start in at 3:00 P.M." Besides, now that he's sixteen years old, enjoying the designated school lunch hour with his girl-friend brings additional contact with the local high school for Derek. He has also attended a couple of proms.

"The children themselves need to work out a way to handle any isolation or distancing from public school friends," Lynda concludes. "It's never been an issue of 'us and them,' so our house is filled with kids who utilize all the various elements of learning."

Steve Feinstein's daughter, Hillary, was happy and learning enough in the San Antonio, Texas, public schools until she hit sixth grade. She not only grew glum but for the first time was failing tests. At teachers' conferences, when Steve explained Hillary's kinesthetic learning style, his words fell on deaf ears. "They flat-out told me that they couldn't cater to the learning style of a student who was one of less than 10 percent of any given class," he remembers. To further complicate things, Hillary was getting throat or ear infections at least once each month and quickly racking up absences.

While in eighth grade, the young girl met two homeschoolers at church. Like a growing number of children, Hillary asked her parents if they would allow her to do the same. "She didn't expect us to take her request seriously," says Steve, "but we did. We spent several months researching options—on the Web, via magazines, and via our friends who homeschooled." The Feinsteins chose self-directed learning while using Clonlara School to keep records and provide advice and eventually a diploma.

Hillary's fraternal twin remains in public school, as the school's teaching method fits her learning style well. "She's a built-in conduit for her sister to meet teens through sleepovers and the like," Steve says. After a year of relative homeschooling isolation, they've found two area support groups, including one that offers some classes for teens that Hillary is excited about.

Hillary misses other teens but understands that she is making a trade-off. Her time isn't empty; rather it fills from other directions. Now that she's not forced to read, she's read more books in six months than she read in her last three years of school. She has resumed the viola lessons that she dropped during "decompression" time. She instant-messages and e-mails peers she has met at camps throughout the United States. She has many adults friends as a result of volunteering at church. Most important, she has realized dramatic improvements in her health since she left school.

SERIOUS STUDENTS HAVE THEIR OWN WORRIES

HAVE YOU heard the old saying "If Mama ain't happy, ain't nobody happy"? This could easily translate into "If Mama is stressed-out over homeschooling, her children will be too." It's the nature of family life that what affects one of us affects all of us, and this phenomenon is especially important to remember during homeschooling.

We as parents can certainly work to control our own stress and worries about homeschooling so that we don't unnecessarily pass them on to our children. But many children harbor their own worries about their studies, especially the more serious types.

"The final time I brought my children home from school, Natalie was seven years old, and Travis was eleven," says homeschooling mom Cindy Allas, of Fairfield, California. "Travis has a more serious personality and continues to have guilt about whether he's learning enough, forgetting too much, paying enough attention."

Cindy discovered that in her dealing with Travis's concerns, her role as homeschooling mom includes becoming his cheerleader or one who must make a point of constantly reminding him of how much he's learned since he's been home from school. "It also helps to be involved right away with a support/play group so that the children can see that there are many other children learning this way," adds Cindy.

Serious Moms Bring Home Too Much School

In many homes, no one is more programmed about the way learning "is supposed to be" than Mom herself. Couple this with a motherly desire to give her child the best, throw in a pinch of pressure from the mother-in-law, and you've got all the incentive necessary to bring home too much school.

In many homes, no one is more programmed about the way learning "is supposed to be" than Mom herself.

If you've done much reading on homeschooling, you've been warned against this time and again, as was Peg Sponable of Schenectady, New York. Still, "there was so much public school inside of me, it kept sneaking out," says Peg. "I was trying to do too much too soon."

WHAT I WISH SOMEONE HAD TOLD ME DURING MY FIRST YEAR OF HOMESCHOOLING

I wish I'd known about homeschooling before I ever sent any of my children to public school. I didn't hear about homeschooling until three years ago. Even though I spent two years researching homeschooling and feel that I could not have been better prepared, there has been a thorn. My eleven-year-old daughter has not adjusted to homeschooling and wants to go back to public school in the fall. My seven-year-old son loves homeschooling and doesn't want to go back to public school. The familiar scenario of "longer in pubic school, harder to adjust" hits right on the money. I know my daughter will resent me if I don't allow her to at least try junior high, as she feels she is missing out on something. At least I know that she can always come home again if that grass is not greener after all.

—MARGARET SPONABLE, SCHENECTADY, NEW YORK

This tendency leads to nagging, pushing, and stress for all, hardly a joyful atmosphere in which to learn. "I was trying to get everything done in a four-hour period, like some books said was an average time," Peg explains. "What was I thinking? It took trial and error to come to a way that works, and it is a totally different schedule than I had ever imagined."

"DECOMPRESSION" TIME FACILITATES A SMOOTH TRANSITION

TO DECOMPRESS means "to relieve of pressure," and no other term could better describe what homeschooling parents have found to be a saving grace for the child coming to intellectual and social freedom from schooling. Pressure created by school attendance comes from many directions and may be subtle or blatant. Often children aren't even aware that the pressure exists, because they hardly remember anything different, may not even understand what has happened to them, and may have trouble coping *without* the pressure. It is frighteningly similar to the way addiction to nicotine, caffeine, alcohol, and other drugs sneaks up on people.

Basically, decompression means relieving the child of pressure to "perform" educational activities. The amount of time needed for decompression varies with each child. Some folks report that after just a few weeks of space to breathe, relax, and veg out, their children eagerly bounce into activities of interest. Others observe that it takes a full year or even longer before their children get their bearings and confidently move forward.

By reading this book and magazine articles that share personal accounts, you will comprehend the indicators of a need for decompression and assist your child, just as the support team helps the deep-sea diver slowly make the transition from the pressure of being underwater before returning to dry land.

Withdrawal from Being Told What to Do

It still brings a smile when I remember my six-year-old, kindergarten schooled son standing in the middle of the kitchen, telling me how I was "doing school" all wrong, and explaining to me my role as teacher. As so many things are at that age, it was simple. "You tell me what to do, then when I'm done, you tell me what to do next," he said.

Karen Bigalke's two daughters did the same when they left public school to learn in their Calgary, Alberta, Canada, home. "I like them to try to figure out subject matter on their own," says Karen. "I'll ask if they need help rather than simply tell them how to do something. Related to this, they also had to get used to managing their time wisely. At first," remembers Karen, "when there was no one holding their hand every minute of the day, they strayed. Four years later, they love it and manage time efficiently enough to assist me and still have the time to participate in their favorite activities. My son, now going into second grade, has been far more self-reliant since day one. He never went to school so never had to be 'deschooled.'"

This transition was most difficult for the oldest of the four of six children Kathy Giddings brought home from an Iowa public school. As an eighth grader, "he was used to being told where to go, when to go, how many to do, redo, redo, redo," says Kathy. "He was used to just getting it done, then along came Mom, who wanted eagerness and willingness to learn. We got bogged down."

Kathy evaluated what was going on and decided she was assigning too much work. "I knew the answers and figured that it would take ten minutes to do this page of work, but that was based on *my* skill level. My expectations did not match the skill level of the child. Now he understands what I want, and I understand his limits. This can come only with practice. We do lots better now, in our fifth year."

Withdrawal from Reading for Pizza

Gold stars, happy-face stickers, free pizza. Ah, the bribes we give children in the name of learning in school. Trouble is, these external rewards steal the limelight from the learning itself, setting up the children to focus on the treats. Any wonder you could study all night for a test, only to forget the material when the test was over?

"I brought two sons home from school, after second and fourth grades," Jeanne Faulconer says. "I had a reluctant reader, and though I was using a curriculum to some extent, somehow I knew what to do to 'fix' this reading problem."

Jeanne had heard nightmare scenarios from parents who, in an attempt to "catch up" lagging children, had pressured themselves right into sending the children back to school, and she wanted no part of that.

WHAT I WISH SOMEONE HAD TOLD ME DURING MY FIRST YEAR OF HOMESCHOOLING

I wish someone had told me that the first year of homeschooling, after having my daughter in "real" school for six years, was not going to be the pleasant mother/daughter bonding experience I had been led to believe would happen when homeschooling. The first year was a nightmare and required a lot of patience and telling ourselves that this was going to work and it was what we both wanted.

As a single mom homeschooling my daughter and a three-year-old in the wings, I found it a challenge. The first few months were crazy. Always hearing "Mom, that's not the way we did it at 'name of last school.'" My dad was always criticizing and trying to tell me she wasn't learning anything, and I was totally frustrated by how little she did know after having been in private school through the fifth grade. How we made it through that year was a miracle, and now it is a family memory to be shared. We all agree we would never go back to regular school.

Best advice I wish I had received? Prepare for at least a year of deschooling before things settle down, relax, and don't worry about covering everything on the "core" curriculum.

—MARY NUNALEY, OLD HICKORY, TENNESSEE

"I didn't require my child to read," says Jeanne. "He no longer read for pizza certificates. He no longer read to score on computer assessments that earned him points and pencils. He no longer read a certain number of minutes that he had to record in a notebook. I simply did not make him read *anything*."

Instead, Jeanne read *to* him . . . and read . . . and read. "By Christmas, I couldn't keep reading material out of his hands," she reports. "He was staying up too late reading, avoiding chores by reading, and driving me crazy retelling me everything he read. When I started reading aloud with his younger brother, he would take the book when we were through and read five more chapters."

Jeanne removed all sources of pressure associated with reading, making the space necessary for it to become an enjoyable activity and, more important, creating the opportunity for her son to consider the act his own. "Now," says Jeanne, "if only he will take off writing . . ."

Withdrawal from Resisting Learning

One of the great ironies of the artificial socialization of schools is that in the hallowed halls of learning, the smartest attendees get the least respect (unless they happen to also be gorgeous or good athletes). It's also incredible how quickly even the youngest children pick up on that irony and learn to hide their proficiencies.

> Children coming home to school may have grown resistant to learning because they've seen the "smart" kids ridiculed, bullied, or otherwise forced into relative misery.

Children coming home to learn may have grown resistant to learning because they've seen the "smart" kids ridiculed, bullied, or otherwise forced into relative misery. Having learned that it's not cool to be smart, they carry this tendency home.

When Ann Weedon took Shane out of the Niles, Michigan, public school after third grade, "he fought every learning experience I presented him," says Ann. "I've since found out that this is very common with children who left school after having problems."

Ann decided to focus less on textbooks, workbooks, and the writing Shane hated, and more on subjects she knew he enjoyed, especially math and science. "I read to him often, and we learned by discussing topics, instead of writing about them. He enrolled in a Spanish class, and we took lots of field trips. By my allowing him time to breathe and just be," Ann says, "he now seeks out learning on his own terms."

Laraine O'Donnell called this the "I don't want to do anything" attitude in her two young daughters. "Hey, we're home, right?" they thought. "We should get to watch TV and sleep all we want!"

Laraine saw that the emotional changes the girls were going through probably made them need more sleep than usual, and since they are a family of night owls, she willingly went along with this. She adjusted the waking-up-and-getting-to-work schedule. "Sometimes we make it and sometimes we don't," Laraine says, "but we get our work done. It's just done at a time that suits us best."

The Decompression Experience Described

Because the decompression process is relatively new—and such a personal one, to boot—our society has more understanding of the withdrawal process of a heroine addict than of the adjustments necessary to withdraw from schooling. The examples above indicate that while it is your child who will experience some or many of the withdrawal symptoms, a compassionate, understanding parent greatly aids the process and helps pave the way for as smooth a transition as possible.

It's not easy to watch your child go through the process, so I conclude this section with Jill Meyer's experience to help you see that decompression doesn't last forever and that once you reach the other side, you'll be happy you made the effort.

Jill's seven-year-old daughter, Olivia, attended school, in Denver, only until April of first grade. Jill recognized the familiar "honeymoon" stage of coming home. "She was so pleased to be out of school, which had become a trial of continual worksheets and coloring in, that she was agreeable to *anything*. She wanted to sit down and 'do school' and worried about 'falling behind.' She expected me to tell her what to do and when," Jill says.

Jill realized that other homeschooling parents she had met, themselves in need of a bit of "deschooling," felt that a similar response from their children validated their decision to homeschool and led to much initial excitement. "For the whole year that I agonized about taking Olivia out of school, I was also 'deschooling' myself by reading everything about homeschooling that I could get my hands on, so I felt prepared for anything," Jill explains. "I was even disappointed to find Olivia so attached to the school model of living, but at least I was prepared to observe how things would change."

The "honeymoon" lasted just a few short weeks. Olivia then wanted to lie around and imagine walking on the ceiling. She wanted to in-line skate. Anything but schoolwork.

"It seemed she expected me to order her around," says Jill, "but at the same time was ready to rebel against it. Since I didn't do any ordering, this reaction eventually went away. I can't help but think this ambivalent response is directly created in the school atmosphere and comes from never being able to determine one's own fate there."

Formerly one of the great readers in her class, Olivia didn't crack open a book for three months. Having prepared herself for this eventuality, Jill put her trust in the decompression process and accepted it. In the meantime, Jill observed that Olivia made strides in ridding herself of negative social behaviors learned in school, only to fall back into them with a vengeance.

"It seemed as if she was losing her compass," says Jill. "She wanted to know what all the kids were wanting and liking. She was obsessed with collecting Beanie Babies and wanted to impress her old school friends by dressing like a Spice Girl. She started teasing her brother more and almost went out of her way to create conflict with us, her parents."

At the same time, though, Olivia could be clingy and unsure of herself, a sign of the emotional impact of schooling. "School had told her who to be, and now she didn't know who to be anymore. She had to find out for herself," says Jill. This led to reaction swings as the tough shell Olivia had worn for school purposes cracked. "She got weepy and more easily hurt," Jill explains. Fortunately this state was also temporary, as Jill notices her daughter now feels safer to ex-

LEARNING ACTIVITY

Creating Common Ground
(across the curriculum; middle and teen years)

One of the favorite things that has happened in our household is sharing what we are reading. Of course we talk about the books we read, but it's been fun seeing my children, especially my oldest son, develop an interest in the newspaper and *Time* magazine. Many mornings there are articles in the paper about things I know will interest him, and he always reads what I suggest. Then we have this great basis for discussion. He has been surprised to discover that the newspaper holds such a variety of information—from the latest dinosaur find to a preview of the much-awaited Harry Potter book. Articles in *Time* have helped us with tough and varied concepts like relativity, sexuality, and steroid use. I like this activity because it involves reading, talking about what's been read, reflecting on the material, and developing broader knowledge about the subject matter. They like it because it's interesting, fresh, in an adult form, and it provides a relaxed way for them to interact with Mom on serious stuff.

—JEANNE POTTS FAULCONER, MOORESVILLE, NORTH CAROLINA

press herself when feelings come, instead of bottling them up only to vent at a later time.

"Gradually, gradually, I saw Olivia return to the child she was before she went to school," says a happy Jill. "She began to regain her sparkle, curiosity, and own opinions. She started picking up books again, but I worried at first, because they seemed too young, like the Beanie Baby cult thing. She got cuddly with stuffed animals and played in a way I thought was young for age. I really think she was catching up on some emotional stages that she had missed while she was in school."

Jill figures it took about a year for Olivia to find herself completely and for the decompression period to work its magic. She can't say with certainty there was any one point at which major changes took place. Rather, Jill observed "a long journey of small shifts in perception and behavior. Olivia lost a sort of jadedness, a desire to manipulate, an avoidance of getting involved. Now she *wants* to get involved and seek out her own learning. Her responses to friends, learning, and disappointments seem more genuine and heartfelt. I'm very proud of her when she can determine on her own the value that some information has, weigh it for its own merits and in comparison to what she has learned elsewhere, rather than just taking information in indiscriminately, only to forget it later."

> Jill figures it took about a year for Olivia to find herself completely and for the decompression period to work its magic.

10

FIRST-YEAR HURDLES

In This Chapter

✦ Doubting Uncle Thomases and
Grandma Thomasinas

✦ A roller coaster of emotions

✦ Spider webs, dust bunnies, and creeping crumbs, oh, my!

✦ How can homeschooling possibly "fit"?

© EyeWire

"Why didn't someone tell me I didn't need to get up at 5:00 A.M. to clean the house so it looked perfect before we started the school day? By 10:00 A.M. I was trying to keep my eyes open while reading to my first grader; how productive was I? It's hard to change a strong tendency toward orderliness, but there is a greater plan where your housework is not as important. It took almost my whole first year to figure it out."

—Julie Bertsch, Piedmont, South Dakota

*Y*OU ASKED FOR it, you're about to get it. I'm setting before you the hurdles that other families faced during their first year of homeschooling despite their best-laid plans. We share them with you not to scare you from homeschooling but to confirm that frequently the everyday families who do this face obstacles to their practice. If you, too, come up against any of them, the experiences of those who went before should help as you decide how you are going to leap over them.

DOUBTING UNCLE THOMASES AND GRANDMA THOMASINAS

IT'S ONE thing to paint your house, only to have your mother-in-law stick up her nose and mutter something about nausea. It's quite another to soul-search, decide that the very best thing you can do for your children is to create a new family lifestyle, then listen to her wail that you will ruin her grandbabies forever. Yes, many families and circles of friends contain one or more well-meaning persons who will question your reasoning skills. This isn't really surprising.

> Many families and circles of friends contain one or more well-meaning persons who will question your reasoning skills.

Isn't just about everyone you know and are related to the product of more than a decade of schooling? Doesn't it make sense that your decision to take a different approach for your children will be seen by some as criticism of their own upbringing? Some might even say, "Hey, I went through all that malarkey, and I turned out okay."

As tempting as it may be, this is not the time to inform Uncle Albert that you think you've pegged his personality disorder.

Instead smile, secure in the knowledge that no matter how miserable they are making your life today, your relatives and friends may

LEARNING ACTIVITY

Money Management (math; early years)

I used this game initially because my second grader needed to increase her speed with handling and counting money. My kindergartner needed to memorize math addition facts with small numbers. (My fifth grader joined in because the others were having so much fun without him.)

Each child gets a pair of dice. Pile up hundreds of pennies in the middle of a circle of play. In the bank, I as banker keep piles of nickels, dimes, and quarters, with one-dollar bills in reserve (enough for each child).

To begin: Children roll dice simultaneously, add their numbers, and collect that many pennies from the center pile. They continue at their own speed. Each time they roll doubles, they can bring pennies to the bank, in exact amounts to obtain silver coins. They continue rolling and collecting pennies. When they've accumulated enough in silver coins to trade for a dollar, they have reached the goal. If you want to add competition, then the first one to get a dollar bill wins. On Friday my children keep the dollar as part of their allowance.

—SUSAN CLAYTON

sing a different tune with the passage of time and the actual reality of homeschooling, as opposed to reacting to their preconceived notions.

"Well-meaning relatives wondered if we weren't depriving our children of opportunities to make friends, if homeschooling was legal, what kinds of textbooks we planned to use, if we would keep up with the public schools," says Kristi Schrampfer. "I even had a family member tell me that we couldn't possibly teach the kids enough, since we weren't experts in everything. (What teacher is?)"

Kristi realized familial concern was natural, "but it certainly was no help to me in dealing with my own self-doubts as a beginning homeschooler," she explains. "At times I felt the need to defend our choice, but most often I simply adopted a wait-and-see attitude in response."

The results? "As the years have passed and family members have seen the results of our efforts, much of the skepticism has given way to approval. Our confidence in what we're doing has grown," Kristi concludes.

Laurie Meyerpeter's relatives approved of homeschooling but still questioned and expressed concerns, especially about socialization. "I found that it really did matter to me if these people approved, and their perception of homeschooling on this matter was not accurate," Laurie says. "We sometimes had so much socialization that it was difficult to accomplish much."

Laurie utilized her support network to quell concerns. "Our homeschool co-op produced a Christmas play, and we invited the relatives. The play was a success, but the additional benefit was that the relatives got to see that there were dozens of homeschooling children in our area, and they seemed perfectly normal and not at all deprived," she says. "I also sent them subscriptions to our co-op newsletter filled with children's work. It helped them see homeschooling in a different light. My children liked to write about what they were doing—sports, 4-H, music lessons, field trips, co-op activities, and more. That encouraged our relatives and showed them that homeschooling kids have busy and active lives." Laurie reports that she is no longer as sensitive about the issue of socialization.

Speaking of Sensitivity

Once we grow more comfortable with homeschooling, many of us begin to admit that at the beginning we were probably just a teensy-weensy bit oversensitive about comments and questions on the subject. After all, it seems that friends and strangers alike suddenly turn into education experts at just the mention of the word, at just the time we harbor the deep doubts that accompany lack of experience.

It's good to remember that everybody isn't necessarily "out to get you" because of your decision.

"I've had to learn that when someone questions our home-schooling, it may not be to criticize but rather to learn more," says Lynn Foster. "I was so worried that the world was out to get us that I was always on the defensive about homeschooling, and that is a definite turnoff to those who support public schooling. The best way to convince others is to educate them and let them see the benefits homeschooling can bestow on a family."

When Doubting Thomas Is Your Husband

I'd love to report that when homeschooling is the topic of spousal discussions, it produces an instant meeting of the minds. This isn't always the case. While in some households Dad tries his darnedest to sway Mom, more often it appears to be the opposite scenario.

Anecdotal evidence suggests that a homeschooling trial period is often an acceptable approach with a doubting spouse. "Let's try it for [insert as many years as you think you can get away with], dear. We'll see if we recognize any benefits for the children and for the family, then revisit the decision when the trial period is over." (It has been reported that this works best when accompanied by a tray of warm chocolate chip cookies.)

A trial period gives you and your children time not only to get comfortable with homeschooling but also to gently increase your spouse's understanding. Dinner can be a time of sharing the day's activities and relating what was learned that day. During the course of a trial year, your spouse can participate in weekend and vacation field trips, read bedtime stories, share his skills and hobbies with the kids, attend evening support-group activities, and meet other home-schoolers. All the while you can help him feel as great a part of the homeschooling experience as possible, by keeping him posted on your activities and soliciting advice and support. Just as you will sprinkle your home with books for your children to pick up, choice books and newspaper and magazine articles about homeschooling can be left around the house for your spouse. (Bathrooms are popular strategic locations.)

"At first, the biggest hurdle to overcome was convincing my husband that this was something I could do," says Karen Bigalke. "Even though I felt homeschooling was the choice to make, it is hard to do if your spouse is not behind you. Once we got going, though, and the children progressed and surpassed expectations, the hurdle faded away."

Doubting Yourself

It's a rare homeschooling parent who can say that he never entertained either subtle or blatant doubt in the decision to homeschool. The decision may initially appear to be about choosing an education for the children, but at the same time, it can feel like one of life's tougher tests for you.

I wish I could give you a magic pill to wipe away all your doubts and fears, but there isn't one. We all move through the doubt in our own way, at our own pace, so naturally it will last longer for some than for others. I've heard a million reasons for new homeschooling parents to doubt themselves; you're not the first with your reason(s), and you surely won't be the last. Experience is the magic that eventually washes doubt away, if not always completely. In the meantime, cherish those additional moments you are getting to spend with your children. Take courage from these.

"Unlike in many families, it was my husband who brought the idea home," says Lori Kephart. "I told him school was the reward for mommies who didn't kill their kids before then! Despite his interest in the idea, I still felt it wasn't right for me. I wasn't patient enough. I wasn't 'that kind' of mom. I barely finished high school. How could I possibly teach?"

> A trial period gives you and your children time not only to get comfortable with homeschooling but also to gently increase your spouse's understanding.

Dear hubby encouraged Lori to spend their son's year before kindergarten in a homeschool experiment to see if it could work. "Our son, Bob, was delighted at the idea of 'playing school' every day." Lori adds, "I had every intention (sort of actual sabotage) of proving to hubby that there was no way that this would work."

Not only was homeschooling easier than Lori expected; it was more fun too. "I'm not a good 'play' mommy, but I'm good at reading aloud, and I like talking about the things we read," she says. "I discovered I had a knack for creating curriculum from field trips and library books. I discovered that as a postcareer mom who had trouble 'fitting in' as a stay-at-home mom, I felt satisfied in my new role as teacher, and I loved seeing the sparkle when something just clicked. It's like their first steps and first words. I'd never want to miss it!"

Today the plan is for Bob and his two younger siblings to spend all of their school years at home. "I am 110 percent convinced that homeschool is the answer for us," Lori asserts, "and Hubby's been gracious enough not to say I told you so."

A ROLLER COASTER OF EMOTIONS

IF YOU planned to move from the United States to Turkey, you would naturally expect to prepare for and encounter major changes in your daily life. Switching from school-schedule–driven to family-centered living isn't as drastic a move, but it does create a new lifestyle, so you should expect some adjustments here as well. Some of these changes are universal, affecting all homeschoolers. Others are more personal.

It's the personal adjustments that can leave us feeling as if we're riding a roller coaster of emotions as we enter our new lifestyle. While you may discover a need for adjustments unique to you, homeschooling parents have already survived many of the loops on this roller coaster ride and share their stories. Fasten your seat belt.

Shouldering Educational Responsibility

The buck stops here. This sentiment is frightening in many scenarios, but when it comes to your own children's education and its relationship to their future well-being, yikes!

Stop. Take a deep breath. Realize that you took on responsibility for your child's life at the moment of conception. While others may send their children to school and, by all appearances, have someone else to blame for any failings, who is ultimately responsible for what happens to the children? Who will live with the consequences of a school's failure to educate? The children's families, of course.

Hopefully this knowledge will help you keep educational responsibility in perspective. By homeschooling, you are not taking on any more responsibility than you already hold. Rather, you are merely deciding that you are also the best person to fulfill this responsibility, instead of passing it on to others.

Karyn Scallorn knew she wanted to be a stay-at-home, home-educating mom before she ever began. Still, during her first year, she found responsibility for her children's entire education "paralyzing." Karyn wasn't going to let this continue forever. "Once I decided that whatever happened, I was just going to do it and fix things as I went, homeschooling was a breeze," she says. "It was a matter of my calming down."

> While others may send their children to school and, by all appearances, have someone else to blame for any failings, who is ultimately responsible for what happens to the children?

Doing Enough? Too Much?

At first glance this issue may not seem to be a particularly emotional one—until you realize that you are really swinging from one fear, pushing your child too hard, to another fear, that your child isn't keeping up with all the little Joneses in school. The key word here is

WHAT I WISH SOMEONE HAD TOLD ME DURING MY FIRST YEAR OF HOMESCHOOLING

I wish someone had reminded me that my son would still be the same child, with the same personality and the same adolescent problems, even though we were now homeschooling.

I had called experienced homeschoolers and read many books on the subject. They all talked about how wonderful it would be (which it is) and how much closer I would be to my son (which I am). No one told me that some days he would say he didn't want to do lessons. No one told me that some days I would have to bribe or threaten to get him to do his work. No one told me that lessons that I'd planned for weeks would be as exciting to him as brushing his teeth (which I also have to beg him to do at times). I was about to give up and decide that I was just a bad parent when I learned at a support-group meeting that many other parents went through the same things and the same feelings.

—BECKY SORRELL, GRETNA, VIRGINIA

fear, and it wastes an awful lot of energy you could be better expending elsewhere. The trick is keeping yourself balanced in a comfortable "middle" of reasonable expectations and confidence in self and child.

"I have to work on patience and expectations daily," explains Diane Burton. "I had a lot of difficulty in the beginning months with boundaries. How much is too much to expect them to absorb in a day and the constant worry of are we keeping up (with whom we are having this imaginary race, I'm not sure). Striking a balance was hard, but limiting my expectations seemed to help things settle down during the later half of our first year."

Kathy Raine, of Newfield, New York, feared she would leave gaps in her children's education through homeschooling. Still, she knew from the start that her goal wasn't to "cram their heads," and she set about overcoming years of fixed beliefs about education.

She realized that "no one comes out of any mode of schooling knowing 'everything.'" She says, "I think a child can spend years in an educational system and come out lost. I hope my children never feel like they're wasting their time and lives and then grow into adulthood just sleepwalking through life, never discovering and acting on their own goals."

Lost Friends

You decide to homeschool; your friends do not. Their preschoolers grow and join the march to school, and/or their older children continue to board the school bus. Your friends' days are filled with the same things as they've always been; extracurricular activities go on. And now you're not free for lunch—or shopping or that swell-sounding yoga class, either. Your availability has changed right along with your priorities. As you ponder learning styles, your friends chatter on about the school's new absentee policy, parent-teacher meetings, and how they will work their schedules around a school closing for teachers' in-service meeting.

Some friendships withstand long absences punctuated only by brief phone conversations. Others do not. In many instances, a homeschooling parent's circle of friends shrinks. Most often, friendships are built and sustained by our commonalties. Your act of homeschooling can definitely take away some or all of these, as does moving to a different neighborhood, taking a new job, or deciding to attend a different church or college. In other words, while losing old friends may happen because of homeschooling, it's the same thing that happens to people every day for many reasons.

And what happens to those who move, take a new job, or attend a different church? They meet different people and make new friends. The same will happen when you begin homeschooling.

WHAT I WISH SOMEONE HAD TOLD ME DURING MY FIRST YEAR OF HOMESCHOOLING

I would have spent a lot less time and energy being anxious about other people's perceptions of my choices. My husband and I know that what we are doing is socially and academically best for our kids, and we need no other assurance than that. I would still have reassured the grandparents, explained our choices to concerned family members, and answered the questions of friends. But I would have spent a lot less energy being defensive, trying to justify myself, and attempting to get validation from others. The health and well-being of my kids is at stake; no other justification is necessary. And life is good.

—ERIKA LEONARD HOLMES, RICHMOND, CALIFORNIA

Quite naturally you will seek out others who share your lifestyle. While you may not believe it yet, they will probably also be seeking out you and your children to join them!

"I noticed my nonhomeschooling friends weren't around as much anymore when we first started," says Stephanie Romero, of Milwaukee, Wisconsin. "It seems like an unavoidable gap comes between you and those who send their children to school. At times it's just been a matter of not having time to get together as much, and other times I think there is some disagreement as to my decision to homeschool." Stephanie adds, "Yes, I've gained new friends who homeschool, but giving up some of my other friends has been difficult."

"Loneliness has cropped up for me; my circle of friends has been small," admits Lisa Bugg, of Huntsville, Alabama. "But I must say this year has brought many interesting people into my life, and that's where I focus. I work at making these new friendships."

Working at friendships is always a good idea, whether you are homeschooling or not.

Focused on Your Personal Liabilities

Once you begin to contemplate the weight of bearing complete responsibility for your children's education, you may already have a well-meaning friend or relative pointing out your shortcomings. Still, you will likely engage in an even more complete self-assessment process. Of course, you will happen upon some qualities you feel will help you homeschool, but by and large you will probably shine a huge spotlight on your personal liabilities. You know what I'm talking about: all those negative things with which you can fill in the blanks in such statements as "I'm not _____ enough"; "I am too _____";"I was never good at_____."

You can waste a whole lot of energy focusing on your shortcomings. You could probably even talk yourself right out of homeschooling if you concentrate on them long and hard enough. This reality is proven every day when people, upon finding out that your family homeschools, question you and then you almost always respond in self-deprecation with one of the blanks filled in.

That we perceive ourselves this way—incapable and/or deficient—may be a result of the training we received in school during our formative years. This thought is definitely worth examining. In fact, if you reach the same conclusions as many schooled-children-turned-homeschooling-parents, this examination might not only help you overcome your negative perceptions of your abilities but also reinforce your decision to homeschool so that the same never happens to your children.

You'll also have assistance once you take the plunge into homeschooling. Believe it or not, your children, with their innate abilities, can help you conquer this sense of inadequacy. Once you get your children out of the confines of schooling, your inadequacies won't magically disappear. Rather, you'll recognize that your deficiencies—real or perceived—don't matter as much as you thought, simply because you've been putting far too much emphasis on teaching, instead of on your children learning.

"I'm not really a patient person," says Dena Terrell, mom of two early-years children, from her home at Yokota Air Base, in Japan. "Considering homeschooling, I wondered if it would be possible for my son and me to sit down together, every day, and actually learn something without my throwing in the towel too early."

Circumstances forced Dena to try home-schooling anyway. "I discovered that my son has a love of learning I never knew about," she says. "He soaks up everything I give him and comes back for more. I'm so awed and grateful to be able to see and mold his wonderful curiosity."

On days when Dena follows her natural inclination not to sit down and get to work, "we learn the most," she says. "That's because when I see trouble, I've learned to take a different aim. We'll make the lesson fun by creating something with our own hands, or make up a song about it. Sometimes we put the 'work' aside, set the table, and pretend to have a fancy dinner; he doesn't realize I'm teaching him etiquette, and my daughter thinks it's a tea party! Or we'll head outdoors, and I'll call out a color to look for, a number of something to bring me."

> That we perceive ourselves as incapable and/or deficient may be a result of the training we received in school during our formative years.

These activities are as important to Dena as they are to her children. "They help diffuse my frustration before it begins," she explains. "At the same time, it gives them a sense of adventure I have to wonder if they'd get from a mainstream school. The end of our first year is fast approaching, and now I can say that homeschooling is definitely for us. I'll continue to teach my children myself for as long as it is feasible for us."

What About My Job?

Thanks in part to homeschooling critics' incessant insistence on telling the media that homeschooling requires the constant presence of a parent—and thereby the sacrifice of one or more jobs—many people still think that homeschooling parents can't be employed.

This isn't true. Sure, it's more challenging to homeschool when employment is desired or necessary, but it's not impossible. Sometimes it takes a little help from your friends, sometimes a lot of creativity. But folks are leaping this hurdle, just as all the others, every day.

Mary Nunaley was a single working mom when her older child began homeschooling, in sixth grade. "Luckily I have the support of family and neighbors," says Mary. "We worked out a schedule where 'teaching' occurs at night and on weekends, and homework happens during the day." Note that Mary was able to turn the typical school schedule totally backward in order to accommodate her situation. "I also found a new job that caused me to leave the field I loved," she adds, "but it allowed me more flexibility and time home to educate both of my children."

When LeAnne Lopez-Carlessi found she needed to work while homeschooling, she and her daughter rose at 5:00 A.M. to get started. After that, her daughter and younger son stayed in a home day care that had lots of homeschooled children in the neighborhood and provided a quiet place for more study during the day.

"I nearly gave up a dozen times," says LeAnne, "but we hung in there, and now I'm able to stay home again. The benefits of homeschooling were well worth the exhaustion I felt during that time."

Erika Leonard Holmes is a working mom who feels her parttime job as a teacher with a nonprofit organization is a piece of her. She lives in California, where educational options are plentiful, and her belief that working moms could not homeschool kept her from researching the subject. All the while, she knew her son could make the changes necessary to function in a school of any kind, but she "couldn't shake the feeling that bringing about those changes would be a huge loss for him personally, as well as for our family."

One day another teacher friend mentioned that she was considering homeschooling, and Erika replied, "I can't look at that option, because I can't leave my job."

"What are you talking about?" the friend asked her. "A lot of people have jobs and homeschool. In fact, you have the perfect job for homeschooling."

Erika was shaken. "Her response was a wake-up call: it highlighted for me that I had made a decision out of ignorance and prejudice. I got some homeschooling books and began reading that night after my husband went to bed," says Erika. "I felt like I was taking seriously something that 'everyone knows' is forbidden. It was a feeling like none I've ever had. My heart pounded, and I could see my hands shaking a bit as I read, and I doubt I've ever soaked up text as quickly as I did that night. I was thinking, 'Please, please, please, give an example of someone who does this in a way that seems healthy and educationally sound while managing a job too. Please.'"

Erika not only got what she wanted; she got a name for everything she believed to be true as a scholar, mother, teacher, and violence prevention educator: unschooling. "The entire landscape of my life shifted in those few days and settled into something as comfortable and 'right' as an old pair of jeans."

Today Erika awakes and works from 5:30 to 7:00 A.M. and an hour in the afternoon. She will go teach classes if an excellent care situation can be found. If not, she reschedules the classes. The organization she works for understands that her children are young for a brief period of time and is willing to wait to have more of her time.

"Yes, I'm up at 5:30 A.M.," says Erika, "but 10:30 finds me at the park or by a creek, coffee in hand, chatting with friends or my children, perhaps drawing. One-thirty finds me snuggled on the couch with my two kids, reading *Horton Hears a Who*. My life has never, never been this relaxed. It doesn't matter if anyone besides my husband and my boss believe I can do this. Exploring homeschooling showed me that I can take charge of my life and that I can make it what I want it to be."

Feeling Alone in Your Choice

When you consider that only 2 to 3 percent of school-aged children learn at home, it's important to be in touch with others who understand homeschooling, if only to have a place to share doubts and not be criticized, to share frustration and not be told, "Well, send your child to school, then."

> It's important to have a place to share frustration and not be told, "Well, send your child to school, then."

While the number of homeschooling support groups continues to swell, it's still sometimes difficult to find an "in person" group with which you feel comfortable. Discomfort may stem from personal incompatibility, essential differences in educational philosophy, or a group's requirement of a signed statement of faith.

If you need to, think about posting notices around town and start your own group. In Leesburg, Virginia, Michelle O'Donnell couldn't find a homeschooling group with children close to kindergarten son Breck's age. "I ran an ad for moms with young children and their siblings," says Michelle, "and before I knew it, we had a waiting list for our new group. We get together for field trips, play dates, and park days that provide social opportunities for kids and moms."

With options exhausted, some homeschooling families learn to go it alone, as did Teri Nine. "We had to learn to rely on ourselves," she explains, "to trust the decision we made and not succumb to feelings of doubt and insecurity just because those around us did not believe the way we did. Eventually I joined support groups online and e-mail loops. These have been a great source of support and friendship."

It may not be "in person" support, but if you have a computer, you are almost sure to find an e-mail list brimming with folks with whom you can relate, feel comfortable, and share what's on your mind. (As of February 2001, there are 1,275 homeschool-related lists at http://www.yahoogroups.com alone.)

SPIDER WEBS, DUST BUNNIES, AND CREEPING CRUMBS, OH, MY!

YOU THINK your house has that "lived-in" look now? Wait until it's actually lived in! But where is the law that says our homes must be void of dust bunnies, and who gave Martha Stewart the final say on it all?

Homeschoolers leap the housework hurdle in their own ways, but many share a relaxation of standards to ensure there's still time for sleep each night.

"I wish I'd worked more on this sort of training and household organization while the children thought I knew everything," says Nicky Jacoby, of Gettysburg, Pennsylvania. Take Nicky's advice to heart, then try to learn to be content with "kid-cleaned." In this way you'll be able to enjoy putting your energy into your fellow inhabitants, instead of into the "box" in which they live.

Clear Out the Clutter

Another way to clear this hurdle is to first clear clutter. When she started homeschooling with a new baby in the house, Kimberly McLamb, of Kensington, Maryland, also brought home her work as a certified public accountant. "I had to choose to simplify or go insane," she says. "Out went items not used, clothes not worn, crafts not completed."

WHAT I WISH SOMEONE HAD TOLD ME DURING MY FIRST YEAR OF HOMESCHOOLING

I wish someone had told me how to balance housework and schoolwork in a twenty-four-hour day. I found that working at the kitchen table worked better for us, as opposed to my two children in separate rooms at their desks. I spent a lot of time running from room to room and couldn't tackle any housework. At the kitchen table, I could run to the basement, put up a load of laundry, go hang it outside, cook, plan meals, do dishes, pay bills, or just sit with my children and read quietly while they worked. This was so much better than constantly running up and down the stairs.

—DIANE BURTON, MAYS LANDING, NEW JERSEY

Kimberly also feels that making it through Christmas without adding to clutter is another victory. "Grandparents are given curriculum lists in place of lists full of toys with short lives or little educational value," Kimberly explains. "It's tough! Nonhomeschooling cousins open gifts containing whatever caught their eyes on television the week after Thanksgiving, then peer curiously at my daughter's CDs, math manipulatives, and educational puzzles."

Three Weeks On, One Week Off

When you're in charge of the schedule, you can shape it in any way that best fits your needs. When Joy Hayden, of Sterling, Virginia, got tired of forgetting to do the laundry during the first two weeks of homeschooling each year, here's how she decided to handle housework.

"We homeschool for three weeks and take one week off," Joy says. "During the week off, my children catch up on any work they failed to finish during the first three weeks. I use the time to run errands, make appointments, and do some heavier cleaning."

The week off has always included visits to Grandma and craft projects, but now the Haydens have added a unit study with another family as well. "We moms take turns leading the unit study, which means I don't have to prepare one every month," says Joy. "This way we don't forfeit our entire week off, and the kids love it."

Prioritizing

On some mornings we wake up and realize that, if given the use of ten extra hands that day, we still couldn't accomplish everything we would like to. While this problem isn't unique to homeschooling parents, our additional responsibility can make some days seem far shorter than twenty-four hours.

"I wish someone had told me that it's okay if your house isn't always picked up or even cleaned up and dusted," Gwena Chavez, of Fort Wayne, Indiana, says. "I wish someone had told me how to juggle a million things all at once—especially pleasing my husband, who doesn't always agree on what should be a day's priorities. I just can't do it all at once, and I had to learn to relax and pray for wisdom and discernment in prioritizing my daily chores—chores, by the way, some of which I now assign to my young children."

A Few More Tips to Help You Get It All Done

Where there's a will there's a way, and homeschoolers must have a lot of will, because they've found a lot of ways to accomplish as much as possible in any given day.

+   Find out more about once-a-month cooking, a real meal-preparation time-saver.

- ✦ Organize—with shelves (and more shelves), plastic bins and baskets, covered containers big and small, and anything else that helps create "a place" for everything.

- ✦ Cut back on nonfamily activities; when the children get older (in what will seem the blink of an eye), you can resume same.

- ✦ Have more activities outside.

- ✦ Find a mother's helper—sometimes neighborhood teens are willing to entertain children for an hour or two for a day or two each week, either for pay or in barter exchange for something you can provide in return.

- ✦ Family and friends may want to help—you don't know if you don't ask.

HOW CAN HOMESCHOOLING POSSIBLY "FIT"?

NOT ONLY can homeschooling bend in a million ways to fit your needs, but the act of bending it often uncovers additional benefits you never imagined your family would realize.

Let Learning Flow around Everyday Activities

Margaret Sanders's hurdle with two early-years children has been "an abundance of speech therapy sessions both at home and at the therapy office." Instead of allowing the frequent appointments to interrupt learning, Margaret learned to center "schooling" around everyday activities. "We read constantly," she says. "When I decided to teach the four-year-old how to read, we had lessons at bedtime for the most part. For formal math lessons, the two-year-old kibbitzed and loved it. Now he asks for math lessons."

Set a Schedule . . .

While it's nice to be able to utilize homeschooling's flexibility, some children are just more comfortable knowing what to expect each day, and this shouldn't be denied them simply to do things differently than the local school.

It took eight-year homeschooling veteran Debbie Brown, of Valinda, California, a few years to realize that her oldest son needed a strict schedule as he got older. "He couldn't concentrate once the schedule was broken," Debbie explains. "Now we have a set time for each subject, and whatever he doesn't complete in the time frame has to be finished at the end of the day, kind of like homework."

> The act of bending homeschooling often uncovers additional benefits you never imagined your family would realize.

Debbie admits that this won't work for all children and notes that finding the best way for each child to learn is the purpose of homeschooling. "The schedule gives my son an incentive to get right to work and not waste time," she has observed. "It also reminds him what subject he should be concentrating on by that time of day."

. . . Or Loosen Up!

As schedules work well for some, others find that a lack of routine works equally well. Sometimes flexibility within structure is the perfect approach for all involved. This happened for Nina Sutcliffe, who found that alternating between parent-suggested activities and those that allow her son to follow his mood results in their getting the most accomplished at the end of a day.

"I schedule things like reading and clarinet playing," says Nina, "but not others, like math, which he thrives on and does daily without prodding. We don't do even those things that are scheduled at the same time every day. We might read in the morning one day, in the afternoon the next, and just before bed on the third day."

The benefits Nina found include "the ability to follow our individual moods and be flexible around other activities that come up." She adds, "I also do work out of the house, and the work occurs at different times of the day. It took me a long time to not try to do things the same time every day—I had this notion that following a routine would allow us to get everything done. But in our case it only created stress, so this 'let's get this done sometime today' works for us."

Seize Teachable Moments

Sometimes, after you've honed your observation skills, you find that this teaching business can be as simple as seizing the moments that our children present to us on a silver platter.

> This teaching business can be as simple as seizing the moments that our children present to us on a silver platter.

Sue Dalangin, of Moreno Valley, California, gave birth to another child just before she started homeschooling kindergarten with her first. "I admit I was tired the first couple of months, and we didn't always do everything the curriculum had laid before us for the day," Sue says. "Lo and behold, I discovered that we didn't have to sit at a table for x number of hours in order to learn! We could do math on the sofa while I nursed the baby, or read in the car—and at all those doctors' appointments—instead of while seated at a desk."

Children want to learn, Sue concluded. "If you look for those open moments when you know they are ready to be taught, you accomplish a lot more than if you spend many hours at a desk, fighting for their attention."

Let the Child's Lead Take You to His Need

Because she's more relaxed than her son, Cindy Allas says it "took a while," but she finally stopped trying to change the way he wanted

LEARNING ACTIVITY

Data Proficiency (math; early and middle years)

Four years ago, when my children were kindergarten- and preschool-age, I started teaching myself a computer database. This happened when our library's summer reading program was kicking off. Part of the program was a contest to see who could log the most books read over the six-week period. Since I needed data to practice my programming skills, I made a small database for the children's book logs, instead of writing them out by hand. The children watched as I typed in the book titles—they helped me find the authors' names—and were delighted to see their logs printing out. Each subsequent year, I slicked up our summer reading database screen with fields like page numbers, type of book read, date, and who did the reading. The reports got fancier, and we even tried graphing some of the data last year. Also, last year my daughter typed in her own book records, and both children watched as I made changes in the screen and pop-up lists. I suspect we will keep finding ways to build on the project in the future.

—RUTH DUNNAVAN, MOULTONBOROUGH, NEW HAMPSHIRE

to go about learning. "He," says Cindy, "having the most in regular school years of my children, likes a daytime school schedule, and I prefer to do it when the mood strikes, especially reading stories snuggled up on my bed at night."

Cindy observed that this just wasn't working out for the boy, so now "my son has me organized on a schedule." She adds, "My daughter leans more to the unschooler side and is happy creating projects and writing stories at all times of the day or night."

Laurae Lyster-Mensh says, "Our first year of homeschooling after my son was born was the most difficult and qualifies as a first-year problem to me, because everything was different."

With a new baby, Daniel, much younger than his big sister, Liana, "the dynamics of home-based learning completely changed," Laurae continues. "Suddenly I couldn't follow Liana's interests as they happened. I was no longer able to react fully and spontaneously to her. My son's healthy need for continual care curtailed my daughter's healthy need to explore—something we had spent years cultivating!"

The family went through a "lifestyle reconstruction," to last until Daniel is old enough to appreciate some of the same things as Liana. "Daniel goes to a few days of structured daycare now," says Laurae, "and Liana takes more classes outside the home. Our schedule as a family has shifted to more divided time, where one parent has one kid at a time. My husband has cut back on work. I suppose in a schooling family the situation may be parallel, but the effect was extreme for us. We feel good about how we have managed it so far, but it takes constant tweaking."

11

GOLD-MEDAL

HURDLE JUMPERS

In This Chapter

+ Lost job, cesarean section, and "forced" socialization

+ Morning sickness

+ Boom!

+ A life-altering accident

+ Back-to-back hurdles

+ Chronic illness

+ Five top tips for avoiding homeschool burnout

© EyeWire

"I wish someone had told me how much I would love homeschooling. I wish someone had told us what it would mean to our family, what it would be like to actually have a family. I did have someone tell me, 'You can do this. You can do this.' That helped tremendously. After all, don't we all question whether to homeschool? 'Can I really do this?' You can do this! I can do this! I am doing this! And things are fine!"

—Melanie Gingras, Florence, Kentucky

*I*T'S AT THE same time we face first-year homeschooling hurdles that we're also filled with the greatest amount of self-doubt that homeschooling will ever create. Yet it is under these conditions that ordinary people go to extraordinary lengths to leap the hurdles into second and subsequent years of homeschooling. Our society spends a lot of energy honoring athletes, politicians, philanthropists, and entertainers, but rarely do we take a moment to appreciate those who overcome adversity in order to live a family-first lifestyle.

> Rarely do we take a moment to appreciate those who overcome adversity in order to live a family-first lifestyle.

In this chapter you will meet just a few of the world's gold-medal homeschooling hurdle jumpers. As we take a moment to honor their commitment and fortitude, let their trials and tribulations make your hurdles appear a little less cumbersome. Let their hard-won lessons teach you also. Allow their stories to enlighten and inspire you to also try one of the most positively life-altering activities available today. You have nothing to lose, and so very much to gain.

LOST JOB, CESAREAN SECTION, AND "FORCED" SOCIALIZATION

AN EMERGENCY cesarean section during the Kenyon family's first year of homeschooling was totally unexpected. When the main breadwinner lost his job a week later, they faced the prospect of an extended period of unemployment.

"This was a wake-up call for us as a homeschooling family," says mom Mary. "We stopped 'doing school' temporarily and decided to just get through this stressful period as best we could."

Mary and her family decided to focus on what was most vital to them at the time, confident they could catch up on schoolwork during the following summer. A few months later, when the crises be-

WHAT I WISH SOMEONE HAD TOLD ME DURING MY FIRST YEAR OF HOMESCHOOLING

I wish someone had assured me that I could do this. We didn't know any homeschoolers, friends and family questioned our decision, so I didn't have a mentor or support system to offer such needed encouragement. When faced with such a new challenge, a person is bound to have questions and concerns. But since we began this journey, four years ago, I have learned the importance of trusting myself and, more important, trusting my children. Today we are thoroughly enjoying our homeschooling lifestyle, and the children are thriving, both socially *and* academically.

—KRISTI SCHRAMPFER, APPLETON, WISCONSIN

came history, the Kenyons dusted off their textbooks to get back to their studies.

"Lo and behold," says Mary, "we found that the children had been learning despite our lack of text reading." She adds, "In fact, without the textbooks, there was no stopping the questions, curiosity, and projects. During this period we made many trips to the library and eventually decided 'real reading' was much more meaningful for some of the subjects, especially history, than the textbooks."

Just to keep things interesting, Mary's relatives were also pressing on her their concerns about socialization. Mary wondered whether her daughter, coming home from fifth grade, would miss daily contact with her peers.

"I hauled my children to every homeschool support-group meeting in the area," says Mary. "They hated it. Only after several months of this 'forced' socialization did I realize we were just happier staying home."

The Kenyons moved from the country into town, where the children were "surrounded by neighbor children, and it seemed the more they played with other children, the less they enjoyed each other!" Mary observed. "We now live in the country again, fairly isolated. We have enough to occupy ourselves, have pen pals and good friends we see occasionally, and the children have fun together." Mary adds, "Funny, how the one thing I worried about the most has become the least important."

MORNING SICKNESS

WITH A seven-year-old just a few months into homeschooling, and three- and one-year-olds along for good measure, Larissa Lee discovered she was pregnant again. Prone to morning sickness, she spent the first four months of pregnancy exhausted and sick. Most mornings Larissa could barely get out of bed, and when she did manage, she felt sick all day.

"I was disappointed that all the plans I had made didn't seem to be working out," says Larissa, "and I was sure that my daughter would want to return to school the next year."

Morning sickness eventually stopped, during the fifth month. As she began feeling better, Larissa realized that even when she felt like they weren't "doing" homeschooling, her daughter was learning a lot. "We had continued trips to the library, so she was reading according to her own interests," Larissa explains. "We had kept going to museums and taking other trips. She had accompanied me to my midwife appointments and read everything they gave me about fetal development and birth. She learned to keep herself busy without an adult's telling her what to do every minute of the day."

Larissa kept a journal during her downtime and discovered how much could be learned from daily activities. "I learned not to be so hard on myself when I felt that we weren't getting as much done as I

LEARNING ACTIVITY

The Unplanned Activity (across the curriculum; all ages)

Throughout the years, my children have stored up much information about the world we live in. The best "learning activity" is still the unplanned one. Yes, I rely on textbooks for the fundamentals (the three R's), but my children get more excited about what is happening around them than what I can show in a textbook. So I allow plenty of time just to explore. Give them the best. Give them free time for the Unplanned Activity.

—JANE KOSSWIG, NEW BRITAIN, CONNECTICUT

had hoped," she says. "There have been times when we have accomplished a lot of 'schoolwork,' and now I have the perspective to know that if we have a bad day or week or month, it isn't the end of the world."

A lovely benefit is that with all her knowledge of the birthing process, big sister was able to attend her sibling's birth, an event that forms bonds to last a lifetime.

> Now I have the perspective to know that if we have a bad day or week or month, it isn't the end of the world.

BOOM!

In their busy New Britain, Connecticut, household Jane and Chris Kosswig's family of eight (including five children and a grandpa) had been homeschooling for one month before Jane slipped and fell. "We thought we would do school at home," says Jane, "but, with my injured back, we worked at the kitchen table, on the couch, from the floor, in the chiropractor's waiting room, and in bed."

Jane's lessons came fast and furious, chief among them that she wasn't really all that organized. "With little ones crawling all over me, and toys and books all over the floor," she says, "I realized that as a family we needed to pull together. It's taken some time, but now our household runs a lot smoother. Now we work as a team."

This mom of five realizes that her family went through an adjustment period. "It was not all peaches and cream," she says. "We laughed, we cried, we worked and prayed. We loved. We appreciate the lifestyle that homeschooling allows us. Some of our best lessons were unplanned. Learning is not just memorizing facts but living life. Taking our children home to school was the best thing we could do for our family morally, spiritually, and academically."

A LIFE-ALTERING ACCIDENT

FORMER PUBLIC school teacher Anita Peterson had known she would homeschool since the birth of her second child, Jackie, born fifteen months after her first child, Aaron. How hard could it be, she reasoned. ("I later came to find having been a teacher a hindrance," adds Anita, "instead of a benefit.")

When Aaron was just over two years old, an exhausted Anita plopped down on the floor one day. "I didn't notice at first," says Anita, "but the children were playing behind a floor lamp made out of plaster. When they accidentally knocked it down, it landed on my head."

At first, Anita experienced migraine headaches and constantly felt more tired than ever. Four months later, she suffered her first grand mal seizure, followed by another four months after that. Anita's doctor put her on antiseizure medications to depress her central nervous system and, further, her energy level. Migraines grew more frequent and severe.

"Over time I switched medications four times. One of them made my hair fall out!" Anita remembers. "All of these factors af-

WHAT I WISH SOMEONE HAD TOLD ME DURING MY FIRST YEAR OF HOMESCHOOLING

I wish someone had told me not to be in such awe of the public schools' way of teaching, so I wouldn't have tried to emulate it so closely. I wish I had realized that they don't have a magic formula for teaching and that their scope and sequence are not sacred. Who are these anointed ones who have the insight to know what my child needs to know and exactly when he needs to learn it?

—LISA RICHARDS, NEVIS, MINNESOTA

fected my reasoning as a person, but mostly as a mother. My temper had a hair trigger, and I couldn't stand loud noises (i.e., children)."

To cope, Anita hired a Mexican woman to help four days each week. "She taught my children Spanish as well as took care of us," says Anita. "I had to learn to let her take over and be 'mom' for a while so that I could take care of myself. I seriously questioned my ability to homeschool many, many times. Thankfully I had read about unschooling early on and decided that whether it suited my children or not, that was the only way we were going to be able to homeschool. Because of my experiences as a public school teacher, sending them to any school was not an option."

Anita believes that this decision gave her the space to heal and helped her children become "independent beings" now that they are seven and five years old. Her health has improved, along with her energy level. "I still have frequent headaches, and the kids can tell just by looking at my face," she says. "Depression comes and goes, but when I'm down, they make special notes, bring me wildflowers, and give me 'magic kisses.'"

Anita sees the consequences of her accident as not a hindrance but rather a blessing. "It taught my children patience, sympathy, and respect for others' feelings," she explains. "It has taught me what is truly important. On the days that my headaches are bad or my mood is down, the best part of the day may be sitting on the sofa and reading to my children. Or taking an hour to tuck them in at night. I'm not so sure I would so appreciate the 'small' things in life and in homeschooling if not for this experience."

BACK-TO-BACK HURDLES

DESPITE DAD'S initial doubts about homeschooling, he gave the Carlson family a year to try it, and two children came home in Yucaipa, California, to be taught by mom Barbara. They began in July, only to discover in October that Barbara's terminally ill father was quickly dying, more than four hundred miles away.

"We grabbed the bin of workbooks and materials and headed to my sister's home, which was nearer to my father," she explains. "We spent the next three months between home and my sister's—with aunts, uncles, cousins, and even my sister's retired special education teacher mother-in-law as 'teachers.' During this time we went from quite structured homeschoolers to *very* relaxed homeschoolers and found that the stresses we'd encountered in trying to homeschool with so much structure were gone!"

Later that school year, a cerebrovascular accident, similar to a stroke but with no bleeding, left Barbara unable to drive. "We took advantage of homeschooling during this tense time to read together in bed while I rested," she says. "We discovered the wide array of Public Broadcasting System programming and videos in areas of interest and didn't have to worry about how to get the kids to and from a traditional school. Both incidents convinced us that homeschooling gives us the flexibility to enjoy learning regardless of where we are or what other events may be happening in our family."

CHRONIC ILLNESS

ANDY, THE oldest of Kim Toll-Brown's three children, came home from first grade last March. Younger brother Jamie wanted to try kindergarten but after four days announced that "school kindergarten" wasn't for him. Within the first homeschooling year, Kim was diagnosed with lupus, a serious, chronic disease. Frequent doctor visits, treatments, and periods of inactivity have become a way of life. Throw into the mix a pregnancy, complete with morning sickness, for good measure.

"When we first started homeschooling, I felt a lot of pressure to get things done when I felt well, to make up for the time I felt terrible," explains Kim, "but I quickly learned that it doesn't work that way. Even when I have been unable to spend a lot of time with the boys, they have always kept learning. I couldn't stop them if I tried."

Kim vividly recalls lying in the hospital before the birth of her youngest, Josephine, worrying about all the time they were losing. "When I got home, there was the elder with his nose in an encyclopedia, and the younger had made his first steps toward becoming a reader, all on his own!"

> The lupus has strengthened the family's resolve to live the lifestyle they believe in.

The illness has also elicited a stream of opposition. Relatives are quick to ask, "What about the boys? Have you been able to teach them anything these last few days?" Still, the lupus has strengthened the family's resolve to live the lifestyle they believe in.

Her personal hurdle taught Kim that while she's not expendable to the homeschooling process, she is not the "key" to her children's learning either. "This is not to say that we still don't struggle with how the illness affects our lives. It does have a profound impact," says Kim. "For instance, we don't have a car during the day. I don't want one. That means we can't go on all those field trips that homeschoolers are so famous for. I don't have the energy to take them.

LEARNING ACTIVITY

Familiarity Breeds Learning (across the curriculum; all ages)

Whenever I want the kids to really internalize something, like the alphabet, multiplication tables, punctuation, etc., I tape up a poster about it on their bedroom wall and just leave it. Over days, weeks, or months, they pick it up, and when it's time to go over it, they learn it easily and quickly. Some think I'm a fool for believing this, but it works!

—TERI NINE, PLANO, TEXAS

I wait until evenings, when my husband can stay with the baby, and then we go, or we go as a family on the weekend."

The family's lifestyle includes more quiet time than the children would prefer—but, thinks Kim, there's a lesson in even this. "Lots of people are trying to learn to simplify and lead a quiet life. Our lifestyle is less fraught with time pressures than anyone I know. We like it this way," says Kim.

FIVE TOP TIPS FOR AVOIDING HOMESCHOOL BURNOUT

ANY OF the parents in these stories could easily have thrown up their hands in surrender and sent their children to school all day, succumbing to what is known in homeschooling circles as "burnout." As with other circumstances, homeschooling burnout occurs most frequently when a person is focused on one life aspect to

PET PEEVE

I admit I sometimes become impatient with the zeal of first-year homeschoolers, and especially irksome is the tendency to justify their decision by denigrating their public school system. Of course, I am occasionally guilty of this as well, but here's my advice on the subject. Never criticize your local school in an attempt to justify homeschooling. Homeschool and public schools are different; both have strengths and weaknesses. Just because your homeschool is not as "bad" as public schools doesn't make it "good," either. There may be a day that your children enroll in school through a change in circumstances or change in needs or interests. Children often have friends who attend public school, they will marry a spouse who attended public school, and they may have children of their own who attend public school. Discriminatory remarks about public school will be remembered in the future as unkind about the educational experiences of friends and loved ones.

—LAURIE MEYERPETER, LINCOLN, CALIFORNIA

the detriment of other life aspects, or when one goes about a pursuit in such a way that accomplishing it creates stress and dissatisfaction.

These burnout circumstances are ones our gold-medal hurdle jumpers refused to allow to exist in their lives. Instead, they examined their true needs under adverse conditions and "bent" homeschooling as necessary to weather crises or adjust to new life circumstances.

You, too, can help prevent homeschool burnout by recognizing it as a possibility and taking steps to avoid it. Consider the suggestions below as preventive medicine that will help no matter if you have clear homeschooling skies or if you need to weather a storm or two during your first year.

Take Time for Self and Spouse

That piece of advice may sound simple, but if you're not alert to the possibility of keeping homeschooling in its rightful perspective, planning, creating, and carrying out homeschooling activities and adventures could take over your life. When this happens, something else will suffer, and the first effects become visible in a lack of time for your own interests as well as time with your spouse. Who could possibly appreciate and enjoy homeschooling under these conditions?

Kate Varley describes a typical first-year experience: "I busily tried to do everything right. I wanted to give our kids the opportunities to explore interests and use their talents in a way that formal school had not," Kate begins. "I wanted everyone—family, friends, evaluator, and school district—to realize that what we were doing was great, and my way of doing that was to subordinate my interests to what I saw as the needs of our homeschooling. I wish that someone had gotten through to me that I would be much better off, as would the whole family, if I maintained some nonhomeschooling interests of my own."

A love of writing withered when preparation of "an incredibly detailed record" of educational activities took up a majority of Kate's spare time. "I didn't engage in the kinds of activities that I might have if I hadn't felt so responsible for our homeschooling," she explains. "With time, I've relaxed. I don't want to prove to others that we're doing good work in homeschooling. I realize we're doing lots of wonderful things, and if others don't recognize it, it's their problem. I particularly gave up the idea of impressing the educational establishment, a fruitless pursuit. I am required by our state (Pennsylvania) to keep a daily log, and I do, but I no longer feel an internal need to document every learning moment of our kids' day (when are they *not* learning?)."

Today Kate makes time for outside interests, which she feels could actually enrich her children's homeschooling experience someday. "What's more, I feel energized by the contacts, which lends excitement to our homeschooling experience," says Kate. "Years ago my husband gave me a sweatshirt that said, 'If Mama ain't happy, ain't nobody happy!' That's true. And giving yourself permission to conduct some aspects of your life without the kids present can be a very good experience for the whole family. Moms are people too."

Begin with the End in Mind

Yes, I'm repeating myself, but this aspect of homeschooling is important enough to repeat. "Begin with the end in mind" was previously mentioned in relation to creating your educational philosophy. It helps throughout all of homeschooling, not just during your first year, to remember where you are going so that you keep your eye on "the big picture." By doing so, a single bad day remains in perspective: It's one day in a lifetime of learning. You'll remember that your kindergartner, in what in retrospect will seem the blink of an eye, will one day be a man who will create his own roof and not always be the young and challenging bundle of energy and mischief, raw emotion, and nonreasoning being that you see today.

> Keeping the big picture in front of you helps you see that even if you don't accomplish all those wonderful things this month or this year, there is still time.

Keeping the big picture in front of you helps you see that even if you don't accomplish all those wonderful things this month or this year, there is still time. Experience will teach you that you can always think of more wonderful things than you will ever have the time (and possibly the money or the energy) to accomplish anyway. Remembering all these things is a nice way to prevent burnout, as it will help you cherish all the little things in your day that are the true gifts of homeschooling: one of your child's *aha!* moments, taking advantage of gorgeous weather to watch the clouds roll by, really knowing your child.

LEARNING ACTIVITY

More than You Ever Wanted to Know about Your Pet
(across the curriculum; early and middle years)

During a unit study on animals, it was recommended to study your dog or cat. We didn't have either, but we did have a guinea pig. My children, ages three and nine at the time, had a blast. They drew pictures, read books, watched videos, poked and prodded our guinea pig, and eventually learned more about guinea pigs than any human being ought to know! (And there has never been a more thoroughly loved and cared for guinea pig than ours.)

—TERRI L. BANDALOS, FREDERICK, MARYLAND

Don't Sign Up for Everything

It just happens. Every activity you hear about sounds better and more educationally valuable than the last, so you sign up for that one *too*. If you're not careful, before you know it, people will be flagging you down on street corners, mistaking you for a taxi as you race between activities all day.

Can you think of anything that will burn you out on the idea of homeschooling any more quickly than physically running yourself ragged in the name of learning? In the name of impressing your mother-in-law with all that your children can do when free of the school schedule? Homeschoolers have seen a lot of miracles in their efforts, but to date no one has reported that it stretched their days beyond twenty-four hours.

"We're fortunate to live in an area where there are many homeschoolers and a number of active support groups organizing many outings and activities," says Sandy Keane, who homeschools in

LEARNING ACTIVITY

Learning on the Move (across the curriculum; all ages)

We live in the country and spend a lot of time driving, so some of our learning takes place in the van. Older siblings read to younger ones, and we use audiotapes so everyone can listen. Also, the creative ones look at cloud formations and "look" for letters, numbers, animals. . . . The list can go on forever.

—JULIE BERTSCH, PIEDMONT, SOUTH DAKOTA

North Vancouver, British Columbia. "I wish someone had told me that first year that I didn't have to do everything just because it was available."

Why should new homeschoolers be cautioned from signing up for everything? "We joined in," says Sandy, "because a) we didn't know what we should be doing, b) we still bought into the 'kids have to be with other kids as much as possible' line of socialization thinking, and c) the contact with other adults with similar philosophies of parenting and learning was important to me." Sandy concludes, "Over the years, point *c* is the only one which I still feel is valid."

Don't Conduct School at Home

You may want to use a curriculum as you begin homeschooling. You may join a homeschool charter school for support. You may choose an online course complete with tests and transcripts. *You still don't have to "do school" at home.* After all, a world of learning awaits you on your own schedule. Why burn out on someone else's?

"When I began homeschooling, most of the homeschooling families I knew did some form of school at home. We started off down that same path," says Sally Farrington, who is just returning to North Carolina after a three-year military stint in Italy. "I went so far as to have a detailed schedule for the day, math from nine to ten o'clock, history from ten to eleven, and so on. It didn't take too long for that to get thrown out the window.

"Looking back," Sally muses, "I wonder why it took me so long to realize I needed to relax; there were a ton of signs along the way."

This mom wishes that someone had given her a shake and told her not to be afraid to just live. "There are so many opportunities out there to learn, but I was afraid at first not to have a lesson plan," says Sally, "and afraid not to follow it. Life, however, has a way of butting in to the best-laid plans."

The Farrington family's days gradually began including opportunities to volunteer, to go places, to spend a rainy day with a good book instead of a textbook. "We've recently become involved with community theater, which can involve late nights—so we don't have early mornings," she adds.

What has this taught Sally about living life without school's schedule? She shares a long list of lessons. "We've all learned things I never could have taught if we were locked into a set schedule: self-confidence, good diction, knowledge of directions, construction, publicity, exposure to lots of good plays, the experience of competition (how to be a gracious winner or a good loser), making friends of all ages and walks of life. Thank God I wised up," Sally says, "and we didn't miss this wonderful opportunity. So to anyone just beginning the journey—don't forget to lighten up, stay flexible, and enjoy the ride!"

Find Support Wherever You Can

In decades past, many homeschooling families took off on this path with nothing but their own convictions to carry them through. Often no other homeschoolers lived nearby. While it's very possible to homeschool in isolation today, why would you?

Since homeschooling evolves into a lifestyle, it's others who live similar lifestyles who can join you in laughing and crying, venting and patting your children on the back, asking questions of others and answering the questions of still others whenever you can. Fellow homeschoolers can empathize, a very handy pick-me-up if or when you need one. They won't let you burn out, be-cause they'll share options (often in the form of "that happened to us, this is what we did, and this is how it turned out for us"), resources, and words of encouragement that "this, too, shall pass."

While it's very possible to homeschool in isola-tion today, why would you?

Even if your life is filled with homeschooling naysayers, you can find support, sometimes in places and people least expected. Enough folks are going to ask why your children aren't in school to give you the op-portunity to tell them about homeschooling. You'll be pleasantly surprised by how many people say nice things, and you may very well find yourself talking to another homeschooler.

"I wish someone had explained the benefits of becoming in-volved in a homeschool group and conventions, even years before we started homeschooling. Being able to learn from others' experiences has helped so much," says Val Vaughn, of Fort Thompson, South Dakota.

"The field trips and other opportunities are great, but it's spend-ing time with other families that really helps," she continues. "Our local homeschool group has a moms' brunch once a month. It has been educational for me as a parent. We visit in someone's home, very relaxed, and I'm free to ask questions about curriculum, child rear-ing—anything. It has given me direction I couldn't get on my own or through books. Conventions always seem to have at least one work-shop on getting started, and the encouragement received is helpful."

12

AFTER YOUR

FIRST YEAR

In This Chapter

✦ Reflections from those who continue the journey

✦ Homeschooling: the ever-changing,
never-ending story

© EyeWire

"I wish someone had told me that a lesson doesn't need to be on the school board's list of required curricula to be important. There are other lessons that are equally or more important that our children learn just by being around us. They learn to be kind to people and animals, to be honest, to be tolerant and respectful of differences, to value themselves, to take care of themselves and their belongings, and so much more. These are the immeasurably important lessons that can be learned much better in the home environment than in an institution."

—Terry Stafford, Fort Langley, British Columbia

*N*O ONE, INCLUDING you, knows at the starting gate just how she will feel about homeschooling when she completes her first year. Hopefully your year will have been filled with

+ observation—utilizing the gift of time with your child to know her better

+ exploration—experimenting and putting what you learn to work for the benefit of your child

+ expanding educational horizons—stretching your thinking about what education is, how it may be scheduled, organized and implemented, and what its goal is.

REFLECTIONS FROM THOSE WHO CONTINUE THE JOURNEY

WHETHER OR not you continue homeschooling, that which you learn during your first year will almost certainly enrich your family life and show that you are far more capable of handling responsibility than you might have previously imagined. These are gifts you will keep with you no matter what the future holds.

> Hopefully your year will have been filled with observation, exploration, and expanding educational horizons.

Reflections on what a continued homeschooling future may hold for your family are this book's parting words. While many of homeschooling's benefits are readily apparent in the first year, others are merely planted during this time. They are nurtured more slowly, tended and encouraged with love and care, and blossom on their own timetable, just as your children do.

These benefits are virtually obscured by the educational establishment's focus on homeschooling's social, academic, and "accountability" issues. However, these aspects of homeschooling (or even their lack thereof) pale in importance compared to the ultimate rewards found in bringing family home for education. The establishment is truly missing the forest for the trees and, worse, failing to hear this important message even as they profess to have children's best interests at heart. As strongly as Mom and Dad have their best interests at heart? Hardly.

Maybe, just maybe, for some reason these folks don't want attention turned to these benefits. Maybe they'd rather we didn't talk about them. Three experienced homeschooling moms, one of whom was homeschooled herself, graciously chose to talk about them anyway and share the additional "perks" they found when they continued on the homeschooling journey.

Growing Togetherness
by Catherine Donnelly

My parents decided to homeschool my two brothers and me for academic reasons when I was ten years old. After a few years their motivation shifted. When asked why they were still homeschooling, they would smile and share how close our family had become and how they valued the opportunity to include God in everything. Homeschooling became an integral part of our spiritual and family heritage.

It was difficult at first. We experienced loneliness and boredom, and I ached for just one girlfriend my own age. But I drew much closer to my brothers—we did everything together. Some families go on vacation once a year to build memories. We constructed them daily.

When I was thirteen years old, my father lost his job. We moved to a town we had never been to before—Kamloops, British Columbia, hours away from relatives and friends. Uprooting is always difficult, but we were also technically homeless. Our old home was sold, and the new one wouldn't be ready for a month. Without Dad, who had traveled ahead of us, we spent those thirty days roaming around the Spokane, Washington, area in our station wagon with our cat, looking for Rags, our lost dog. Sometimes we stayed with friends, sometimes in motels. It was an adventure that taught resourcefulness as well as how important it is to really cooperate with one another.

When our new home was ready, we had to give up on finding Rags. Heartbroken, we set out without him on an eight-hour journey to the home we'd never seen before. We cried together and consoled one another and prayed that God would keep him safe.

On our arrival in Kamloops, Dad greeted us with "Rags has been found!" We headed back to the Humane Society in Spokane the very next day. Returning to our new home with our family intact once again, we knew we had been tested on one of life's challenges—and passed—together. We learned how important each one of us is, how much we needed to help one another through problems big or small.

As we grew into teens, my brothers and I cemented bonds started long ago. At fifteen, I was still comfortable running around the neighborhood, playing hide-and-seek with my brothers, while many girls my age scorned such activity. We worked in the garden together, read and made up stories, went for long bike rides, and sometimes just sat and talked or listened to music. My childhood is filled with memories that center around family.

I grew up, became a mother to three children, and now desire that we, too, can build a strong sense of togetherness in our family. The constancy of a strong family relationship cannot be replicated, and sadly is undermined, by school attendance. Through homeschooling, my husband and I have focused on two keys to achieve this.

First is time, simply spending time together on a daily basis, through good and rough times. Homeschooling lets us work, play, and learn together. The second key is sharing a common family heritage. Homeschooling is an opportunity to cultivate one's own cultural heritage. By reading the same stories, knowing and making one's family history, sharing inside jokes, and really knowing one another, a family draws closer together over the long haul.

It takes at least a year to grow this kind of closeness, but it's worth the wait. When my son, Benjamin, was five years old, I told him not to worry; reading would get easier for him. It was a good year later when he reminded me of our conversation.

"You were right, Mom," he said, smiling, as we snuggled on the couch, and he confidently read me a story about dinosaurs.

Unlocking the Box

by Lisa Bugg

What do my grandfather, grandmother, and homeschoolers have in common? They've all held the key to something important. Grandmother's cedar chest held the family stories, the triumphs and tragedies.

"Papaw's" locked toolbox held magazines with "pictures" of 1940 pinup girls my grandmother pretended not to know about. And homeschoolers, by taking education out of the box, have unleashed a powerful force, a secret that will help heal our culture.

Jonathan Mooney says, in *Learning Outside the Lines* (Simon and Schuster, 2000), "The assumption is that when given equal instruction, intelligent people will learn and unintelligent people won't." But what is equal instruction? And who gets to define intelligence? Howard Gardner tells us there are eight or more kinds of intelligences. How do we integrate this with the fact that schools have only one acceptable form of instruction, only one way to be successful? If you cannot function within their rigid form, you, too, are labeled unintelligent. What becomes of all other gifts and ways of being?

> Homeschoolers have unleashed a powerful force, a secret that will help heal our culture.

In many cases our children will be labeled with some sort of pathology to explain away why they are not learning. Worse, they will function but still be overlooked, just because they can conform and do their work adequately. Yet these children are not truly engaged in anything going on around them, much less exploring and developing their own, unique potential.

It's very hard for first-year homeschoolers to believe that the most important aspect of this journey has almost nothing to do with academics. In the beginning, getting out of the box keeps us prowling both the parenting and education sections of the public library. We search for just the right books, materials for projects (which are mostly left undone, so don't feel guilty), and events to take our children to. We are convinced that without our providing a science lab at home, Johnny's shot at college is severely handicapped. While excited about the freedom to learn in meaningful ways, we miss freedom's point.

What homeschoolers let fly out of the box are the freedom to think and to feel and the freedom to control our time. This gift takes a while to understand and appreciate. These are the freedoms with the potential to heal our society. Right now many in society can't even be sure what life could look like, so prevalent is the idea that education means "being schooled." But when children grow as the masters of their own time, they honor life instead of academic success. When free to be their true selves, to give voice to their thoughts, and to create lives which nurture them, children grow into strong, self-confident, peaceful human beings.

This aspect of homeschooling strikes terror in our entrenched educational establishment. After all, when we exercise the freedom not to value its rigid definition of academic success, a multibillion-dollar industry stands in jeopardy. As you live and learn with your children, you will discover the emperor is naked and fat, fat with all manner of "experts" and useless and mind-numbing rituals, such as endless testing and evaluation. Just like those 1940 pinup pictures in Papaw's toolbox, homeschooling shows us the naked truth about our current educational system. In fact, it shows us we do not need an "educational system" at all.

Homeschoolers are a nucleus of empowered individuals creating an educational revolution. We live our lives outside the lines, and it's apparent we are raising vibrant, innovative, and caring children. Our active kinesthetic learners are not locked into in-school suspension rooms. Our children with learning differences are not forced to assume the persona of a bad or stupid child. Our quiet children do not lose their most precious of gifts to indifference.

In a summer 2000 *Whole Earth Magazine* article by Peter Warshall, titled "Interview with Rachel Naomi Remen," the author of the nonfiction *My Grandfather's Blessings* (Riverhead, 2000) says that "you heal a dominant culture by forming a subculture of credible people in the middle of it who value something new, who reinforce and reward something that the dominant culture represses." This is the hope homeschooling brings. Our children will be a nucleus of young adults who will speak to a different way of living and learning. It's a way of living where family bonds are strong and healthy, where time is slowed so that passions may be birthed and nurtured. It's a way of living that rebuilds and sustains a culture dedicated to human beings rather than to corporate profits and expert opinions.

And that's the key.

Homeschooling Produces Confident Kids

by Tammy Drennan

I was fortunate to have grown up in a family that fostered self-confidence. My brothers and sisters and I were led to believe that we were competent human beings and as likely to be right about something as the next guy, maybe even more likely. That this attitude I inherited was so strong is probably what helped me come through my schooling experience with my self-confidence intact. I had more than one long discussion with a teacher because I felt he or she had misgraded a paper, and I routinely added choices to multiple-choice tests. While I respected the opinions and experience of others, I completely trusted my own judgment.

I am always amazed at most people's lack of confidence in themselves. I once talked to a man who had just taken a state-required exam related to his profession.

"How did you do?" I asked.

"I don't know," he responded. "The results won't be in for a few weeks."

I pressed him, "But surely you have a general idea of how you did. Did you know the material on the test?"

He insisted that he could not possibly know how he did, not even if he had passed or failed, until he got the results back.

I've encountered this same thinking while tutoring math students. A student will do a problem, then look to me to learn if it was right or wrong. I always ask, "What do you think?" And the student almost always insists he does not know, does not even have a clue.

Institutional schooling is designed to squeeze the self-confidence out of kids. It is a natural by-product of the system. It happens at the college level too. When the school is done with us, it confers upon us a diploma which grants us permission to feel competent in particular areas (ironically whether we actually are competent or not). The high school diploma grants permission to feel confident enough to pursue college or low-level employment.

> Institutional schooling is designed to squeeze the self-confidence out of kids.

Think about school, starting with kindergarten or first grade. The first thing you learn in school is that the teacher is always right. Next you learn that parents are not as smart as teachers. You may not be taught this directly, but few children end first grade without being sure of it. Next, you learn that the only opinion that counts is the teacher's and that nothing is right until teacher says it is. At five or six years old, you have no defense against this attack on yourself and your family. You learn right off the bat not to trust yourself, not to trust your senses, your observations, or your intuition. This attitude is reinforced for twelve years. Now you are an adult with a persistent worry that you might be doing it all wrong. You spend a good portion of your life seeking "expert" opinion on everything from raising your kids to health care to decorating your house, because you have been trained not to trust yourself.

Homeschoolers are not immune to this problem. After all, most homeschooling parents have been raised in institutional schools. But it is amazing how strongly confident most homeschooled kids remain even if their parents struggle with self-confidence.

I have headed up many dozens of homeschool events, and I am always struck by the total self-confidence of the kids at these events. Having never had their competence to learn or their value as human beings challenged, they are relaxed and confident and completely comfortable affording others the same respect they have come to expect themselves.

Institutional school settings destroy self-confidence on many fronts. At the instructional level, kids learn they should not trust themselves as learners. They are taught directly and indirectly to doubt their senses and their ability to draw sound conclusions about evidence. Also at this level, children are denied the opportunity to verbalize serious thoughts and to work through ideas by interacting with others. Further, they are denied the confidence-building habit of choosing a course of study (and the amount of time they will spend on it) for themselves.

At the social level, institutional school creates an atmosphere that fosters an "every man for himself" attitude. The main cause of this is the unnatural grouping of children by age and the practice of forced association. In a natural community or family setting, the variety of ages and the fact that the people spend time together by choice fosters an atmosphere of support and mutual respect. Adults look out for children and step in when children are having difficulty acting civil. Older children look out for little ones. And everyone tends to be engaged in meaningful activity. It is nearly impossible for people who have not experienced this, people whose lives revolve around institutional schooling and the troubled children it produces, to believe it could be true. When schools try even small imitations of this natural arrangement, they see improvements. One school in my neck of the woods was surprised to see how eagerly older children read to younger ones when given the opportunity. Why should it be surprising? These children were allowed to feel competent again, and it did their souls good.

Finally, school inculcates insecurity, which in turn promotes cruelty. The insecure child is the self-centered child. He is focused on his own survival, his own interests. No one else really matters. His confidence in himself is under attack, and he must find a way to survive and feel worthwhile. The answer is often to make others feel or look inferior. He protects himself (or so it seems to him) by attacking the security of others, either by taunting and teasing or by ostracizing, or in dozens of other big and little ways.

All of these institutional attacks on the personhood of children are born of the unnaturalness of the institutional setting. This explains the high level of self-confidence we witness in homeschooled kids—they grow up in natural circumstances where they are cherished, respected, and trusted. Homeschooling provides the opportunity for your children to grow up free from persistent instructional and social assault, free from emotional battery, free to become self-confident, independent, happy adults.

HOMESCHOOLING: THE EVER-CHANGING, NEVER-ENDING STORY

THROUGHOUT THIS book, experienced homeschoolers have shared with you what they wish someone had told them when they were new to homeschooling, not only hoping to save you time and money but to help your homeschooling journey become a successful and happy one as soon as possible. I firmly believe that the more intimate knowledge you have about homeschooling, the more successful will be your personal decisions regarding it. Successful decisions create the happiest practitioners, and my heartfelt wish for you and your family is that you can join this merry band.

I couldn't have asked for and received so many answers to the important question "What do you wish someone had told you about homeschooling?" without considering how I, too, might answer. Many ideas crossed my mind, but I think the most useful tidbit would have been to know that homeschooling is an ever-changing, never-ending story, its script so amazing that it is an honor to play even a small role.

WHAT I WISH SOMEONE HAD TOLD ME DURING MY FIRST YEAR OF HOMESCHOOLING

I wish I'd realized how much I'd love spending so much time with my children, enjoying them as people, not just my offspring. They are funny, loving, inquisitive, thought provoking, silly, happy. Not that they're not also at times self-centered, rude, lazy, whiny, or argumentative, but the former outweigh the latter by far.

I love going someplace and spending the time to let my children fully enjoy what they see, instead of rushing them through because our time is limited. I love sitting on the couch reading in our pajamas at noon. I love when my daughter says to me, "How come you don't make us do dioramas like in school?" so I assign her one and she's excited to do it. I loved when my then-five-year-old son sat at a table with a doubting step-grandfather and out of the blue asked him, "Do you

Children grow, family circumstances change, life takes unexpected twists and turns. One day the scenery is set for a homeschooling adventure in which your family travels to parts previously unknown, meeting interesting people who share new ideas. Turn around and homeschooling is an unfolding drama in which your rapidly maturing daughter flaps her wings in preparation for flight. A horror story plays out as the washing machine dumps gallons of sudsy water on your new kitchen floor just as you planned to enjoy a nature walk, but that doesn't matter at the moment, because your toddler is screaming. You suspect big brother may have pulled her shoulder out of joint while helping you get her out of the water, and if the doctor is going to help, you've got to get to his of-

> Homeschooling is an ever-changing, never-ending story, its script so amazing that it is an honor to play even a small role.

know about DNA?" (I thought the step-grandfather was going to fall out of his chair.) I love sitting on the floor of our "project room" (garage with indoor/outdoor carpet) listening to classical or African or new-age music while putting together a Legos or a K'Nex project. I love it that I was there with my son a couple of weeks ago, when his first tooth fell out—and knowing that no matter what time of day it happened, I wouldn't have to miss it. I love it when they wake up and come into my bed in the morning and go back to sleep after my husband leaves for work.

If I'd known all this sooner, if society didn't make us believe that the "normal" thing to do is to let someone else share all these joys with our children for more than thirty hours each week (or more, if we're working full-time) . . . if only I could help more parents see the joy in these simple moments in our lives. This is what I would try to tell those who are starting to homeschool, or thinking about home-schooling, and that I wish someone had helped me to understand years ago."

— ROBIN NORELL, ORLANDO, FLORIDA

fice now. Someday you and your children will laugh together about the horror, much the same way you chuckle during days that lay before you a comedy of errors.

Some days fill with how-to stories, otherwise known as crash courses in making Play-Doh, finding someone to answer your child's question about a rare meteorological event, and learning creative uses for parts left over after you manage to put the clock back together.

Permeating it all is a magnificent love story, one that gently guides the plot through its twists and turns. The love story wraps warmly around your family, yes, but it grows to envelop the greater world as the homeschooling lifestyle exposes truths previously forgotten. There's the truth that knowledge is not the purview of a few who train to dispense it but, rather, possessed by all individuals and stamped with their own unique brand. Most are willing to share it, too, if only someone asks. The homeschooling lifestyle exposes children to the world not as a place to enter "someday" but as a joy- and learning-filled classroom ripe for exploration. Revealed when our children grow as part of the world instead of corralled away from it, the truth is that people of all ages can and should participate in the dance of life together.

The love story doesn't end here. It's so compelling it follows the players far into the future, unfolding as a lifelong appreciation of learning that becomes part of the journey, instead of simply the means to an end.

Before I actually started homeschooling, would these words put forth by others have conveyed the depth and breadth of the experi- ence about to unfold? Ha. How could mere words do that? Words could not have made me understand, because I was not yet capable of "thinking outside the box." I was still confusing "schooling" with "education," which prevented my thinking on the subject from flying toward a new place, a place where education transcends the schedule, organi- zation, and methods of others so that its possessor may lay full claim to it.

> Only your attention can give you the tools you need; only your time can hone them.

The ability to think outside the box develops over time, a result of study, observation, thought, and a valuable collection of abject failures and stunning successes. Only your attention can give you the tools you need; only your time can hone them. If upon completion of your first year of homeschooling you are on your way to thinking outside the box, if your children are uncovering and following interests with the time available to them, if education is emerging as something you all do for yourselves instead of having it done "to" you, congratulations.

You are a homeschooling success.

HOMESCHOOLING RESOURCES

In This Appendix

✦ General homeschooling information

✦ Finding state-specific information online

✦ Special interest e-mail list sampler

✦ Is money tight?

✦ Organizational aids

✦ Learning differences and special needs

✦ Study helps

✦ Kate Montanio's favorites for online learning

+ National academic contests in which
homeschoolers have participated

+ Home education research

+ Just for kids

+ Teens (college, work, and more)

+ Diploma-granting, independent-learning organizations

+ Information to help you create your own curriculum

+ General resources

+ Just don't tell the kids these are learning materials

+ Standardized-test suppliers

+ Transcript preparation

$\mathcal{A}$s homeschooling's popularity increases, so does the list of materials created for this "market." The following list of resources is by no means all-inclusive but is intended to provide a starting point to familiarize you with just how much is available for homeschooling parents.

A sign of the times, Internet contact information is provided for most of the resources herein, sometimes exclusively. While many companies make a concerted effort to reach out to potential customers through more traditional marketing means, commerce on the Internet is here to stay. If you do not own a computer, you should be able to gather information via your local library's computer, at a cybercafe, or at a friend's home. After performing your initial research, you just may find that a home computer is advantageous, not only because it's always available but because you can use it at your convenience, even if that means at 5:00 A.M.

For a homeschooler in the Information Age, access to the Internet is emerging as a vital tool. It's not a tool to be used exclusively—you wouldn't exclusively use a hammer for all your home repairs—but like a hammer, it sure is nice to have it there when you need it for dozens of odd reasons from time to time.

At the same time, for the convenience of the many who still do not utilize the computer tool, I devote as much space as possible to contact information for resources that are available offline. Therefore, you will not find precious space given to long lists of Web pages under subject headings, as these are available in other books and referred to in practically all homeschooling state newsletters and national magazines. For those who are online, you know where to go for reviews that you trust and how to conduct searches to broaden exposure to the many sources available to you.

Inclusion of a resource in this list does not imply personal endorsement or recommendation. Its value for your family must be determined by you.

GENERAL HOMESCHOOLING INFORMATION

✦ Beginner's quick access to specific information on the Web: search on http://www.google.com

✦ Beginner's quick access to e-mail lists, message boards, and chat rooms: go to http://www.yahoogroups.com

✦ To find a homeschooling group, click on "Reference and Education." Click on "Education." Click on "Homeschooling." Here available groups are sorted by categories. Click on a category that interests you, and you will be provided with a list that includes brief descriptions of each entry. To begin the short process of joining, click on the name of one you like.

Books

Cohen, Cafi. *Homeschooling the Teen Years: Your Complete Guide to Successfully Homeschooling the 13- to 18-Year-Old.* Prima, 2000.

Dobson, Linda. *The Homeschooling Book of Answers: The 88 Most Important Questions Answered by Homeschooling's Most Respected Voices.* Prima, 1998.

————. *Homeschooling the Early Years: Your Complete Guide to Successfully Homeschooling the 3- to 8-Year-Old Child.* Prima, 1999.

Griffith, Mary. *The Homeschooing Handbook.* Prima, 1999.

Hegener, Mark and Helen, eds. *The Homeschool Reader: Perspectives on Homeschooling.* Home Education, 1995.

Henry, Shari. *Homeschooling the Middle Years: Your Complete Guide to Successfully Homeschooling the 8- to 12-Year-Old Child.* Prima, 1999.

Holt, John. *Teach Your Own: A Hopeful Path for Education.* Delacorte, 1989.

————. *How Children Learn*. Addison-Wesley, 1995.

Layne, Marty. *Learning at Home: A Mother's Guide to Homeschooling* (revised). Sea Change, 2000.

Moore, Raymond and Dorothy. *The Successful Homeschooling Family Handbook*. Thomas Nelson, 1994.

Ransom, Marsha. *The Complete Idiot's Guide to Homeschooling*. Alpha, 2001.

Rupp, Rebecca. *Home Learning Year by Year*. Three Rivers, 2000.

Magazines

Family Times; bimonthly; 888-300-8434; http://www.Home Educator.com/FamilyTimes

F.U.N. News; quarterly; 888-FUN-7020; http://www.unschooling .org/funnews.htm

Growing Without Schooling; bimonthly; 617-864-9235; http://www .holtgws.com

Home Education Magazine; bimonthly; 509-486-1351; http://www .home-ed-magazine.com

Homefires; 888-4-HOME-ED; http://www.homefires.com

Link; bimonthly; fax, 805-493-9216; http://www.homeschoolnews link.com

Voices: The Journal of the National Home Education Network; quarterly, free online; www.nhen.org; e-mail: info@nhen.org

Internet

A to Z Homeschool: http://www.gomilpitas.com/homeschooling

Best Homeschooling: http://www.besthomeschooling.org

Eclectic Homeschoolers Online: http://eho.org

Internet Homeschool Support: http://www.geocities.com/Athens /8259/

Home Education Learning Magazine: http://www.helmonline.com

Home Education Magazine: http://www.home-ed-magazine.com

Homeschool.com: http://www.homeschool.com

Homeschooling in the News: http://www.geocities.com/mmoy /hsitn.html

The Homeschool Zone: http://www.homeschoolzone.com

Jon's Homeschool Resource Page: http://www.midnightbeach.com/hs/

Kaleidoscapes: http://www.kaleidoscapes.com

National Home Education Network: http://www.nhen.org

Native American Homeschool Association: http://expage.com/page /nahomeschool

School Is Dead; Learn in Freedom!: http://learninfreedom.org

Teach-At-Home: http://www.teach-at-home.com

Unschooling.com: http://www.unschooling.com

FINDING STATE-SPECIFIC INFORMATION ONLINE

National, State, and Local Support Groups

National Home Education Network: http://www.nhen.org/leginfo/

Sites for National, State, and Local Support: http://www.geocities .com/Athens/8259/local.html

States

Alabama: http://members.aol.com/kaekaeb/AHEN/Ahen.htm

Alaska: http://ChartnCompass.com/

Arizona: http://members.tripod.com/home4school/: (a local Phoenix group that can help you)

Arkansas: http://www.geocities.com/Heartland/Garden/4555/ahrd98/groups.html

California: http://www.hsc.org/: http://www.comenius.org/chn/

Colorado: http://members.aol.com/treonelain or http://members.iex.net/~mkantor/SHSSH_Frame_Set.htm

Connecticut: http://members.iex.net/~mkantor/SHSSH_Frame_Set.htm

Delaware: http://home-educate.com/DE/

Florida: http://www.angelfire.com/fl3/teachingourown/: http://helps online .org/support/

Georgia: http://llg.freeyellow.com/

Hawaii: http://www.geocities.com/Heartland/Hollow/4239/

Idaho: http://nav.webring.yahoo.com/hub?ring=idahome&list

Illinois: http://www.geocities.com/Athens/Acropolis/7804/

Indiana: http://members.aol.com/usteach/in.htm

Iowa: http://home.plutonium.net/~pdiltz/idea/

Kansas: http://eagle.cc.ukans.edu/~tpeters/laugh/

Kentucky: http://cdaffy.tripod.com/kyhome.html

Louisiana: http://www.la-home-education.com/

Maine: http://members.aol.com/Cmslhomeschool/resources.html

Maryland: http://www.mhea.com/

Massachusetts: http://mhla.org/

Michigan: http://www.angelfire.com/mi/SMHA/index.html

Minnesota: http://www.homeschoolers.org/

Mississippi: http://www.home-ed-magazine.com/groups/7.html #Mississippi

Missouri: http://www.microlink.net/~fhe/index.htm

Montana: http://www.mtche.org/

Nebraska: http://missionjoy.org/homeschool/area_groups.htm

Nevada: http://members.aol.com/nnhs/info/nnhspage.html

New Hampshire: http://www.nhhomeschooling.org/

New Jersey: http://www.geocities.com/Athens/Agora/3009/

New Mexico: http://expage.com/NewMexicoHomeschooling

New York: http://www.nyhen.org

North Carolina: http://www.mindspring.com/~flt-nc/

North Dakota: http://www.nhen.org/LegInfo/northdakota/north dakota.htm

Ohio: http://members.dencity.com/HiO/

Oklahoma: http://oklahomahomeschooling.org/

Oregon: http://www.teleport.com/~ohen/

Pennsylvania: http://www.phen.org/

Rhode Island: http://www.home-ed-magazine.com/groups/10.html #Rhode Island

South Carolina: http://www.icpn.com/homeschool/index.html

South Dakota: http://beta.communities.msn.com/southdakota homeschoolers

Tennessee: http://personal.bna.bellsouth.net/bna/j/k/jkbrooks/Tn HomeEd.htm

Texas: http://www.startlooking.com/homeschool/thi/: http://www .jsoft.com/archive/taffie/

Utah: http://www.itsnet.com/~uhea/

Vermont: http://www.yahoogroups.com/group/vthomeschoolers (email list)

Virginia: http://poe.acc.virginia.edu/~pm6f/vhea.html

Washington: http://homestead.com/WaHomeEdNet/WHENmain .html

Washington, D.C.: http://www.yahoogroups.com/group/BWHE (email list)

West Virginia: http://members.tripod.com/~WVHEA/

Wisconsin: http://www.homeschooling-wpa.org/

Wyoming: http://www.eho.org/states5.htm#wyoming

Canada (all provinces): http://www.gomilpitas.com/homeschooling/regional/Canada.htm

SPECIAL INTEREST E-MAIL LIST SAMPLER

Charlotte Mason Literature: CMLit@yahoogroups.com

Deschooling Adults: DeschoolingAdults@yahoogroups.com

Homeschoolers Who Are Single: HomeschoolingSingle@yahoogroups.com

Homeschooling Blind Children: Blindhomeschoolers@yahoogroups.com

Homeschooling Internationally Adopted Children: hsoic@yahoogroups.com

Homeschooling Special Needs Children: Homeschoolspecneeds@yahoogroups.com

Parents Who Work and Homeschool: WORKandHOMESCHOOL@yahoogroups.com

Swapping Curriculum: curriculumswap@yahoogroups.com

IS MONEY TIGHT?

Books

Dominguez, Joe, and Vicki Robin. *Your Money or Your Life: Transforming Your Relationship with Money and Achieving Financial Independence.* Penguin USA, 1993.

Gold, LauraMaery, and Zielinski, Joan M. *Homeschool Your Child for Free* [Internet resources]. Prima, 2000.

Hendrickson, Borg. *How to Write a Low Cost, No Cost Curriculum.* Mountain Meadow, 1998.

Kenyon, Mary Potter. *Homeschooling from Scratch: Simple Living— Super Learning.* Gazelle, 1996.

Morgan, Melissa L., and Allee, Judith Waite. *Homeschooling on a Shoestring.* Harold Shaw, 1999.

Williams, Jane. *How to Stock a Home Library Inexpensively.* Bluestocking, 1995.

Internet

Cheapskate Monthly Online: http://www.cheapskatemonthly.com

Frugal Moms: http://www.frugal-moms.com

Homeschooling on a Shoestring: http://www.geocities.com/Athens/4663

Free Online Classes

3-D Animation Workshop: http://webreference.com/3d/indexa.html

Acting Workshop: http://www.execpc.com/~blankda/acting2.html

Art: http://www 2.evansville.edu/studiochalkboard/

Astronomy Classes: http://www.cnde.iastate.edu/staff/jtroeger/astronomy.html

Basic Guide to Essay Writing: http://members.tripod.com/~lkliving ston/essay/

Entrepreneurial Basics: http://www.myownbusiness.org/index.html

Genealogy Classes: http://www.rootsweb.com/~genclass/index.html

Marine Biology Learning Center: http://www.marinebiology.org/

Music Theory: http://www.musictheory.halifax.ns.ca/

Phonics: http://billjanaecooksey.tripod.com/Classes.html

Thousands of Free Step-by-Step Tutorials: http://www.learn2.com

Web Site Design: http://www.shire.net/learnwebdesign/map.html

Used-Curriculum Sources

http://www.clevermoms.com

http://www.homeschool-curriculum.com

http://www.insidetheweb.com/mbs.cgi/mb395652

http://www.ebay.com (search homeschooling)

http://www.rsts.net/home/recycler/

http://bbs.homeschool.com/cgi-bin/agnes.exe?Used01Agnes+Used
01AgnesHTML

http://eho.org/garagesale.htm

http://theswap.com/

Free E-Books

The Internet Classics Archive: http://www.classics.mit.edu

The Online Books Page: http://www.digital.library.upenn.edu/books

Project Gutenberg: http://www.promo.net/pg

Freeware

Tucows (for ages 2–12): http://go.concepts.tukids.tucows.com/

Freeware Humpherlinks: http://www.humph3.freeserve.co.uk/free
waresites.html

Kids Freeware : http://www.kidsfreeware.com/

Softseek (PC only): http://www.softseek.com/Education_and_ Science/Childrens_Education

Other Freebies

Internet Field Trips: teacher.scholastic.com/fieldtrp/index.htm

School Express (free worksheets): http://www.schoolexpress.com

Unit Studies: http://www.alaska.net/~ccandc/free.htm

Worksheets: http://www.freeworksheets.com

ORGANIZATIONAL AIDS

Books

Aslett, Don. *Clutter's Last Stand: It's Time to De-Junk Your Life.* Writer's Digest, 1984.

Bykofsky, Sheree. *500 Terrific Ideas for Organizing Everything.* Budget Book Service, 1997.

Taylor-Hough, Deborah. *Frozen Assets: How to Cook for a Day and Eat for a Month.* Champion, 1998.

Internet

Home Organization: http://www.learnfree-home.com/home organization/

List Organizers: http://www.listorganizer.com/products.htm

Organized Times: http://www.organizedtimes.com

LEARNING DIFFERENCES AND SPECIAL NEEDS

Books

Armstrong, Thomas. *The Myth of the A.D.D. Child: 50 Ways to Improve Your Child's Behavior and Attention Span without Drugs, Labels, or Coercion.* Plume, 1997.

Davis, Ronald D. *The Gift of Dyslexia: Why Some of the Smartest People Can't Read and How They Can Learn.* Fireside, 1998.

Diller, Dr. Lawrence. *Running on Ritalin: A Physician Reflects on Children, Society, and Performance in a Pill.* Bantam, 1998.

Freed, Jeffrey, and Parsons, Laurie. *Right-Brained Children in a Left-Brained World.* Perigree, 1997.

Reichenburg-Ullman, Judyth. *Ritalin-Free Kids.* Prima, 1996.

Rosner, Jerome. *Helping Children Overcome Learning Difficulties.* Walker, 1993.

Shore, Kenneth, Psy.D. *Special Kids Problem Solve: Ready-To-Use Interventions for Helping All Students with Academic, Behavioral & Physical Problems.* Prentice Hall, 1999.

Yahnke, Sally. *The Survival Guide for Parenting Gifted Kids.* Free Spirit, 1991.

Curricula

Greenwood School; 802-387-4545; e-mail, grnwood@sover.net: http://www.greenwoodinstitute.org

Power Learning Network (fourth grade and up): http://www.power learningnetwork.com

Internet

Autism (Spectrum Children's Support): http://www.homestead.com /wholefamily/wholefamily1.html

Brightword Creations: http://www.brightword.com

Davidson Foundation: http://www.davidsonfoundation.org

Education by Design: http://www.edbydesign.com/specneedsres /index.html

Gift of Dyslexia: http://dyslexia.com/index.htm

Homeschooling Children with Special Needs: http://www.geocities .com/Athens/8259/special.html

Homeschooling Kids with Disabilities: http://www.members .tripod.com/~Maaja/index.htm

Learning Disabilities Online: http://www.ldonline.org

Lindamood-Bell Learning Processes: http://www.lblp.com/

Links on Special Needs and Homeschooling: http://www.gomilpitas .com/homeschooling/weblinks/specialneeds.htm#Dyslexia

Prufrock Press (gifted education resources): http://www.prufrock .com

Resource Room: http://www.resourceroom.net/index.asp

Unschooling Special-Needs Children: http://www.inspirit.com.au /unschooling/resources/hsspecialneeds.html

E-mail Lists

ADD/ADHD Homeschool List: Send e-mail to deborahbowman @xc.org; use ADHD HS list as the subject line.

Aut-2b-Home: Send e-mail to Tamglsr@sgi.net; send bio along with request to be added.

Homeschooling Gifted Children: Send e-mail to majordomo@ teleport.com; use HGC-1 as the body of message.

Newsgroup

alt.education.home-school.disabilities.

Newsletters

At Our Own Pace (Hard-copy newsletter free with request for donation)
Jean Kulczyk
102 Willow Drive
Waukegan, IL 60087

NATHHAN News
National Challenged Homeschoolers Association Network
P.O. Box 39
Porthill, ID 83853
208-267-6246
http://www.nathhan.com

STUDY HELPS

Bartlett's Familiar Quotations: http://www.columbia.edu/acis/bartleby/bartlett/

Britannica Encyclopedia: http://www.britannica.com

Elements of Style: http://www.bartleby.com/141/index.html

Encyclopedia Smithsonian: http://www.si.edu/resource/faq/start.htm

Kids' Almanac, Atlas, and More: www.factmonster.com

Library of Congress: http://www.loc.gov/

Library Index (browse or search for libraries): http://www.libdex.com/

Library Spot: http://libraryspot.com/librariesonline.htm

Martindale's Reference Desk: http://www-sci.lib.uci.edu/HSG/Ref.html

State Libraries: http://www.dpi.state.wi.us/dpi/dlcl/pld/statelib.html

Webster's Revised Unabridged Dictionary: http://humanities.uchicago.edu/forms_unrest/webster.form.html

Online "Tutors"

Fact Monster: http://www.factmonster.com

Tutor.com: http://www.tutor.com

Tutor Net.com, Inc.: http://www.tutornet.com

KATE MONTANIO'S FAVORITES FOR ONLINE LEARNING

Art Ideas for Kids: http://artforkids.about.com/kids/artforkids/?once=true&

Art to Go: http://www.mfah.org

Everyday Art: http://www.everydayart.com/

Free Lesson Plans: http://www.schoolexpress.com/

Guide to Government: http://bensguide.gpo.gov/

The History Channel Classroom: http://www.historychannel.com/classroom/index.html

Interactive Math (grades 1–6): http://www.sbgmath.com/index.html

Links to homepages for 3,000 colleges and universities: http://www.mit.edu:8001/people/cdemello/univ.html

Support for first-year homeschoolers: http://smoothingtheway.homestead.com/home.html

NATIONAL ACADEMIC CONTESTS IN WHICH HOMESCHOOLERS HAVE PARTICIPATED

Lego Mindstorms: http://www.legomindstorms.com/fll/

Math Olympiad
    2154 Bellmore Avenue
    Bellmore, NY 11710
    http://www.moems.org

MathCounts
    1420 King Street
    Alexandria, VA 22314
    http://www.mathcounts.org

National Geography Bee
    1145 17 St. NW
    Washington, DC 20036
    http://www.nationalgeographic.com/geographybee/
      basics.html

National History Day
    0119 Cecil Hall
    University of Maryland
    College Park, MD 20742
    301-314-9739
    http://www.nationalhistoryday.org

Odyssey of the Mind
    P.O. Box 547
    Glassboro, NJ 08028
    http://www.odyssey.org

Pizza Hut "Book It": http://www.bookit.com

Scripps Howard National Spelling Bee
    P.O. Box 371541
    Pittsburgh, PA 15251
    http://www.spellingbee.com

Siemens Westinghouse Science and Technology Competition
    877-822-5233
    http://www.siemens-foundation.org/science/science
    _and_technology.htm

ThinkQuest
    Advanced Network and Services, Inc.
    200 Business Park Drive
    Armonk, NY 10504
    http://www.thinkquest.org

HOME EDUCATION RESEARCH

Dr. Larry Shyers socialization research: http://learninfreedom.org
/socialization.html

Holt Associates: http://www.holtgws.com/RESEARCH.HTM

Lots of links at http://www.gomilpitas.com/homeschooling/weblinks
/research.htm

JUST FOR KIDS

Magazines

Boomerang! (audio magazine/cassette tape)
P.O. Box 261
La Honda, CA 94020
800-333-7858

Cobblestone/Faces/Odyssey/Calliope/Babybug/Ladybug/Cricket/Muse
7 School Street
Petersborough, NH 03458
800-821-0115
http://cobblestonepub.com/

Contact Kids Magazine:
http://www.sesameworkshop.org/promo/offers
/contactkids/0,2417,,00.html

Dragonfly: http://mizvx1.acs.muohio.edu/~dragnfly/index.html

GAMES Magazine
P.O. Box 10147
Des Moines, IA 50347-0147

New Moon: http://newmoon.org

National Wildlife Federation's *Ranger Rick* and *Your Big Backyard*
 8925 Leesburg Pike
 Vienna, VA 22184
 800-588-1650
 http://www.nwf.org/rrick/

Science at Home*:* http://www.scienceathome.com

Scientific American Explorations
 800-333-1199

Skipping Stones
 P.O. Box 3939
 Eugene, OR 97403-0939
 http://www.treelink.com/skipping/form.htm

Stone Soup
 P.O. Box 83
 Santa Cruz, CA 95063
 800-447-4569
 http://www.stonesoup.com

World
 National Geographic Society
 P.O. Box 63002
 Tampa, FL 33663-3002
 800-647-5463
 (also: National Geographic videos, order 800-627-5162)
 http://www.nationalgeographic.com/world

Zoobooks
 12233 Thatcher
 Poway, CA 92064
 800-992-5034
 http://www.zoobooks.com

Internet

Carpentry for Kids: http://www.b4ubuild.com/books/kidsbooks .shtml

Children's stories in English and Spanish (The Children's Digital Library): http://www.storyplace.org

Complete online typing course: http://www.easytype.com

Enchanted Learning: http://www.EnchantedLearning.com

Scout School: http://www.cis.net/~cmmeyer/ScoutSchool

Terra Server Homepage: http://terraserver.microsoft.com

E-Mail Groups

All Homeschool Kids (ages 10–15): http://www.yahoogroups.com /subscribe/All_Homeschool_Kids

Free Teens (ages under 21, not in school, or looking to not be): http://www.yahoogroups.com/subscribe/Free_teens

Highschool Home-Ed: Send e-mail to Listserv@listserv.aol.com with following command in body of message: subscribe highschool-home-ed Your Name

Home Learning Teens (ages 11+): http://www.yahoogroups.com /subscribe/homelearningteens

Homeschoolers International Pals (ages 8–18): http://www.yahoo groups.com/group/homeschoolers_international_pals

Homeschool Kids (all ages): http://www.yahoogroups.com/subscribe /homeschool-kids

Homeschooled Scouts: Send blank e-mail to homeschooledscouts subscribe@yahoogroups.com

TEENS (COLLEGE, WORK, AND MORE)

Books

Cohen, Cafi. *And What about College: How Homeschooling Can Lead to Admissions to the Best Colleges and Universities.* Holt, 2000.

————. *Homeschoolers' College Admissions Handbook.* Prima, 2000.

Dobson, Linda. *Homeschoolers' Success Stories: 15 Adults and 12 Young People Share the Impact That Homeschooling Has Made on Their Lives.* Prima, 2000.

Llewellyn, Grace. *The Teenage Liberation Handbook: How to Quit School and Get a Real Life and Education.* Lowry House, 1998.

Peterson's Guides—(Various) information on educational travel, internships, summer opportunities, and more

Sheffer, Susannah. *A Sense of Self: Listening to Homeschooled Adolescent Girls.* Heinemann, 1997.

Internet

Back to College: http://www.back2college.com

Colleges That Admit Homeschoolers: http://learninfreedom.org /colleges_4_hmsc.html

The Collegiate Homeschooler: http://www.eatbug.com/homeschool /html/the_collegiate_homeschooler.htm

Guide to Unconventional Colleges: http://home.pacifier.com/~vcamp be/list/

High School Hub: http://www.highschoolhub.org

National Collegiate Athletic Association (NCAA) Homeschooled Student Guidelines: http://www.ncaa.org/cbsa/home_school.html

Homeschooling Foreign Exchange Students
   Nacel Open Door, Inc.
   800-856-2411 pin 576
   http://www.nacelopendoor.org

Overseas Study Program: http://www.iiepassport.org

People to People Student Ambassador Program: http://www.student
   ambassadors.org

E-Mail Lists

Teens from New York and neighboring states: Send blank e-mail to
   NYteenunhomeschoolers-subscribe@yahoogroups.com

Pregnant teens/teen moms: Send blank e-mail to: the-net@yahoo
   groups.com

DIPLOMA-GRANTING, INDEPENDENT-LEARNING ORGANIZATIONS

Courtesy of Cafi Cohen, from her online list: http://www.homeschool
teenscollege.net/diplomaisp.htm. Accreditations vary; not all are accredited.

Abbington Hills School (K–12)
   Suite 6-152
   2140 Route 88
   Bricktown, NJ 08724
   732-892-4475; http://www.abbingtonhillschool.com

Alpha-Omega Academy (K–12)
   300 North McKemy Avenue
   Chandler, AZ 85226
   800-682-7396
   http://www.home-schooling.com/Academy.htm

Alpha-Omega Academy Online [Switched-On Schoolhouse
    CD-ROM Curriculum & Program] (grades 3–12)
    300 North McKemy Avenue
    Chandler, AZ 85226-2681
    877-688-2652
    http://www.switched-onschoolhouse.com/aoao/index.html

American School (grades 9–12)
    2200 East 170th Street
    Lansing, IL 60438-9909
    708-418-2800 or 800-531-9268
    http://www.iit.edu/~american/

Branford Grove School (grades 1–12)
    P.O. Box 341172
    Arleta, CA 91334
    818-890-0350
    http://www.branfordgrove.com/

Brigham Young University Independent Study High School
    (grades 9–12)
    206 Harman Building
    P.O. Box 21514
    Provo, UT 84602-1514
    801-378-2868
    http://coned.byu.edu/is

Cambridge Academy (grades 6–12)
    33000 SW 34th Avenue
    Suite 102
    Ocala, FL 34474
    800-252-3777
    http://www.home-school.com/Mall/Cambridge/Cambridge
        Acad.html

Christa McAuliffe Academy (K–12)
3601 West Washington Avenue
Yakima, WA 98903
509-575-4989
http://www.cmacademy.org/

Christian Liberty Academy Satellite Schools (CLASS) (K–12)
502 West Euclid Avenue
Arlington Heights, IL 60004
800-348-0899
http://www.homeschools.org/

Chrysalis School, Inc.
14241 NE Woodinville-Duvall Road, #243
Woodinville, WA 98072
425-481-2228
http://www.chrysalis-school.com/

Citizen's High School
188 College Drive
Orange Park, FL 32067
904-276-1700
http://www.citizenschool.com

Clonlara Home Based Education Program and
    Clonlara CompuHigh (K–12)
1289 Jewett Street
Ann Arbor, MI 48104
313-769-4515
http://www.clonlara.org

Crossroads Christian School (K–12)
P.O. Box 757
Baker, FL 32531-0757
850-423-1291
http://www.crossroadschristianschool.com/

Dennison Online Internet School (grades 7–12)
P.O. Box 29781
Los Angeles, CA 90029-0781
323-662-3226
http://www.dennisononline.com/

Eagle Christian School (grades 7–12), distance learning ministry of
Valley Christian School
2526 Sunset Lane
Missoula, MT 59804
888-EAGLE4U
http://www.eaglechristian.org/

Great Books Academy Homeschool Program (K–12)
1213 North Piedmont Road
P.O. Box 360
Piedmont, OK 73078
800-521-4004
http://www.greatbooksacademy.org/

Harcourt High School (grades 9–12)
P.O. Box 1900
Scranton, PA 18505-1900
800-275-4409
http://www.harcourt-learning.com/programs/diploma/index.html

HCL Boston School
P.O. Box 2920
Big Bear City, CA, 92314-2920
909-585-7188
http://www.harcourt-learning.com/programs/diploma/index.html

Hewitt Homeschooling Resources (K–12)
P.O. Box 9
Washougal, WA 98671
800-348-1750
http://www.homeeducation.org/

Home Study International (preschool–college level)
    12501 Old Columbia Pike
    Silver Spring, MD 20904
    800-782-4769
    http://www.hsi.edu/index.asp

ICS Newport/Pacific High School (grades 9–12)
    925 Oak Street
    Scranton, PA 18515
    800-238-9525, ext. 7496
    http://www.icslearn.com/ICS/courses.htm

Indiana University High School (grades 9–12)
    Owen Hall 002
    790 East Kirkwood Avenue
    Bloomington, IN 47405-7101
    800-334-1011
    http://scs.indiana.edu/

Institute for the Study of the Liberal Arts and Sciences (grades
        7–12–adult; includes Scholar's Online Academy and Regina
        Coeli Academy)
    9755 East McAndrew Court, Tucson, AZ 85748
    520-751-1942
    http://www.islas.org/

Internet Academy (K–12)
    32020 First Avenue South
    Federal Way, WA 98003
    253-945-2004

Keystone National High School (grades 9–12)
    School House Station
    420 West Fifth Street
    Bloomsburg, PA 17815
    800-255-4937
    http://www.keystonehighschool.com/

Kolbe Academy (K–12)
  1600 F Street
  Napa, CA 94559
  707-255-6499
  http://www.community.net/~kolbe/

Laurel Springs School; grades K–12
  1002 East Ojai Avenue
  Ojai, CA 93024-1440
  800-377-5890
  http://www.laurelsprings.com/

Malibu Cove Private School (grades 9–12)
  P.O. Box 1074
  Thousand Oaks, CA 91358
  805-446-1917
  http://SeascapeCenter.com

North Atlantic Regional High School (grades 9–12)
  116 Third Avenue
  Auburn, ME 04210
  800-882-2828, ext. 16, or 207-777-1700, ext. 16
  http://homeschoolassociates.com/NARS/

North Dakota Division of Independent Study (grades 5–12)
  http://www.dis.dpi.state.nd.us/

NorthStar Academy (grades 7–12)
  22571 Wye Road
  Sherwood Park, Alberta, Canada T8C 1H9
  888-464-6280
  http://www.northstar-academy.org/

Oak Meadow School (K–12)
  P.O. Box 740
  Putney, VT 05346
  802-387-2021
  http://www.oakmeadow.com/

Phoenix Academies (grades 7–12)
  1717 West Northern Avenue
  Suite 104
  Phoenix, Arizona 8501-5469
  602-674-5555 or 800-426-4952
  http://www.phoenixacademies.org

Royal Academy (K–12)
  Home Education & Family Services
  P.O. Box 1056
  Gray, ME 04039
  207-657-2800
  http://www.homeeducator.com/HEFS/royalacademy.htm

School for Educational Enrichment (grades 9–12)
  P.O. Box 221365
  El Paso, TX 79913
  915-584-9499
  http://www.diplomahighschool.com

School of Tomorrow (K–12)
  P.O. Box 299000
  Lewisville, TX 75029-9000
  800-925-7777
  http://www.schooloftomorrow.com/

Seton Home Study School (K–12)
  1350 Progress Drive
  Front Royal, VA 22630
  540-636-9990
  http://www.setonhome.org/

St. Thomas Aquinas Academy (K–12)
  P.O. Box 630
  Ripon, CA 95366
  209-599-0665
  http://www.staa-homeschool.com

Summit Christian Academy (K–12)
   2100 North Highway 360
   Suite 503
   Grand Prairie, TX 75050
   800-362-9180 or 972-602-8050
   www.scahomeschool.com

Sycamore Tree (K–12)
   2179 Meyer Place
   Costa Mesa, CA 92627
   949-650-4466
   http://www.sycamoretree.com/

Texas Tech University Division of Continuing Education
   (grades 9–12)
   P.O. Box 42191
   Lubbock, TX 79409-2191
   800-692-6877, ext. 320
   http://www.dce.ttu.edu/

University of Missouri–Columbia High School (MU High School)
      (grades 9–12)
   136 Clark Hall
   Columbia, MO 65211-4200
   573-884-2620 or 800-858-6413
   http://cdis.missouri.edu/MUHighSchool/HShome.htm

University of Nebraska (Lincoln) Independent Study High School
      (grades 9–12)
   33rd and Holdredge Streets
   Lincoln, NE 68583-9800
   402-472-4321
   http://dcs.unl.edu/disted/ishs.html

University of Texas at Austin High School Diploma Program
    (grades 9–12)
    P. O. Box 7700
    Austin, TX 78713-7700
    512-232-1872
    http://www.utexas.edu/cee/dec/diploma/

Westbridge Academy (K–12)
    1610 West Highland Avenue
    P.O. Box 228
    Chicago, IL 60660
    773-743-3312
    http://www.flash.net/~wx3o/westbridge

West River Academy (K–12)
    2420 North First Street
    Grand Junction, CO 81501
    970-241-4137; or, toll-free, 800-400-1528, ext. 2848

Willoway Academy (grades 7–12)
    610-678-0214
    http://www.willoway.com/

Additional Sources of Distance Learning

Center for Talent Development Northwestern University
    (math and science online for grades 6–12)
    847-491-3782
    e-mail, ctd@nwu.edu
    http://ctdnet.acns.nwu.edu

ChildU (to grade 8): 877-4ChildU; http://www.homeschool.com
    /childu

Distance Learning at About.com: http://www.distancelearn.about
    .com

Distance Learning Resource Network: http://www.dlrn.org/adult/higher.html

K12 (grades K–2 initially): http://www.K12.com

McGuffey Academy International (K–12)
P.O. Box 109
Lakemont, GA 30552
706-782-7709

Northern Virginia Community College: http://eli.nv.cc.va.us/vc/randa.htm

PCS Edventures
800-429-3110
http://www.edventures.com

Southeast Academy (grades 1–12)
P.O. Box MM
Ball Park Avenue, Saltville, VA 24370
703-496-7777

University of Arkansas (grades 9–12)
Division of Continuing Education
#2 University Center
Fayetteville, AR 72701
800-638-1217 or 501-575-7232

University of Houston Distance Education: http://www.uh.edu/academics/de

University of Oklahoma (grades 9–12)
Independent Study Department
1600 South Jenkins, Room 101
Norman, OK 73072-6507
800-942-5702 or 405-325-1921
http://cce.occe.ou.edu; ibergeron@cce.occe.ou.edu

Yahoo Distance Learning: dir.yahoo.com/Education/Distance Learning

College Level Distance Learning

Books

Bear, John. *College Degrees by Mail and Modem.* Ten Speed, 2000.

Peterson's. *Guide to Distance Learning Programs 2001 (Peterson's Guide to Distance Learning Programs, 5th Edition).* Peterson's Guides, 2000.

Thorson, Marcie K. *Campus-Free College Degrees: Thorson's Guide to Accredited College Degrees Through Distance Learning.* Careers Unlimited, 2000.

INFORMATION TO HELP YOU CREATE YOUR OWN CURRICULUM

Books

Hirsch, E. D. *What Your _____ Grader Needs to Know: Fundamentals of Good _____ Grade Education.* (For grades K–6.) Delta, various publication dates.

Rupp, Rebecca. *Home Learning Year by Year: How to Design a Home school Curriculum.* Three Rivers, 2000.

Traditional

Birchwood Homeschool & Teacher Training Program
    877-700-1056
    http://www.serveunet.com/birchwood
Calvert School
    888-487-4652
    http://www.calvertschool.org
Curriculum Services
    877-702-1419
    http://www.curriculumservices.com

ESP Books
  800-643-0280
  http://www.espbooks.com

Motivation Plus
  732-469-6864
  http://www.motivationplus.net

World Book Encyclopedia's "Typical Course of Study": http://www
  .worldbook.com/ptrc/html/curr.htm

Classical

Books

Berquist, Laura. *Designing Your Own Classical Curriculum: A Guide to Catholic Home Education.* Ignatius, 1998.

Wilson, Douglas et al. *Classical Education and the Home School.* Publisher Unknown, 1996.

Wise, Jessie and Bauer, Susan Wise. *The Well-Trained Mind: A Guide to Classical Education at Home.* W. W. Norton & Co., 1999.

Internet

Classical Christian Homeschooling: www.classicalhomeschooling.org

Links: http://www.geocities.com/Athens/8259/classic.html

Well-Trained Mind: www.welltrainedmind.com

Charlotte Mason

Books

Gardner, Penny. *Charlotte Mason Study Guide.* Penny Gardner, 1997.

Mason, Charlotte. *Charlotte Mason's Original Homeschooling Series* Charlotte Mason Research & Supply Company, 1993.

Rackliffe, Karen Skidmore. *Wild Days: Creating Discovery Journals.* Karen Skidmore Rackliffe, 1999.

Internet

Interested in Charlotte Mason?: http://www.geocities.com/Heartland
/Meadows/4380/cmason.html

Links: http://www.geocities.com/Athens/8259/classic.html

Unit Studies

Books

Bendt, Valerie. *How to Create Your Own Unit Study.* Common Sense,
1997.

Bennett, Amanda. *Oceans: Unit Study Adventure.* Holly Hall, 1997.

Buchberg, Wendy. *Quilting Activities Across the Curriculum: A Thematic Unit Filled With Activities Linked to Math, Language Arts, Social Studies, and Science.* Scholastic Trade, 1997.

Internet

Homeschool in the Woods: http://home.rochester.rr.com/inwoods/

Homeschooling with Frugal Unit Studies: http://www.stretcher.com
/stories/990726h.cfm (money saving)

Links: http://www.geocities.com/Athens/Aegean/3446/unitstudies
.html

Unit Studies for Everyone: http://www.gulftel.com/~lvhmskl/unit.htm

Unit Studies Message Boards: http://www.kaleidoscapes.com/unit
studies/index.cgi

Eclectic

Internet

Eclectic Homeschool Online: http://www.eho.org

Links: http://www.gomilpitas.com/homeschooling/methods
/Eclectic.htm

Interest Initiated, or Unschooling

Books

Boyars, Marion and Illich, Ivan. *Deschooling Society: Social Questions.* Marion Boyars, 1999.

Brown, Teri with Elissa Wahl. *Christian Unschooling: Growing Your Child in the Freedom of Christ.* Champion, 2001.

Griffin, Mary. *The Unschooling Handbook: How to Use the Whole World as Your Child's Classroom.* Prima, 1998.

Hayes, Charles D. *Self-University: The Price of Tuition Is the Desire to Learn.* Autodidactic Press, 1989.

Holt, John. *Teach Your Own.* Delacorte, 1981.

Internet

Family Unschoolers Network: www.unschooling.org

Gleanings of Wisdom on Unschooling: http://home-educate.com /unschooling/unschoolquotes.htm

Self-University Campus: http://www.autodidactic.com/campus.htm

Unschooling: http://www.unschooling.com

Unschooling List Frequently Asked Questions: http://user.mc.net /~kwentz/ULfaq.html

Independent Cooperative Learning Situations

Books

Albert, David H. *And the Skylark Sings with Me—Adventures in Home-schooling and Community-Based Education.* New Society, 1999.

Hegener, Mark and Helen, editors. *Alternatives in Education: Family Choices in Learning.* Home Education Press, 1992.

Miller, Ron, ed. *Creating Learning Communities.* Foundation for Educational Renewal, 2000.

Williams, Jane. *Family Learning Cooperatives: Getting Started.* Bluestocking Press. Available from Alliance for Parental Involvement in Education (http://www.croton.com/allpie)

Internet

Alternative Education Resource Organization: www.EDREV.org

Creating Learning Communities: http://www.creatinglearningcommunities.org/

Home Education Resource Center of Central Ohio: http://www.qn.net/~sandbar/HERCCO.html

HomeSource (OR): www.betheltech.com

National Coalition of Alternative Community Schools: www.ncacs.org

Pathfinder Learning Center (MA): www.pathfindercenter.org

Public School Programs for Homeschoolers
Books

Coyne, John, and Hebert, Tom. *This Way Out.* E. P. Dutton, 1972.

Mintz, Jerry, et al. *The Almanac of Education Choices.* Macmillan, 1995.

Internet

National Association of Charter Schools: www.chartereducation.org

Oregon Association for Alternatives in Education: http://www.teleport.com/~oaae/oae_int.htm

U.S. Charter Schools: http://www.uscharterschools.org

GENERAL RESOURCES

For all the subjects listed on the following pages, please don't forget related real books (fiction and nonfiction), television documentaries, movies, field trips, arts and crafts, and everything you can think of to help keep learning fun and rewarding.

Books

Leppert, Mary and Michael. *Homeschooling Almanac, 2002–2003.* Prima, 2001.

Reed, Donn and Jean. *The Home School Source Book.* Brook Farm, 2001.

Rupp, Rebecca. *The Home Learning Source Book.* Three Rivers, 1999.

———. *Good Stuff: Learning Tools for All Ages.* Holt, 1997.

Catalogs

F.U.N. Books 1688 Belhaven Woods Court
    Pasadena, MD 21122-3727
    http://www.fun-books.com
    888-FUN-7020

The Education Connection
    P.O. Box 910367
    St. George, UT 84791
    800-863-3828
    http://www.educationconnection.com

John Holt Bookstore
    2380 Massachusetts Avenue, Suite 104
    Cambridge, MA 02140-1884
    888-925-9298
    http://www.holtgws.com

The Home School
    P.O. Box 308
    North Chelmsford, MA 01863-0308
    800-788-1221
    http://www.thehomeschool.com

Michael Olaf's Essential Montessori for Ages 3–12+
65 Ericson Court
Arcata, CA 95521
707-826-1557
http://www.michaelolaf.com

Rainbow Resource Center
Route 1, Box 159A
50 North 500 East Road
Toulon, IL 61483
309-695-3200
http://www.rainbowresource.com

The Sycamore Tree
2179 Meyer Place
Costa Mesa, CA 92627
http://www.sycamoretree.com
800-770-6750

Reading

Ball-Stick-Bird Publications (learning to read)
P.O. Box 13
Colebrook, CT 06021
860-738-8871
http://www.ballstickbird.com

Chinaberry Book Service
2780 Via Ornage Way, Suite B
Spring Valley, CA 91978
800-776-2242
http://www.chinaberry.com

Sonlight Curriculum, Ltd.
8185 South Grant Way
Littleton, CO 80127
http://www.sonlight.com

Van Doren, Charles. *How to Read a Book.* Simon & Schuster, 1972.

Zephyr Press
P.O. Box 66006
Tucson, Arizona 85732
800-232-2187
http://www.zephyrpress.com

Book Review and Recommendations

American Library Association Resources for Parents, Teens, and Kids: http://www.ala.org/parents/index.html

Book Links
434 West Downer Place
Aurora, IL 60506-9954
630-892-7465
http://www.ala.org/BookLinks

Carol Hurst's Children's Literature Site: http://www.carolhurst.com

Eager Readers: http://www.eagerreaders.com

Hoagie's Kids and Teens: http://www.hoagieskids.org

Writing

AccuWrite
4536 SW 14 Avenue
Cape Coral, FL 33914
941-549-4400
http://www.homeschoolfun.com/

Italic Handwriting Series
Portland State University
Division of Continuing Education
P.O. Box 1394
Portland, OR 97207
503-725-4846
http://www.extended.pdx.edu/press/italic/italic.htm

National Writing Institute
   7946 Wright Road
   Niles, MI 49120
   800-688-5375
   http://www.writingstrands.com/
Zaner-Bloser (workbooks)
   2200 West Fifth Avenue
   P.O. Box 16764
   Columbus, OH 43216-6764
   800-421-3018

Math

ETA/Cuisensaire Company of America
   500 Greenview Court
   Vernon Hills, Illinois 60061
   800-445-5985
   http://www.etacuisenaire.com
Family Math
   Lawrence Hall of Science
   University of California
   Berkeley, CA 94720
   415-642-1026
   http://www.toc.lcs.mit.edu/~emjordan/famMath.html
Modern Curriculum
   P.O. Box 2649
   Columbus, OH 43216-2649
   http://www.pearsonlearning.com
Saxon Math (phonics programs also available)
   Saxon Publishers, Inc.
   2450 John Saxon Blvd.
   Norman, OK 73071
   800-284-7019
   http://www.saxonpub.com

Science

American Science & Surplus
   3605 Howard Street
   Skokie, IL 60076
   800-934-0722
   http://www.sciplus.com

Carolina Biological Supply Company
   2700 York Road
   Burlington, NC 27215
   800-334-5551
   http://www.carolina.com

Edmund Scientific Company
   101 East Gloucester Pike
   Barrington, NJ 08007-1380
   800-728-6999
   http://www.edsci.com

Insect Lore
   P.O. Box 1535
   Shafter, CA 93263
   800-LIVE-BUG
   http://www.insectlore.com

Schoolmasters Science
   745 State Circle
   P.O. Box 1941
   Ann Arbor, MI 48106-1941
   http://www.school-tech.com

Smithsonian Center for Educational and Museum Studies
   http://web7.si.edu/ftlr/index.html

Wild Goose Company
   375 Whitney Avenue
   Salt Lake City, UT 84115
   800-373-1498
   http://www.wildgoosescience.com

History and Social Studies

American Girl (Pleasant Company)
    8400 Fairway Place
    P.O. Box 620190
    Middleton, Wi 53562-0190
    800-845-0005

Audio Memory
    800-365-SING
    http://www.audiomemory.com

Bellerophon Books
    P.O. Box 21307
    Santa Barbara CA 93121
    800-253-9943
    http://www.bellerophonbooks.com

Bluestocking Press
    P.O. Box 2030
    Shingle Springs, CA 95682
    800-959-8586
    http://www.bluestockingpress.com

Critical Thinking Press
    P.O. Box 448
    Pacific Grove, CA 93950-0448
    800-458-4849
    http://www.criticalthinking.com

Greenleaf Press
    3761 Highway 109 N, Unit D
    Lebanon, TN 37087
    615-449-1617
    http://www.greenleafpress.com

Jackdaw Publications
    P.O. Box 503
    Amawalk, NY 10501
    800-789-0022
    http://www.jackdaw.com

Knowledge Unlimited
P.O. Box 52
Madison, WI 53701-0052
800-356-2303
http://www.ku.com

National Geographic Society
P.O. Box 10543
Des Moines, IA 50340
888-225-5647
http://www.nationalgeographic.com

U.S. Geological Survey
Federal Center, Bldg. 41
P.O. Box 25286
Denver, CO 80225
303-236-7477
http://www.usgs.gov

Foreign Language

Audio Forum
96 Broad Street
Guilford, CT 06437-2635
800-243-1234
http://www.audioforum.com

Bolchazy-Carducci Publishers, Inc. (Latin)
1000 Brown Street
Wauconda, IL 60084
800-392-6453
http://www.bolchazy.com

International Linguistics Corporation
3505 East Red Bridge
Kansas City, MO 64137
800-237-1830
http://learnables.com

Muzzy, The BBC Language Course for Children
  Early Advantage
  270 Monroe Turnpike
  P.O. Box 4063
  Monroe, CT 06468-4063
  888-248-0480
  http://www.early-advantage.com

Penton Overseas, Inc.
  2470 Impala Drive
  Carlsbad, CA 92008
  800-748-5804
  http://www.pentonoverseas.com

Power-Glide
  1682 West 820 North
  Provo, UT 84601
  http://www.power-glide.com

Software

Blaster Learning Series: http://www.mathblaster.com

Broderbund (see The Learning Company)

Edmark Corporation (PreK–8; special needs)
  P.O. Box 97021
  Redmond, WA 98073
  800-362-2890
  http://www.edmark.com

The Edutainment Catalog
  One Martha's Way
  Hiawatha, IA 52233
  800-338-3844
  http://www.ShopMattel.com/education.htm

Knowledge Adventure (includes Blaster, Dr. Brain, and
    JumpStart series)
  800-545-7677
  http://www.knowledgeadventure.com

The Learning Company (now includes Broderbund)
    800-395-0277
    http://www.learningco.com

Smart Kids Software
    P.O. Box 590464
    Houston, TX 77259-0464
    888-881-6001
    http://www.smartkidssoftware.com

Software Reviews

Children's Software Revue
    44 Main Street
    Flemington, NJ 08822
    800-993-9499
    http://www.childrenssoftware.com

Super Kids' Software Review: http://www.superkids.com/aweb/pages
    /reviews

JUST DON'T TELL THE KIDS THESE ARE LEARNING MATERIALS

A Gentle Wind (young children's music)
    P.O. Box 3103
    Albany, NY 12203
    888-386-7664
    http://www.gentlewind.com

Aristoplay (games)
    8122 Main Street
    Dexter, MI 48130
    800-634-7738
    http://www.aristoplay.com

Bits and Pieces (puzzles)
One Puzzle Place
Stevens Point, WI 54481-7199
800-544-7297
http://www.bitsandpieces.com

Blitz Art Products, Inc.
http://www.bruceblitz.com
Curiosity Kits
P.O. Box 811
Cockeysville, MD 21030
800-584-5487
http://www.curiositykits.com

Dick Blick Art Materials
P.O. Box 1267
Galesburg, IL 61402-1267
800-447-8192
http://www.dickblick.com

Dover Publications, Inc. (inexpensive classics, coloring books,
    and more; preparing to accept phone orders and credit cards)
31 East 2nd St.
Mineola, NY 11501-3582

Hearthsong (games)
1950 Waldorf NW
Grand Rapids, MI 49550-7100
800-325-2502
http://www.hearthsong.com

Lark in the Morning (instruments, recordings, instructional
    materials)
P.O. Box 799
Fort Bragg, CA 95437
707-964-5569
http://www.larkinam.com

Mindware
121 5th Avenue NW
New Brighton, MN 55112
800-999-0398
http://www.mindwareonline.com

Music for Little People
P.O. Box 757
Greenland, NH 03840
800-409-2457
http://www.mflp.com

Rosie Hippos (wooden toys, books, games)
P.O. Box 2068
Port Townsend, WA 98368
800-385-2620
http://www.rosiehippo.com

STANDARDIZED-TEST SUPPLIERS

Abbreviations used below include: CAT: California Achievement Test (K–12); CTBS: Comprehensive Test of Basic Skills (K–12); MAT: Metropolitan Achievement Test (K–12); and PASS: Personalized Achievement Summary System (3–8 homeschoolers).

Bayside School Services
P.O. Box 250
Kill Devil Hills, NC 27948
800-723-3057
e-mail, ballfam@interpath.com

Test: CAT; parent certification to order or administer not necessary; grading and diagnostic services; price: $25

Christian Liberty Academy
  502 West Euclid Avenue
  Arlington Heights, IL 60004
  847-259-8736

  Test: CAT (1970 version)

Family Learning Organization Testing Service
  P.O. Box 7247
  Spokane, WA 99207-0247
  509-467-2552
  e-mail, homeschool@familylearning.org

  Test: CAT; parent certification to order or administer not required; grading and assessment services; price: $25

  Test: MAT; parent certification to order or administer not required grading and assessment services; price: $22

  Also available: CSL—Checklist for Skills Learned (K–8)—list of skills and topics arranged so parent may check off which skills a child has mastered; price: $24

  Also available: FAF—Freestyle (K–12)—List of Washington state's 11 required subjects that homeschoolers must cover, with space for parent to briefly describe the child's progress in each subject over the past year; price: $19

Hewitt Educational Resources
  P.O. Box 9
  2103 B Street
  Washougal, WA 98671
  360-835-8708

  Test: PASS; parent certification to order or administer not necessary; grading and diagnostic services; administered twice per year

Lord's Heritage Christian School
   5813 Papaya Drive
   Fort Pierce, FL 34982
   407-465-1685
   Test: CAT
   Parent certification to order or administer not necessary; grading and diagnostic services; price: from $20 for one test to $12.50 for seven or more

Seton School
   1350 Progress Drive
   Front Royal, VA 22630
   540-636-9990
   e-mail, testing@setonhome.org
   Test: CTBS; price: $20 (fourth edition)

Sycamore Tree
   2179 Mayer Place
   Costa Mesa, CA 92627
   Test: CTBS; price: $50 plus shipping and handling

Thurber's Educational Assessments
   400 Clayton Road
   Chapel Hill, NC 27514
   919-967-5282
   e-mail, thurbersnc@aol.com
   Test: CAT; parent certification to order or administer not necessary; grading and diagnostic services; price: from $22 for one test to group rates of $16 per test

TRANSCRIPT PREPARATION

Books

Cohen, Cafi. *Homeschoolers' College Admissions Handbook: Preparing Your 12- to 18-Year-Old for a Smooth Transition.* Prima, 2000.

Heuer, Loretta. *The Homeschooler's Guide to Portfolios and Transcripts.* Arco, 2000.

McKee, Alison. *From Homeschool to College and Work: Turning Your Homeschool Experiences into College and Job Portfolios.* Bittersweet House, 1997.

Internet

Older Kids: http://www.gomilpitas.com/homeschooling/olderkids/Transcripts.htm

Royal Academy: http://www.Home Educator.com (find "Royal Academy" link)

North Atlantic Regional Schools: http://www.narsonline.com

APPENDIX B

STATE-BY-STATE INFORMATION

Homeschooling Requirements in the United States*

	Statutory language describing nonschool options	Statutory requirements for the home teacher	Does statute give education officials discretion to judge and disallow program?	Does statute require standardized tests for pupil?	Home School or compulsory education law—citations
Alabama	(1) Instruction by tutor; or (2) Qualify as church school	Certification of tutor under option 1 only	Yes, under option 1 only	No	Alabama Code 16-28-3
Alaska	(1) Tutored by certified teacher; or (2) Enrolled in full-time approved correspondence course; or (3) Educational experience approved by LEA**; or (4) Meet requirements for private or religious schools (current SEA policy)	Teacher certificate under option 1	LEA approval under option 3 only	Yes, for options 2 and 4 only; testing at grades 4, 6, and 8	Alaska Statutes 14-30.010; 14.45-120(a)
Arizona	Home instruction by parent or other tutor	None	No	No	Ariz. Rev. Stat. 15-802 through 805; 15-745

continues

*Adapted from Patricia Lines, "Homeschooling: An Overview for Education Policy Makers," Working Paper for the U.S. Department of Education, Office of Educational Research and Improvement (Rev. March 1997).

**Abbreviations: "LEA" means local education agency—either a designated official or board at the local level. "SEA" means state education agency and can mean either the state board or the state school chief. "Parent" includes guardians. "H.S." means high school. "NTE" means National Teachers Examination. The phrase "home can be a school" is consistently used to mean that some administrative or judicial authority in the state has ruled that a home can qualify as a private school under the requirements for private schools in the state. This may also be true in other states, but if there is no formal ruling on the matter, it is not included.

	Statutory language describing nonschool options	Statutory requirements for the home teacher	Does statute give education officials discretion to judge and disallow program?	Does statute require standardized tests for pupil?	Home School or compulsory education law—citations
Arkansas	Home school	None (except for special needs students)	No (sec. 6-15-503(b): Reports to SEA are for statistical purposes only)	Yes. Children seven and older are to take a standardized test from an SBA list; children at age 14 also must take state's eighth-grade minimal competency test. Remediation required if below standard.	Ark. Stat. Ann. 6-18-201, 6-15-501
California	(1) Instruction by tutor; or (2) Independent study arranged through school; or (3) Submit documents as a private school	Tutor's certificate under option 1	No	No	Calif. Educ. Code sec. 48222; 48224; 51745
Colorado	(1) Instructed by certified teacher; or (2) "Home-based education"; or (3) Enrolled in private school that permits independent study at home (People in re D.B., 767 P2d 801 (Colo. App. 1988)	Teacher certificate under option 1	No	Option 2 (which is structured as an exemption from compulsory requirements) depends on child testing above 13th percentile, at grades 3, 5, 7, 9, and 11. Child has opportunity for re-test before exemption is denied.	Col. Rev. Stat. 22-33-104 and 104.5
Connecticut	"Equivalent" instruction "elsewhere"	None	No	The SEA guidelines recommend a portfolio review; all LEAs require it	Conn. Gen. Stat. Ann. 10-184

State			Law authorizes SEA to set approval standards, but it does not do so	Law authorizes SEA to require examinations, but SEA does not do so	
Delaware	"Regular and thorough" instruction "elsewhere"	None	None		Delaware Code 14-2702 through 2703
Florida	"Sequentially progressive instruction . . . by . . . parent"	None	No	Law requires an evaluation. It can be by means of testing, portfolio assessment, evaluation by trained third party, or any valid method authorized by the LEA.	Fla. Stat. Ann. 232.01
Georgia	"Home study"	Parent must have H.S. degree or GED; teacher who is not a parent must have college degree	No	Yes, but law specifies that parents are not required to submit test (§20-2-690[7]); reevaluation required if pupil does not show progress after one year of remediation at home	Official Code of Georgia Ann. 20-2-690
Hawaii	(1) "Appropriate alternate educational program"; or (2) "Home school" filing certain papers; or (3) Instruction by tutor	Under option 3, tutor must have B.A. degree	SEA approval required under option 1 only	Yes; standardized testing in grades 3, 6, 8, and 10	Hawaii Rev. Stat. 298-9
Idaho	"Comparably instructed"	None	No	No	Idaho Code 33-202

continues

	Statutory language describing nonschool options	Statutory requirements for the home teacher	Does statute give education officials discretion to judge and disallow program?	Does statute require standardized tests for pupil?	Home School or compulsory education law—citations
Illinois	School attendance only, but home can be a school; People v. Levison, 404 Ill. 574, 90 N.E. 2d 213 (1950)	None	No	No	Ill. Rev. Stat. ch. 122, par. 26-1
Indiana	"Equivalent" instruction	None	No	No	Ind. Stat. Ann. 20-8.1-3-17 and 20-8.1-3-34
Iowa	"Competent private instruction," which the statute defines as instruction for 37 days per quarter, resulting in student progress	Teacher certificate unless parent enrolls child in a home school assistance program or otherwise offers "competent private instruction"	No	Yes, standardized test or other evaluation, including portfolio review. Must be above 30th percentile or make six months progress in year.	Iowa Code Ann. 299A.1
Kansas	School attendance only, but several unpublished court decisions have ruled that home can be a school	None	No	No	Kan. Stat. Ann. 72-1111 through 72-1113
Kentucky	School attendance only, but state board regs. allow home to be a school	None	No	No	Ky. Rev. Stat. 159-010 through 159.990
Louisiana	"Home study"	None	No, so long as parent certifies that the curriculum is equal in quality to that offered in the public schools	Yes, or evaluation by a certified teacher	LA. Rev. Stat. 17:221(A) and 17.236

State				
Maine	"Equivalent instruction through home instruction"	None	SEA approval. Copy of application must go to LEA, which has opportunity to comment	Yes, or evaluation by a certified teacher, an LEA advisory panel, or a home school panel that includes a certified teacher	Me. Rev. Stat. Ann. 20A-5001A
Maryland	"Otherwise receiving regular, thorough instruction" in subjects usually taught in public school	None	No	No (voluntary testing at local public schools)	Ann. Code of Md., ch. 22, 7-301(a)
Massachusetts	"Otherwise instructed in a manner approved in advance by the superintendent or school committee"	None	LEA approval	Not by statute, but LEA may do so (several evaluation options available)	Mass. Gen. Laws 76-1
Michigan	Nonstatutory option: Attorney General opinion holds home can be a school. A.G. Op. 5579 9/27/79). New statutory option as of July, 1996: A child is in compliance with compulsory education laws if he or she is "being educated by his or her parent . . . at . . . home in an organized educational program that is appropriate" to the child's age and ability, and that covers specified subject areas.	None	No	No	S.B. 679, Amendment A, signed into Law Jan. 9, 1996 with effective date of July 1, 1996

continues

	Statutory language describing nonschool options	Statutory requirements for the home teacher	Does statute give education officials discretion to judge and disallow program?	Does statute require standardized tests for pupil?	Home School or compulsory education law—citations
Minnesota	"Home-school" is included in definition of school	(1) Teacher certificate; or (2) Supervised by certified teacher; or (3) Pass teacher competency exam; or (4) Use of accredited program approved by board; or (5) College degree; or (6) Be a parent teaching a child who complies with pupil testing requirements	No	Yes, option 6 only; children below 30th percentile must be evaluated for learning problems	Minn. Stat. Ann. 120.101 and 127.20
Mississippi	Home instruction	None	No	No	Miss. Code Ann. 37-13-91
Missouri	"Home school"	None	No	No	Ann. Mo. Stat. 167-031 and 167.042
Montana	"Home school"	None	No	No	Mont. Code Ann. 20-5-102 and 20-5-109

State					
Nebraska	School attendance only, but SEA allows home to qualify as (1) An "approved" private school; or (2) "Exempt" private school where parents have sincere religious objection	(1) Teacher certificate; or (2) Meet board standards for exempt private school	No, but SEA approval required for option 1	Statute gives board discretion to require tests but it does not require them	Neb. Rev. Stat. 79-201, 79-1701, 85-607
Nevada	"Equivalent instruction" at home	(1) Teacher certificate or (2) Parent must consult with certified teacher (requirement waived after one year of pupil progress); or (3) Use approved correspondence program; or (4) Board waiver	No. Statute requires "satisfactory written evidence" of kind approved by SEA, but SEA regs. leave no discretion if specified information is submitted	Not by statute, but SEA regs. requires testing at grades 2, 3, 4, 7, and 8 for options 1 and 2	Nev. Rev. Stat. 392.070
New Hampshire	"Home education," which consists of "planned and supervised instructional and related educational activities . . . "	None	SEA approval (sec. 193A)	Yes; or take a district test; or obtain a teacher evaluation or other valid evaluation of child's portfolio	N.H. Rev. Stat. Ann. 193:1 and 193-A

continues

	Statutory language describing nonschool options	Statutory requirements for the home teacher	Does statute give education officials discretion to judge and disallow program?	Does statute require standardized tests for pupil?	Home School or compulsory education law—citations
New Jersey	"Equivalent instruction elsewhere"	None	No. LEA limited to verifying subject matter coverage, Cf. State v. Massa, 95 N.J. Super. 382, 231 A.2d 252 (Morris County Ct. Law Div. 1967)	No	N.J. Stat. Ann. 18A.38-25
New Mexico	"A home study program that provides a basic academic educational program" operated by parent	High school diploma or equivalent	No	Yes	N.M. Stat. Ann. 22-1-2 and 21-1-2.1
New York	Attendance "elsewhere" and instruction that is "substantially equivalent" by "competent" teacher	Must be "competent"	LEA has authority to determine equivalency	Not by statute, but SEA requires taking test from list of SEA-approved tests	N.Y. Educ. Law 3204, 3205, 3210, 3212
North Carolina	"Home school" serving children from no more than two families	Must be parent or member of household of one of two families forming home school; and have high school degree or equivalent	No	Yes; annually	N.C. Gen. Stat. 115C-378, 115C-547, 115C-563 through 565

State	Definition	Teacher Qualifications	Notification	Testing	Citation
North Dakota	"Home-based instruction"	Parent must be (1) Certified; or (2) Have high school education and be supervised by certified teacher; or (3) Pass national teacher exam	Parent reports to LEA; may determine if child is making satisfactory progress for children testing below 30th percentile	Yes	N.D. Cent. Code 15-34.1-03 and 15-34.1-04
Ohio	"Instructed at home by a person qualified to teach the branches on which instruction is required . . ."	(1) H.S. degree or equivalent; or (2) Satisfactory test scores showing equivalence; or (3) Supervised by person with college degree until child shows proficiency on test	LEA approval, as delimited by State Board Regulations	Yes; or evaluation by a certified teacher; an agreed-upon person, or undergo alternative assessment	Ohio Rev. Code 3301-34-04, 3321.03, and 3321.04
Oklahoma	"Other means of education . . . for the full term the schools of the district are in session"	None	No	No	Okla. Stat. Ann., Title 70 10-105(A) and (B)
Oregon	Instruction by a parent or other qualified person	None	No	Yes. Parents may choose among a list of standardized tests.	Oregon Rev. Stat 339.010, 339.030, and 339.035

continues

	Statutory language describing nonschool options	Statutory requirements for the home teacher	Does statute give education officials discretion to judge and disallow program?	Does statute require standardized tests for pupil?	Home School or compulsory education law—citations
Pennsylvania	(1) "Regular daily instruction . . . by a properly qualified private tutor" and satisfactory to district superintendent; or (2) "Home education program"	Certificaton for option 1; H.S. degree or equivalent for option 2	LEA approval	Yes, at grades 3, 5, and 8, plus annual evaluation of portfolio by certified teacher or other specified professional	Pa. Stat. Ann., Title 24, 13-1326 and 13-1327
Rhode Island	"At-home instruction approved by the school committee . . ."	None	LEA approval	No, but SEA gives LEA authority to require an evaluation	R.I. Gen. Laws 16-19-1
South Carolina	Parents "may teach their children at home"; must meet specific requirements listed in statute	H.S. degree or equivalent	Approval by LEA, So. Carolina Ass'n. of Indep. Home Schools, or other association with 50 or more members and meets other requirements in statute (state reviews association standards periodically)	Yes	Code of Laws of S.C. Ann. 59-65-10, 40, 45, and 47
South Dakota	"Alternative instruction for an equivalent period of time . . . in the basic skills"	None	If probable cause exists to believe family is not in compliance, SEA may deny status	Yes. Parents may choose any nationally standardized test.	S.D. Comp. Law 13-27-2, 13-27-3 and 49-6-3001

State	Definition	Teacher Qualification	Approval	Testing	Citation
Tennessee	(1) "Home school" "conducted by parents . . . for their own children . . ."; or (2) Affiliated with and supervised by church school	H.S. degree or GED required to teach grades K–8, and college degree for grades 7–12 under option 1; no requirement for option 2. SEA has authority to grant exemptions to requirements.	No	Yes; at grades 2, 5, 7, and 9. If child is 6 to 9 months behind in core subjects, parent must work with certified teacher to develop remedial course.	Tenn. Code Ann. 49-6-3001 and 49-6-3050
Texas	School attendance, "which includes home schools"	None	No	No	Tex. Educ. Code 4.25, 21.032 through 21.040
Utah	"Taught at home in the subjects prescribed by the state board . . ."	None	LEA approval	No	Utah Code Ann. 53A-11-1012
Vermont	A "home study program"	None	SEA approval	Yes; or other assessment among various options listed in statute	Vt. Stat. Ann. Title 16, 1121; 16(11); 166b

continues

	Statutory language describing nonschool options	Statutory requirements for the home teacher	Does statute give education officials discretion to judge and disallow program?	Does statute require standardized tests for pupil?	Home School or compulsory education law—citations
Virginia	(1) "Instruction of children by their parents in their home"; or (2) Child enrolled in approved correspondence course; or (3) Program approved by division superintendent; or (4) Bona fide religious objection to school attendance (§22.1–254.1D); or (5) Use of certified teacher	For option 1, parent must hold college degree, or qualify as teacher	Yes, under option 4	Yes (must achieve 4th stanine on test) or undergo alternative assessment approved by LEA. Law allows 1 year probation if test results are unsatisfactory.	Va. Code 22.1-254.1
Washington	"Home-based" instruction with "planned and supervised activities" and which covers basic skills provided by parent to their own children only	(1) Parent has 45 college credits or completes a course on home instruction at a postsecondary institution or a vocational technical institute; or (2) Parent teaches under supervision of state certified teacher; or (3) LEA deems parent qualified to teach	No	Yes; SEA-approved tests taken annually; or annual assessment by a certified person currently working in education	Wash. Rev. Code 28A.200.200; 28A.225.10

State	Requirements			Citation
West Virginia	(1) "Instruction . . . in the home" or place approved by the LEA and by a "qualified" person; or (2) File report on home school program	Under option 1, home teacher must be qualified to teach public elementary school. Under option 2, teacher must have H.S. degree and a) 4 years formal education above the pupil's; or b) achieve acceptable score on NTE. NOTE: The 4-year rule has been waived for year 2000–2001 pending a study on the effects of home instruction exemption by the oversight commission on education accountability.	Yes, under option 1; no, under option 2	Yes. In addition, SEA has authority to adopt guidelines for alternative assessments for special education students.	W. Va. 18-18-1
Wisconsin	"Homebased educational program provided . . . by the child's parents . . . or by a person designated by the parent . . ."	None	No	No	Wis. Stat. Ann. 118.15 and 118.165
Wyoming	"Basic academic education program" at home, and approved by LEA	None	Yes	No	Wyo. Stat. 21-4-101

continues

Other Jurisdictions:

	Statutory language describing nonschool options	Statutory requirements for the home teacher	Does statute give education officials discretion to judge and disallow program?	Does statute require standardized tests for pupil?	Home School or compulsory education law—citations
District of Columbia	"Equivalent" instruction	None	Yes	No	D.C. Code 31-401 and 402
American Samoa	No statutory provision	If qualifying as private school, certified teacher required	Yes, if qualifying as private school	No	American Samoa Code 16.0302 through 16.0308
Guam	Home instruction by parent or tutor	None quarterly	No, but Guam board rules require approval	No, but Guam board regulations require testing or other assessment	Guam Code Ann. Tit. 17, 6101 through 6109
Virgin Islands	Home instruction by parent	None	Commissioner of Education must approve program and teacher	No, but Dept. of Education meets with parents and children quarterly	V.I. Code Ann. Tit. 17, 81 through 97
Puerto Rico	No statutory provision	None for private schools	None for private schools	No	P.R. laws Ann. Tit. 18, secs. 71–81
Northern Marianas	Home study	To be set by board	Yes	No	Mariana Code 3-1141

Author's Notes on Table

✦ The table is based on statutory analysis; check with your State Board of Education to verify information or to obtain updated information.

✦ Column three, "Does statute require approval" indicates that approval is needed if the SEA or LEA has authority to do something more than simply verify that the required documents are filed and provide the required information. Note all states except Texas and Oklahoma have mandatory or voluntary filing requirements. Typically, a parent must provide the name, age, grade of child instructed, and often material on the curriculum are part of information reported. Many states identify the form as a "notice of intent to home school."

✦ The table does not include information applicable to all children, whether in home school or other school, e.g., age of compulsory education, and durational requirements for the school day and school year. Most states mandate the same requirements for all children, regardless of where they are educated.

✦ The table does not attempt to resolve legal ambiguities. Where a state or local education agency adopts rules that are not specifically authorized by the statute, there is always a question of the extent to which the rules are authorized. The table does attempt to indicate the situation where the agency is the source of a policy, if only to note the possibility of a legal challenge. Of course, a board with express authority to approve a home program will be in a better position to defend its more stringent requirements.

INDEX